Daytrips

HOLLAND, BELGIUM
and LUXEMBOURG

SECOND EDITION

HOLLAND, BELGIUM and LUXEMBOURG

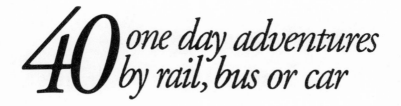

40 one day adventures by rail, bus or car

EARL STEINBICKER

HASTINGS HOUSE
Book Publishers
Mamaroneck, New York

While every effort has been made to insure accuracy, neither the author nor the publisher assume legal responsibility for any consequences arising from the use of this book or the information it contains.

We are always grateful for comments from readers, which are extremely helpful in preparing future editions. Please write directly to the author, Earl Steinbicker, c/o Hastings House, 141 Halstead Avenue, Mamaroneck, NY 10543; or FAX (914) 835-1037. Thank you.

All photos and maps are by the author.

Distributed to the trade by Publishers Group West, Emeryville, CA

ISBN: 0-8038-9368-X
Library of Congress Catalog Card Number 94-072930

Printed in the United States of America
10 9 8 7 6 5 4 3 2 1

Contents

Introduction

Holland, Belgium, and Luxembourg together make up one of the most enchanting little corners of Europe, with more outstanding attractions per square mile than just about anywhere else on earth. Known collectively by that awful acronym *Benelux* and historically as the Low Countries, they offer scores of pleasurable and all-too-little-known adventures for those willing to probe beyond the obvious delights of the capital cities. This book takes a careful look at 40 of the most intriguing destinations and tells you, in step-by-step detail, exactly how to go about exploring them on your own.

What is especially appealing about these compact lands is that virtually *all* of their most enjoyable sights can easily be savored on simple one-day excursions from either Amsterdam, Brussels, or Luxembourg City. Distances are remarkably short, the roads superb, and the modern trains run so frequently to just about everywhere that reference to timetables is hardly necessary.

Daytrips have many advantages over the usual point-to-point touring, particularly for short-term visitors. You can sample a far greater range of experiences in the same amount of time by seeing only those places that really interest you, instead of "doing" each country region by region. They also lead to a more varied diet of sights, such as spending one day in the most un-Dutch of cities, Maastricht, the next back in Amsterdam, and the third on a bucolic island off the northern coast.

The benefits of remaining in one hotel for a while are obvious. Weekly rates are often more economical than overnight stays, especially in conjunction with airline package plans. You also gain a sense of place, of having established a temporary home-away-from-home in a large city where you can get to know the restaurants and enjoy the nightlife. Then, too, you won't waste time searching for a room every night. Your luggage remains in one place while you go out on carefree daytrips.

There is no need to pre-plan every moment of your vacation since with daytrips you are always free to venture wherever you please. Feel like seeing Leiden this morning? Ah, but this is Monday, so you may be better off heading for Volendam instead, or taking a delightful cruise to the island of Texel. Is rain predicted for the entire day? You certainly don't want to be in Bokrijk in a shower, so why not try the wonderful museums in Liège? Is the day just too glorious to spend in Luxembourg City, regardless of its many charms? You can always take off for an outdoor adventure at Vianden and enjoy the sunshine. Then again, you might not want to go anywhere today. Walking tours of the three base cities are included, as well as for the daytrip destinations. The operative word here is flexibility, the freedom of not being tied to a schedule or route.

All of the daytrips in this book may be taken by public transportation, and all by car as well. Full information for doing this is given in the "Getting There" section of each trip. A suggested do-it-yourself tour is outlined in both the text and on the local map provided. Time and weather considerations are included, along with price-keyed restaurant recommendations, background data, and sources of additional information.

The trips have been arranged in a geographic sequence following convenient transportation routes. In several cases it is possible to combine two trips in the same day. These opportunities are noted whenever they are practical.

Destinations were chosen to appeal to a wide variety of interests. In addition to the usual cathedrals, castles, and museums, there are also boat cruises, cheese markets, windmills, canals, caves, exquisite gardens, preserved medieval towns, bustling cities, great seaports, quaint fishing villages, outdoor folk museums, homes of famous artists, locations where history was made, places of natural beauty, plus an exciting railfan excursion, and much, much more.

It may come as a surprise to discover just how much these three small countries have to offer! As you read through this book you may very well decide to spend more than just a few days within their boundaries, or to even join the growing number of knowledgeable travelers who make the Low Countries the focus of an entire vacation.

Finally, a gentle disclaimer. Places have a way of changing without warning, and errors do creep into print. If your heart is absolutely set on a particular sight, you may want to check first to make sure that it isn't closed for renovations, or that the opening times are still valid. Phone numbers for the local tourist information offices are included for this purpose.

Happy Daytripping!

Getting Around Holland

There is a lot more to Holland than just Amsterdam, wooden shoes, tulips, cheese, and windmills—delightful though these most certainly are. The 23 daytrips described in the next section cover some of the very best sights in the nation, with a little something for every taste. That they can be comfortably enjoyed on easy daytrips from Amsterdam should make them all the more appealing.

THE COUNTRY:

But first, there is that slight confusion over the name. Officially, the country is known as the Kingdom of the Netherlands. The term *Holland* refers only to the two western provinces, stretching roughly from Dordrecht in the south to Texel in the north, embracing Amsterdam, The Hague, and Rotterdam. In actual practice, however, just about everyone calls the whole country Holland—and so will this book.

That this fascinating land—whatever its name—should exist at all in its present form is nothing short of amazing. To paraphrase an old saying, God may have created the earth, but it was the Dutch who made Holland. Over half of it lies below sea level at high tide and is kept dry only by an intricate system of dikes, drainage canals, and ceaseless pumping. Much of this land has been reclaimed from the sea, a process that is still going on; and the rest was once a soggy marshland. The thousands of windmills that dotted the landscape in years gone by were mostly put there to pump water. Although quite a few of these have been preserved, their former task is now performed by motors. The Dutch must continually guard the land from the encroaching sea, since any breakdown in the system could result in catastrophic floods—as happened as recently as 1953, when over 1,800 people drowned.

THE PEOPLE:

This long struggle against the elements has endowed the people with certain characteristics. They tend to be hardworking, methodical, and rather serious, and they have an intense regard for order and community despite their fierce individualism. Centuries of overseas trade have developed their sense of liberal toleration, a trait that is readily apparent in the streets of Amsterdam today, and that serves them well in the face of an extremely high population density. It has also made them exceptionally willing to accept foreign ideas, races, and languages. With rare exceptions, they are an unusually honest people whose words mean exactly what they say. And, oh yes, they can be a lot of fun when they let their hair down over a friendly beer.

A LITTLE BIT OF HISTORY:

Although the history of Holland goes back to prehistoric times and includes a long period of Roman domination, this once-inhospitable land did not achieve any real degree of importance until the Middle Ages. It was the rise of the merchant class in the developing towns that brought about an envious level of prosperity. During the 15th century, power came into the hands of the Burgundians and was later transferred to the Austrian Hapsburgs, and through them to the king of Spain.

The Reformation of the 16th century spread rapidly throughout the northern Netherlands. This was regarded as heresy by the bigoted Spanish king, Philip II, who took drastic measures to stamp it out with an army of 10,000 led by the duke of Alba. The rebellious Dutch, under their greatest hero, Prince William of Orange-Nassau (also known as "the Silent" for his diplomatic skills), eventually turned the tide, although the religious struggles continued until the mid-17th century.

With peace came the "Golden Age." Amsterdam flourished as Europe's great center for overseas trade. Dutch fleets sailed the world's oceans and established colonies in distant lands. A flood of refugees from all over Europe, taking advantage of the new religious freedom and soaring economy, brought with them a wide range of talents that further fueled the boom.

By the end of the century, however, a decadence had set in. Wars with England and other European powers left Holland exhausted, and soon a new conservatism put a stop to the creative energies unleashed only decades earlier. The French Revolution led to the founding of the Batavian Republic and eventually to direct rule by Napoleon.

Dutch sovereignty was reestablished in 1814, but by 1830 the Catholic south rebelled and formed the new Kingdom of Belgium. With little in common, the two countries have remained apart ever since.

Holland was neutral throughout World War I, falling victim to Nazi tyranny in 1940. Its major port of Rotterdam was almost totally destroyed, and its large Jewish population virtually annihilated. A brave Dutch Resistance helped to bring about final liberation by 1945. Although it soon lost its major colonies, Holland has regained its prosperity and is now among the most advanced nations in the world.

PRACTICALITIES:

The 23 daytrips described in the next section assume that you are making Amsterdam your base of operations. This is the most logical and convenient choice, especially for those traveling by rail. There are, of course, other possibilities, including The Hague, Haarlem, Utrecht, or even smaller towns such as Hilversum. To use another city or town as your base, you will have to study a rail or highway map and adjust the travel directions accordingly. But first, take a look at the practical information that follows.

TRANSPORTATION:

Nearly all of the daytrips in Holland described in this book can be made by rail, all by car, and some by bus. Which of these you choose depends on purely personal factors, but you may want to consider the following information before deciding.

BY RAIL:

Probably no other country on earth is as well suited to train travel as Holland. Its extremely high population density demands frequent departures, while its flat terrain and relatively short distances insure speedy travel time. All in all, trains are almost invariably the fastest way of getting around.

Serving more than 400 destinations with some 4,000 trains a day, the **Netherlands Railways** (*Nederlandse Spoorwegen* or NS) carries over a half-million passengers every working day in its clean and comfortable cars. Fares are quite reasonable and can be considerably reduced by purchasing one-day return tickets or by using one of the economical railpasses described later on.

There are very few places of tourist interest in Holland that cannot be reached by train, and even those secluded spots invariably have a connecting bus to the nearest rail line. Stations are usually located right in the heart of town, so close to the major attractions that most of the walking tours outlined in this book start right at the station.

Seasoned travelers often consider riding trains to be one of the very best ways of meeting the local people and making new friends. It is not at all unusual to strike up an engaging conversation that makes your trip all the more memorable. You will also get a marvelous view of the passing countryside from the large windows, especially enhanced by the fact that Dutch trains usually ride atop embankments designed to prevent floods.

All trains operated by the Netherlands Railways belong to one of the following categories, as indicated on schedules and departure platforms:

EC — *EuroCity*. A new category of international expresses with special comforts, replacing the former TEE trains. Both first- and second-class seating is offered, and there is a supplementary fare, which is covered by the Eurailpass but not by national passes.

INT — International express trains with both first- and second-class seating. A supplementary fare is often charged on these, but not to holders of the Eurailpass.

IC — *InterCity*. These comfortable expresses are usually your best bet for travel within Holland. Most of them are made up of very modern cars and operate on frequently recurring schedules. Those on the Amsterdam-The Hague-Rotterdam-Dordrecht-Antwerp-Brussels route use the latest *Beneluxtrein* equipment, featuring such niceties as on-board pay phones. There is no supplementary fare, and both classes are provided for.

Sneltrein — Semi-express trains used within Holland. Both classes are available.

Stoptrein — The name says it all. These locals connect very rural areas with cities and sometimes offer only second-class seating. A few are diesel operated.

Schedules are really not necessary as you will seldom, if ever, have more than a half-hour wait for a train going your way. Tables of departure are posted on yellow boards in each station, arranged by route and final destination and showing the platform number, while signs on the platform itself indicate the stops the train will make. Times are expressed using the 24-hour clock; thus a departure at 4:52 p.m. would be marked as 16.52.

A condensed schedule booklet listing most services of interest to tourists is available free at the information counters. Real rail fans will, of course, want to add the complete annual schedule book, called a *spoorboekje,* to their collection. There is a modest charge for this. Those traveling in other European countries as well as Holland may want to invest in the handy ***Thomas Cook European Timetable***, sold in some travel book stores in America, by mail from the Forsyth Travel Library (P.O. Box 2975, Shawnee Mission, Kansas 66201; phone toll-free 1-800-FORSYTH for credit-card orders), or at Thomas Cook offices in Britain.

Reservations are neither necessary nor possible for travel within

Holland, although you might want to consider them for long international journeys.

Most station **platforms** have both an "A" and a "B" end. Be sure you go to the correct one, as shown on the departure boards, since the same platform often handles two different trains simultaneously. A few trains split en route, making it essential that you get on the right set of cars. If in doubt, ask—just about everyone speaks English. **Destinations** are sometimes—but not always—marked on the cars themselves. First-class cars are indicated with the numeral "1" near the door, and occasionally with a yellow or blue stripe above the windows.

There is no regular **food service** on trains within Holland, although many have a roving mini-bar offering snacks, sandwiches, and beverages. The restaurants and cafeterias in the stations are usually quite good and offer excellent value for your money, especially in the smaller cities.

All but the most local of trains carry both first- and second-class accommodations. First class is, of course, a bit more comfortable and a whole lot less crowded during peak travel times, but most people will find second class to be perfectly adequate for the short journeys involved.

RAILPASSES can be a bargain if you intend to do a substantial amount of train travel The Netherlands Railways (NS) accepts the following passes:

EURAILPASS — The best-known pass, it allows unlimited first-class travel throughout 17 European countries, excluding Great Britain. It is available for periods of 15 or 21 days, or 1, 2, or 3 months. The Eurailpass offers a variety of fringe benefits, mostly in countries other than Holland. This is the best pass to use if your travels will take you *beyond* Holland, Belgium, and Luxembourg. It is available from most travel agents outside Europe, from overseas offices of some European railroads, or from some mail-order sources such as the Forsyth Travel Library mentioned above.

EURAIL FLEXIPASS — Allows unlimited first-class travel on *any* 5, 10, or 15 days within a 2-month period. It is valid in the same 17 countries and is sold by the same agents as the regular Eurailpass. This is an attractive deal if you intend to spend time exploring your base cities as well as making daytrips from them.

EURAIL SAVERPASS — An economical version of the regular Eurailpass offering the same first-class benefits for groups of three or more people traveling together. Between October 1st and March 31st the group size can be as small as two persons. This pass is available for a period of 15 or 21 days, or 1 month, and is sold by Eurailpass agents.

EURAIL YOUTHPASS — This low-cost version of the Eurailpass is available to anyone under the age of 26 and allows unlimited *second-class* travel in the same 17 countries for periods of 15 days, or 1 or 2 months. There is also a **Eurail Youth Flexipass** valid for any 5, 10, or 15 days within a 2-month period.

BENELUX TOURRAIL PASS — This handy pass allows unlimited train travel on any 5 days within a 1-month period. Valid for travel throughout Holland, Belgium, and Luxembourg only, it is sold in both first- and second-class versions for adults and for juniors under 26. It is sold by Netherlands tourist offices in North America, and by the Forsyth Travel Library mentioned above.

DOMINO PASS — Valid only in the Netherlands, this economical pass covers unlimited train travel on any 3, 5, or 10 days during a 1-month period. It is available in both first- and second-class versions for adults, or second-class only for juniors under 26, from Netherlands tourist offices in North America, or from the Forsyth Travel Library.

RAIL ROVER — A real bargain for trips within the Netherlands only, this pass is sold at train stations in the Netherlands for either 1 or 7 days of unlimited travel. The 7-day version is also sold by Netherlands tourist offices in North America. Either way, it comes in either first- or second-class versions. A wonderful feature unique to this pass is the **Public Transport Link Rover**, an option that costs little extra and allows the unlimited use of virtually all public transportation in Holland—including country and city buses, trams, and subways—during the same period. *Those confining their trips exclusively to Holland will probably find the Rail Rover with the Public Transport Link to be the least expensive way of exploring the country.*

Remember that all railpasses must be used in accordance with the rules and instructions accompanying them, and that you must always be prepared to show your passport. When having passes validated, be certain that you agree with the dates *before* allowing the agent to write them in.

If you intend to take several of the daytrips in this book, and especially if one or two of them are to more distant places such as Maastricht or Middelburg, a railpass (especially the Rail Rover) will probably wind up saving you a considerable amount of money. Even if the savings are less than that, a pass should still be considered for the convenience it affords in not having to line up for tickets, and for the freedom of just hopping aboard trains at whim. Possession of a railpass will also encourage you to become more adventurous in seeking out offbeat destinations. It allows you to take longer and more circuitous routes, which might be more interesting. Should you ever manage to get on the wrong train by mistake, your only cost will be your lost time. Railpasses can even be used to cut your dining expenses just by riding to a nearby small town for dinner, where restaurants are usually less expensive than in large cities. The same reasoning also holds true for hotels.

The Netherlands Railways (NS) offers an interesting program of one-day do-it-yourself trips that can be used with or without railpasses. Called **NS-Rail-Idee**, it combines rail fares, local transportation, entrance fees, refreshments, and other features into economical packages. A number of these trips are currently available and are described in a free colorful catalog available at train information offices. Unfortunately, this is in Dutch only, but several of the most popular excursions are also outlined in the free booklet *Touring Holland by Rail,* yours for the asking at major stations or from the overseas offices of the Netherlands Board of Tourism. Since quite a few of the trips are to the same places described in this book, the packages could be used in conjunction with it—a nice little savings for those who haven't bought a railpass.

Those buying individual tickets should note that **one-day return fares** (*dagretour*) are available and will save you money over the regular one-way fares.

While virtually everyone in Holland speaks English, the signs in stations and on trains, as well as the words used on schedules, are in Dutch. The **glossary** on pages 16–17 should help you understand these. Travelers in the Flemish-speaking parts of Belgium will find it handy also.

Passengers flying in or out of Amsterdam's Schiphol Airport will be happy to know that there is a new train station right at the terminal, connected by a moving sidewalk. From here, a train leaves every few minutes for Amsterdam's Centraal Station, while other frequent departures serve many cities in Holland and a few in Belgium and Germany.

Additional information about the Netherlands Railways is available from the overseas offices of the Netherlands Board of Tourism, whose addresses are listed at the end of this section.

BY BUS:

With such a wonderful rail service there would seem to be little need for buses outside the cities themselves, yet there are still some small towns and isolated areas to which the tracks do not lead. In nearly every such case you can simply take a train to the station nearest your destination, then transfer to a connecting bus. One trip, to Volendam, must be made entirely by bus, but that's only a 30-minute ride. Full details are given for each daytrip in this book.

A DUTCH
RAIL TRAVELER'S GLOSSARY

Aankomst. . . . . Arrival
Aansluiting . . . . Connection
Alleen Werkdagen . . . . Weekdays only
Alleen Zon en Feestdagen . . . . . . Sundays and holidays only
Bagagedepot . . . . Left luggage office
Bagagekluizen . . . . Baggage locker
Bespreking . . . . Reservation
Binnenland . . . . Inland
Boot . . . . Boat, ferry
Buitenland . . . . Foreign
Conducteur . . . . Conductor, ticket collector
Dagretour. . . . . One-day return excursion
Dagtocht . . . . Daytrip
Damen . . . . Women
Dienst. . . . . Service
Dienst voor Toerisme . . . . Local tourist information office (Belgium)
Doorgaande Trein . . . . Through train to destination
Douane. . . . . Customs
Eerste Hulp . . . . First aid
Eerste Klas . . . . First class
Enkele . . . . To go one way
Feestdagen . . . . Public holidays
Fietsen te Huur . . . . Bicycle rental (in station)
Geen. . . . . No, forbidden
Geen Doorgang . . . . No entrance
Geldig. . . . . Valid
Gesloten. Closed
Gevaarlijk. . . . . Danger
Gevonden Voorwerpen . . . . Lost-and-found
Heren . . . . Men
Hoofdlijn . . . . Main line
Ingang . . . . Entrance
Inlichtingen . . . . Information
Instappen. . . . . Get on (the train)
Kaartje . . . . Ticket
Kruier. . . . . Porter
Ligplaats . . . . Couchette, inexpensive sleeping car
with bunks
Luchthaven . . . . Airport
Metro . . . . Subway, Underground
Naar . . . . To
Niet. . . . . Not
Niet Instappen . . . . Don't board this train
Niet Roken . . . . No smoking

NMBS	Belgian National Railways, also called SNCB
NS	Netherlands Railways
Overstappen	Change of train
Overstapverbinding	Change to connecting train
Perron	Platform
Prijzen	Price
Reis	Journey
Reisbureau	Travel agency
Reizen	To travel
Reiziger	Traveler
Retour	Return (round-trip ticket)
Roker	Smoking car
Slaapwagen	Sleeping car
Spoor	Track
Spoorbaan	Railroad
Spoorboekje	Timetable book
Spoorkaartjes	Tickets
Spoorweg	Railroad
Stilte! Werkcoupe	Do not disturb, Quiet compartment
Stoomtrein	Steam train
Strippenkaarten	Multiple ride public transport ticket
Terugbetaling	Refund
Toegang	Entrance
Toeslag	Suplementary fare, surcharge
Trein	Train
Tweede Klas	Second class
Uitgang	Exit
Van	From
Verboden	Forbidden
Verboden te Roken	No smoking
Verloren Voorwerpen	Lost-and-found
Vertraging	Delay
Vertrek	Departure
VVV	Local tourist information office (Holland)
Wachtkamer, Wachtzaal	Waiting room
Werkdag	Workday
Wisselkantoor	Money exchange
Zitplaats	Seat
Zon en Feestdagen	Sundays and holidays

All of the bus companies in Holland—except the KLM airport bus—accept the Netherlands Rail Rover pass *with* the Public Transport Link option attached, making this the easiest way to get around. There is also a national one-day pass and a national *"Strippenkaart"* for multiple rides over a longer time period, both available at the GVB office in front of Amsterdam's Centraal Station and elsewhere. Ask for their brochure in English that explains everything. You can also just pay the driver for a single ride.

BY CAR:

Holland has what is arguably the most intensive road network in Europe, and it's all free with the exception of a few tolls at major bridges and tunnels. Driving is exceptionally easy outside the big cities; the roads everywhere are smooth and well marked with signposts. You will, however, have problems parking in Amsterdam and in coping with that city's notorious traffic congestion.

All that's needed to drive in Holland is a valid driver's license and a registration for your car. The minimum age is 18 years. Members of the American AAA, British AA or RAC, as well as some other automobile clubs are entitled to the services of the **ANWB** (Royal Dutch Touring Club), whose yellow phones alongside major roads can be used to summon breakdown help. You will also find phone boxes marked *"Politie,"* which bring the police and should be used in case of an accident. Seat belts must be worn in the front seat(s) at all times. Unless otherwise marked, speed limits are 100 kph (60 mph) on motorways, 80 kph (50 mph) on other highways, 50 kph (30 mph) in built-up areas, and even less in residential areas.

Holland is filled with bicycles, which usually have their own lanes or separate paths as well as their own traffic lights. You must always be alert to their presence. Pedestrians have the right-of-way at marked crossings, as do passengers getting on or off trams.

Up-to-the-minute reports on traffic and road conditions are available at any time by phoning (070) 31-31-31.

WHEN TO GO:

Holland may be enjoyed at any time, but note that many of the attractions outside the big cities are closed between mid-autumn and early spring. Specific details are given for each daytrip. The best time to visit is undoubtedly between mid-spring and early autumn. June, with its longer days, offers the most sunshine. Whatever the season, be prepared for rapidly changing weather—and always carry a folding umbrella to insure that it won't rain. A light jacket or sweater will come in handy, even in August.

Amsterdam seems to be a popular summer destination for all of

Europe's youth. This does not seriously affect the hotel situation, although confirmed reservations are still wise. The tourist hordes thin out considerably once you get beyond the downtown area.

HOLIDAYS:

Public holidays (*Feestdagen*) in Holland are more or less as follows:

New Year's Day
Good Friday (many places open)
Easter Sunday
Easter Monday
Queen's Day (April 30th)
Liberation Day (May 5th) (most places open)
Ascension Day (6th Thursday after Easter)
Whit Sunday
Whit Monday (7th Monday after Easter)
Christmas
Second Christmas Day (December 26th)

Trains operate on holiday schedules on most but not all of these days.

LANGUAGE:

Dutch is related to German, with similar spellings but quite different pronunciations. No one will expect you to understand it, however, so don't worry. Virtually everyone in the country speaks fairly fluent English, and does so with pleasure. The pocket-size *Dutch-English Dictionary* by Berlitz has a handy menu-translator section.

MONEY:

The Dutch guilder (*gulden*) is sometimes called the florin, and is variously abbreviated as f., fl., hfl., and Dfl. It is divided into 100 cents. Coins are minted in 5-cent (*stuiver*), 10-cent (*dubbeltje*), 25-cent (*kwartje*), 1-guilder, and 2½-guilder (*rijksdaalder*) denominations. Bills come in values of 5, 10, 25, 50, and 100 guilders, all in different colors for easy identification. There are also higher banknotes, but you're not likely to see them.

It is always advisable to do your money exchange transactions at a commercial bank, where you will get the best rate. The GWK offices in train stations, airports, and at border crossings, as well as some tourist information offices (VVVs), are handy places to change money when the banks are closed. Other money changers often charge outrageous commissions.

A DUTCH
DRIVER'S GLOSSARY

Afdaling . . . . Steep hill
Afgesloten Rijweg . . . . No through road
Allen voor Voetgangers . . . . Pedestrians only
Alle Richtingen . . . . All directions
ANWB. . . . . Royal Dutch Touring Club
Autoweg . . . . Motorway
Band . . . . Tire
Benzine . . . . Gasoline (Petrol)
Benzinestation . . . . Gas (Petrol) station
Bromfietsen . . . . Mopeds
Bushalte . . . . Bus stop
Centrum . . . . To the center of town
Doorgand Verkeer . . . . Through traffic
Douane . . . . Customs
Eenrichtingsverkeer . . . . One-way traffic
Eigen Weg . . . . Private road
Fietsen . . . . Bicycle
Fietsers Oversteken . . . . Cycle crossing
Fietspad . . . . Bicycle path
Filevorming . . . . Get into lane
Geen . . . . No
Geopend . . . . Open
Gesloten . . . . Closed
Gestremd . . . . Forbidden
Gevaar . . . . Danger
Gevaarlijke Bocht! . . . . Dangerous curves ahead
Gladde Weg . . . . Slippery road
Halte . . . . Tram stop
Ingang . . . . Entrance
Inhaalverbod . . . . No passing
Langzaam Rijden . . . . Drive slowly
Let Op! . . . . Attention!
Links . . . . Left
Lucht . . . . Air
Naar Links . . . . To the left
Naar Rechts . . . . To the right
Niet Brommen! . . . . No mopeds!
Olie . . . . Oil
Omleiding . . . . Detour
Onbewaakte Overweg . . . . Unattended railway crosing
Parkeerplaats . . . . Parking place
Parkeren Verboden . . . . No parking
Pas Op! . . . . Attention!
Politie . . . . Police

Rechts	Right
Rechts Houden	Keep to the right
Rem	Brakes
Rijbewijs	Driver's license
Rijksweg	National road
Rijwielpad	Bicycle path
Slecht Wegdek.	Rough surface
Slop-Doodlopende Weg	Dead end road (Cul-de-sac)
Smalle Brug	Narrow bridge
Snelheid Verminderen.	Reduce speed
Spoorweg Kruising	Railway crossing
Steenslag.	Gravel road
Stoplichten	Traffic lights
Straat met Eenrichtingsverkeer	One-way street
Toegang.	Access to
Tegenliggers	Two-way traffic
Tol	Toll
Tweesprong.	Fork in road
Tussen	Between
Uitgang	Exit
Uitrit Vrachtwagens.	Truck exit
Verboden Toegang	No entry
Verkeerslichten	Traffic lights
Voetgangers	Pedestrians only
Voetpad	Footpath
Weg Omlegging.	Detour
Werk in Uitveoring.	Road construction work
Zachte Berm	Soft shoulders

DAYS OF THE WEEK

Maandag	Monday
Dinsdag	Tuesday
Woensdag	Wednesday
Donderdag.	Thursday
Vrijdag	Friday
Zaterdag	Saturday
Zondag.	Sunday
Vandaag.	Today
Morgen.	Tomorrow

SEASONS:

Seizoen	Season
Voorjaar	Spring
Zomer	Summer
Herfst.	Autumn
Winter	Winter

MUSEUM CARD:

If you intend to visit eight or more museums during your stay in Holland it will pay you to invest in the **Museum Card** *(Museum Jaarkaart),* giving you free admission to some 350 museums around the country—including the best and most famous. Although it's good for an entire calendar year, the cost is so reasonable that it can pay for itself in just a few days. Available for adults or children, the card will encourage you to stop into many museums for just a short peek without having to justify the admission charge. It is sold at most museum entrances and local tourist offices throughout Holland, and requires a passport-size photo.

TELEPHONES:

Two types of **public telephones** are used throughout Holland; green ones that accept coins and blue ones that use the convenient **Telecard**, a pre-paid debit card from which the cost of each call is subtracted until its face value is all used up. These cards are available in 5-, 10-, and 25-guilder denominations at train stations, post offices, tourist offices, and many shops. Several tourist information offices are now using phone numbers prefixed with (06); these are toll calls costing 50c (one-half guilder) per minute, so talk fast.

FOOD AND DRINK:

Several choice restaurants are listed for each destination in this section. Most of these are longtime favorites of experienced travelers and serve typically Dutch food unless otherwise noted. All are open for lunch, while many other Dutch restaurants are not. Their approximate price range, based on the least expensive complete meal offered, is indicated by the following symbols:

$ — Inexpensive, but may have fancier dishes available.

$$ — Reasonable. These establishments may also feature daily specials or "Tourist Menus."

$$$ — Luxurious and expensive.

X: — Days or periods closed.

Those who take dining *very* seriously should consult an up-to-date restaurant and hotel guide such as the classic red-cover *Michelin Benelux,* issued annually around the beginning of each year. It is always wise to check the posted menus before entering, paying particular attention to any daily set-meal specials.

Dutch breakfasts, often included in your hotel rate, tend to be enormous. After filling up on eggs, ham, cheese, cold cuts, bread, juice, and coffee, you may not have much room left for lunch. This is just as well, as you can then enjoy a light meal of *uitsmijter* (a fancy open egg-and-meat sandwich), *broodje* (a simple sandwich), *braadworst* (sausage), *pannekoeken* or *poffertjes* (pancakes), *patates* (French fries) or—Heaven forbid—*nieuwe haring* (a raw herring). The latter, with or without the chopped onions, is definitely an acquired taste and is a favorite with the Dutch people. All of these are quite inexpensive, quick to eat, and often sold from streetside stands or at outdoor cafés.

A busy afternoon's sightseeing should work up a healthy appetite for dinner, which the Dutch tend to eat rather early—usually between 6 and 8 p.m. No one ever goes away hungry from one of these repasts. Traditional Dutch cuisine is simple and quite substantial, relying on the quality of its ingredients rather than culinary tricks for its delicious taste. Some specialties are: *erwtensoep* (a thick pea soup with sausages, usually served in winter), *gerookte paling* (smoked eel), *hutspot* (beef stew), and *gebraden kip* (roast chicken). *Hollandse biefstuk* is an excellent beefsteak, while *Duitse biefstuk* is more like a Salisbury steak. Potatoes (*aardappelen*) and vegetables (*groente*) come with virtually every meal. Holland, of course, is famous for its fine cheeses (*kaas*), including Gouda, Edam, and Leidse—which seem to be tastier here than when exported.

The best of traditional Dutch cuisine can be savored at reasonable prices in over 200 restaurants that display the "**Neerlands Dis**" sign with its red, white, and blue soup tureen. Ask at a tourist office for a list of these.

Always a seafaring people, the Dutch have long embraced the exotic cooking of their overseas trading partners and former colonies. Foremost among these are the various Indonesian specialties such as *rijsttafel* (a miniature feast of many spicy dishes), *nasi goreng* (rice with meats, fish, vegetables, and more), and *bami goreng* (the same, with noodles). In many neighborhood restaurants these tend to get mixed up with Chinese dishes, creating a uniquely Dutch "Oriental" style. You'll also come across a tremendous range of other restaurants, featuring just about every kind of international cooking there is, so your palate need never get bored.

More than 280 restaurants now participate in the time-proven "**Tourist Menu**" plan sponsored by the tourist office. These quality establishments offer a three-course meal of their own specialties at one fixed, nationwide price. They can be identified by the blue sign with a fork between the words "Tourist Menu." A free brochure listing all of them is available at VVV and NBT tourist offices in Holland and abroad. Some other restaurants offer a "tourist menu," often at the same price, but unless they have the blue sign they are not part of the official plan and might not live up to the quality standards.

Another good way to cut dining costs is to always check out the daily specials, identified by the word *dagschotel.* Your restaurant bill will almost invariably include a service charge and tax. It is customary to round out the amount to the next guilder, leaving the small change and perhaps an additional tip if the service was exceptional.

Dutch beers are justly famous throughout the world, and if you're a beer drinker you are probably already familiar with them. They are usually referred to as *pils* on menus. It is always interesting to experiment with local brands other than the well-known export labels. Among distilled spirits, the most noted Dutch firewater is a type of gin known as *jenever,* which comes as *jonge* (young) or *oude* (old), and is always drunk neat. Beware.

SUGGESTED TOURS:

The do-it-yourself walking tours in this section are relatively short and easy to follow. On the assumption that most readers will be traveling by public transportation, they always begin at the local train station or bus stop. Those going by car can make a simple adjustment. Suggested routes are shown by heavy broken lines on the maps, while the circled numbers refer to attractions or points of reference along the way, with corresponding numbers in the text.

Trying to see everything in any given town could easily become an exhausting marathon. You will certainly enjoy yourself more by being selective and passing up anything that doesn't catch your fancy in favor of a friendly café. Forgiveness will be granted if you fail to visit *every* museum.

Practical information, such as the opening times of various attractions, is as accurate as was possible at the time of writing. Everything is, of course, subject to change. You should always check with the local tourist office if seeing a particular sight is crucially important to you.

As a way of estimating the time any segment of a walking tour will take, you can look at the scale on the map and figure that the average person covers about 100 yards per minute. The maps, by the way, were drawn to best fit the page size. North does not necessarily point to the top, but is always indicated by an arrow.

* OUTSTANDING ATTRACTIONS:

An * asterisk before any attraction, be it an entire daytrip or just one exhibit in a museum, denotes a special treat that in the author's opinion should not be missed.

TOURIST INFORMATION:

Virtually every town of interest to tourists in Holland has its own information office, which can help you with specific questions or perhaps book local accommodations. These are always known by the letters **VVV** (often depicted as a blue-and-white triangle) which stand for words you couldn't possibly pronounce. The locations of these offices are shown on the town maps in this book by the word "**info.**," and repeated along with the phone number under the "Tourist Information" section for each trip. To phone ahead from another town in Holland you must first dial the area code, which always begins with 0 and is shown in parentheses, followed by the local number. Pay phones use coins and have operating instructions in English on them. VVV offices displaying the **i-Netherland** sign can provide information for the entire country.

ADVANCE PLANNING INFORMATION:

The **Netherlands Board of Tourism (NBT)** has branches throughout the world that will gladly provide help in planning your trip. In North America these are located at:

225 North Michigan Avenue, Suite 326
Chicago, IL 60601
☎ (312) 819-0300, FAX (312) 819-1740

25 Adelaide Street East, Suite 710
Toronto, Ont. M5C 1Y2
Canada
☎ (416) 363-1577, FAX (416) 363-1470

In England, they are at 25-28 Buckingham Gate, **London** SW1E 6NT, ☎ (0171) 828-7900, FAX (0171) 828-7941.

In Australia, the address is 5 Elizabeth Street, **Sydney** NSW 2000, ☎ (02) 247-6921, FAX (02) 223-6665.

*Amsterdam

Other European cities may be exciting, glamorous, sophisticated, or even unique. Amsterdam alone is *gezellig*. This untranslatable word, which more or less means cozy, also connotes intimacy, friendliness, and warmth. Perhaps that is why a city of only 700,000 souls should consistently capture fourth place among all of Europe's many tourist meccas, yielding in popularity only to London, Paris, and Rome.

Despite its delightfully human scale and old-fashioned charm, Amsterdam is a worldly place, filled with people of every imaginable origin. It is very different from the rest of Holland, of which it is the nominal capital—although the government actually resides at The Hague. Being the hub of an extremely efficient rail and highway network makes it the perfect base from which to explore the entire country on remarkably easy daytrips. This plan has the added attraction of returning you each evening to a city noted for its fine restaurants, cultural activities, and exciting night life, as well as for its wide selection of accommodations in every possible price range.

Amsterdam began as a tiny fishing village located near the point where the Amstel River flowed into the IJ and the Zuider Zee. In the late 13th century its inhabitants built a dam across the river to control flooding, thus the origin of the old name, *Amstelledamme*, recognized on a tax exemption agreement of 1275. The town received its charter in 1300 and was a rich trading port as early as the 15th century.

Both the Reformation and a period of Spanish rule temporarily halted its growth, but after 1578 its liberal attitudes attracted refugees fleeing the terrors of the Inquisition. It was their talents and hard work that culminated in the "Golden Age" of the 17th century, during which the city expanded with the addition of the concentric rings of canals that today lend so much color to Amsterdam. Trade declined during the French occupation of the late 18th and early 19th centuries, only to rebound after the opening of the North Sea Canal in 1876.

A wise series of zoning laws has since protected the inner city's essentially 17th-century appearance, preserving that wonderful coziness the Dutch love so well. Their own long tradition of tolerance has led in recent decades to problems with drugs and counter-culture excesses, most of which will probably be solved in time.

There is far more in Amsterdam than can possibly be seen in one day. The "get acquainted" walking tour described in this chapter will give you a good sampling of the treats that await you after that, which can be enjoyed between daytrips to the rest of Holland.

GETTING THERE:

Trains link Amsterdam's Centraal Station with just about every other town in Holland, and operate at such frequent intervals that reference to schedules is rarely necessary. Some typical running times are: Haarlem—15 minutes, Utrecht—30 minutes, Alkmaar—35 minutes, The Hague—45 minutes, Delft—55 minutes, Rotterdam—1 hour, and (about as far as you can possibly go) Maastricht—$2\frac{1}{2}$ hours. There are also good international services to Belgium (Brussels in under 3 hours), Germany (Cologne in 3 hours), France (Paris in under $5\frac{1}{2}$ hours), and other European cities as well.

By car, Amsterdam is only 15 miles from Haarlem, 22 miles from Utrecht, 25 miles from Alkmaar, 34 miles from The Hague, 36 miles from Delft, 47 miles from Rotterdam, and the tremendously long distance of 132 miles from Maastricht—all by superb modern highways. Recommended routes are shown in the chapters for these and other towns.

By air, Amsterdam is served with direct flights from every corner of Europe and the world. Its magnificent Schiphol Airport is only 6 miles from the city center and has its own train station right at the terminal, with very frequent departures for Amsterdam's Centraal Station (17 minutes away) as well as to other cities in Holland, Belgium, and beyond.

GETTING AROUND:

Amsterdam has an amazingly good public transit system, easily one of the best in Europe. Consisting of trams, buses, and a subway (*Metro*), it operates between about 6 a.m. and midnight, with night buses (*nachtbussen*) taking over the main routes after that. Most of the routes begin or end right in front of Centraal Station.

To make effective use of the system, you will need a pocket-size **transit map**, which is available free at the **GVB** office in front of Cen-

traal Station, on the Leidseplein, and at other locations. This explains—in clear English—exactly how to use public transportation in
Amsterdam and describes the several ticketing and pass options available to you, some of which can cut your costs considerably. Buying
a single ticket from the driver is convenient, but is always the most
expensive way to travel. Don't forget to stamp your ticket in the yellow stamping machine upon boarding—there are occasional inspec-
tions, and failure to have a time-stamped ticket will result in a fine.
Those using the **Netherlands Rail Rover** pass *with* the **Public Transport Link** option attached can, of course, ride free.

The **trams** (streetcars) are a particularly enjoyable way of getting
around and give you a wonderful view of the passing street scenes.
Don't miss out on this urban treat.

WHEN TO GO:

Some of Amsterdam's main attractions, especially the Rijksmuseum, can be very crowded during the peak summer season. Things
are much calmer during late spring and early fall, when the weather
is still fine.

A few of the major museums are closed on Mondays, and most do
not open until 1 p.m. on Sundays and holidays.

FOOD AND DRINK:

You can satisfy virtually any appetite in Amsterdam, regardless of
how exotic it may be. The wide choice of cuisines reflects the diverse
ethnic mixture of the city's population, and offers the Dutch a welcome alternative to their tasty but sometimes monotonous diet.

The choice of restaurants listed below, all open for lunch, are
along or near the suggested walking tour route. Other parts of the
city are blessed with equally fine establishments—as you will quickly
discover.

> **Swarte Schaep** (Korte Leidsedwarsstraat 24, just off the Leid-
> seplein) 17th-century interior, with a huge wine selection.
> Phone (020) 622-3021. $$$
>
> **Les Quatre Canetons** (Prinsengracht 1111, 2 blocks southwest
> of the Magere Brug) Light French cuisine, fresh fish. Phone
> (020) 624-6307. X: Sun. $$$
>
> **Oesterbar** (Leidseplein 10) An upstairs/downstairs place spe-
> cializing in seafood, open very late. Phone (020) 623-2988. $$
> and $$$
>
> **Port van Cleve** (N.Z. Voorburgwal 178, near the Nieuwe Kerk)
> Steaks and traditional Dutch cooking. Phone (020) 624-0047.
> $$
>
> **Kopenhagen** (Rokin 84, a block east of the Historical Museum)

Danish cuisine, especially good for fish. Phone (020) 624-2614. X: Sun. $$

Dikker en Thijs (Leidsestraat 80, 2 blocks east of Leidseplein) A gourmet brasserie with Dutch and French cuisine. Phone (020) 627-7721. $$

Bodega Keijzer (Van Baerlestraat 96, just southwest of the Stedelijk Museum) Traditional Dutch cuisine. Phone (020) 671-1441. $$

Mirafiori Hobbemastraat 2, 2 blocks northwest of the Rijksmuseum) Simple but good Italian food. Phone (020) 662-3013. $$

Haesje Claes (Spuistraat 275, a block west of the Begijnhof) An old favorite for traditional fare. Phone (020) 624-99-98. $ and $$

Sama Sebu (P.C. Hooftstraat 27, 1 block northwest of the Rijksmuseum) A favorite Indonesian restaurant noted for *rijsttafel*. Phone (020) 662-8146. $ and $$

Kueken van 1870 (Spuistraat 4, 4 blocks southwest of Centraal Station) Dutch food at rock-bottom prices, interesting clientele. $

Scheltema (N.Z. Voorburgwal 242, 3 blocks southwest of the Royal Palace) A traditional café with good food. $

Egg Cream (St. Jacobstraat 19, 5 blocks southwest of Centraal Station, west of Damrak) A very popular vegetarian restaurant. $

Those in a hurry or still stuffed from an enormous Dutch breakfast will find a multitude of sandwich shops (*broodjeswinkels*) and pancake houses (*pannekoekhuysje*) for a small, inexpensive snack. The cafeterias in the major museums are also good time- and money-savers. Familiar fast-food outlets are quite common, particularly around Kalverstraat, Leidseplein, and Rembrandtsplein.

The venerable **brown cafés** (*bruine kroegen*) are an Amsterdam institution where you can get a friendly drink along with a maximum of Dutch atmosphere. They're located just about everywhere, and are so called because their walls are often stained brown after centuries of tobacco smoke. Each has its own peculiar ambiance, so you'll be sure to find one you like.

TOURIST INFORMATION:

Amsterdam's main tourist office (**VVV**), phone (06) 3403-4066 (toll call) is located just outside Centraal Station. Besides answering your questions, it also provides an accommodations booking service, changes money, and sells maps and guidebooks. It is often very crowded during the peak tourist season, so you may want to use the branch office on Leidseplein instead.

Amsterdam's Centraal Station

SUGGESTED TOUR:

Begin your walk at **Centraal Station** (1), easily reached from anywhere in Amsterdam. Built in 1885 by the noted architect P. J. H. Cuypers, its ornate exterior is a fanciful mix of Gothic and Renaissance elements. It sits atop 8,687 piles on three artificial islands, an arrangement similar to that used by virtually all large buildings in this very water-logged city. Over 1,000 trains a day stop at its elevated platforms and radiate out to nearly all points in Holland. A classic among the railway stations of the world, it even served in 1900 as a model for Tokyo's central station.

The large open area in front of the station is called **Stationsplein**, the suffix *plein* meaning square. It may strike you as being more of a zoo during the summer, when it is often populated with as weird an assemblage of oddballs as you're likely to find anywhere. Among the crowds there are usually several performing street musicians, adding a joyful character to an already exuberant scene. Some of them are quite good and deserve a listening—and a tip. A multitude of tram lines and many buses begin their routes here, as does the Metro. The main tourist office (**VVV**) is located in an historic old coffeehouse building on the water's edge. From this point all of Amsterdam lies spread out before you.

Continue straight ahead onto **Damrak**, a wide shopping street bor-

Crowds in Front of the Station

dering the inner harbor. Several companies along the jetties both here and elsewhere offer **canal cruises**, a wonderful way to spend an hour or so seeing Amsterdam from a unique angle. The evening cruises, often featuring wine and cheese along with the views, are the most enjoyable. Following the old course of the Amstel River, Damrak leads past the Stock Exchange *(Beurs)*, an early example of modern architecture, which dates from 1903 and is noted for its decorative brickwork.

Dam Square, usually just called *Dam*, is on the site of the original dam around which the town developed in the late 13th century. Still the heart of the city, this large open area is frequently crowded with a fascinating assortment of people. The National Monument, near its center, commemorates the Dutch role in World War II, while standing nearby is the world-famous 19th-century Hotel Krasnapolsky as well as several large department stores.

The massive **Royal Palace** *(Koninklijk Paleis)* (2) dominates the entire west side of Dam. Once regarded as the eighth wonder of the world, it was built in the mid-17th-century as a town hall and was adopted as a royal residence in 1808 by Louis Bonaparte, appointed King of the Netherlands by his brother, Napoleon. He left behind a magnificent collection of Empire furniture, which is still there along with all of the wonderful art. It may seem surprising that such a regal

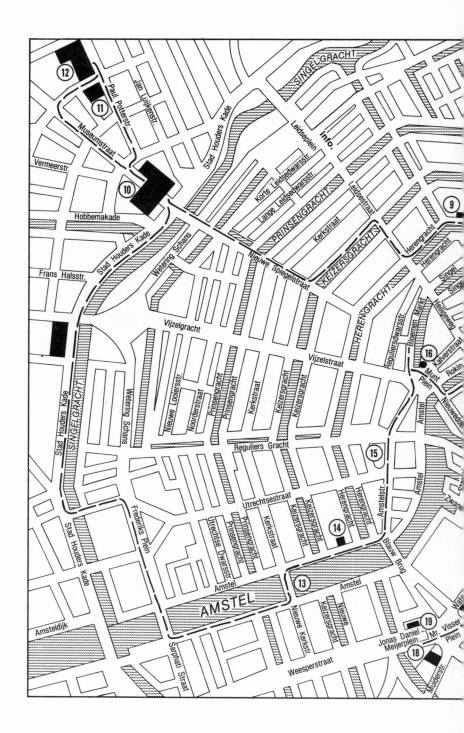

structure has no formal entrance, but this was deliberately done to keep rioting mobs from breaking in. Today, the palace is only occasionally used by the queen, and is open to the public at other times. Visits may usually be made daily from 12:30–5 p.m.

Next to this is the **New Church** *(Nieuwe Kerk)* (3), which actually dates from the early 15th century and which has been heavily altered many times since. Traditionally used for royal investitures, its principal function today is as a venue for concerts and exhibitions. The interior is noted for its baroque woodcarving, 16th- and 17th-century organs, and stained-glass windows. There are also tombs of several of Holland's national heroes. It is usually open daily from 11 a.m. to 5 p.m.

Across the square is **Madame Tussaud's Scenerama** (4), the Dutch answer to the British original. Ever-changing exhibitions here depict famous people and events from both the past and the present, all modeled in wax and enhanced with the latest in special effects technology. Although this is a commercial enterprise, it is thoroughly enjoyable and gives you a chance to view history from a popular Dutch perspective. It is open daily, from 10 a.m. until 5:30 p.m. or later.

At this point you may want to make a little **side trip** to one of Holland's most interesting—and poignant—attractions. The route on the map crosses three major canals: the **Singel**, once the town's outer defensive moat; the aristocratic **Herengracht**, where the richest merchants had their homes; and the **Keizersgracht**, where the slightly less wealthy lived in elegance. The 17th-century houses along these waterways are remarkably well preserved today, and many are used as offices, museums, and the like, as well as for highly desirable residences.

In former times, the merely prosperous had to make do with the **Prinsengracht**, along which you will find the *Anne Frank House (5).
Much has been written about the heart-rending tragedy that occurred here, but words can never convey the touching experience of an actual visit. The Frank family were Jews who had fled Nazi Germany in 1933 and set up a business in Amsterdam. Holland was occupied by Hitler's forces in 1940, and by 1942 the situation had become so grim that the Franks went into hiding in secret, hidden quarters at the rear of the shop. They were discovered in 1944 and sent to concentration camps, where all except Mr. Frank perished. Left behind was the diary of their teenage daughter, Anne, which was returned to the father after the war and later published. Translated into a multitude of languages and made into plays and movies, *The Diary of Anne Frank* is an eloquent testimony to the spirit of mankind. The tiny quarters in which the family lived have been preserved, and the rest of the house now serves as a center for the study of racism and fascism. Visits may

be made Mondays through Saturdays, from 9 a.m. to 5 p.m.; and on Sundays and holidays from 10 a.m. to 5 p.m. It is closed on Yom Kippur, Christmas, and New Year's Day.

Continue on to the nearby **Westerkerk** (6), a beautiful early-17th-century church with the highest tower in town. You may climb all 279 feet of it for an astonishing *view across the city, but only from April through September, on Mondays through Saturdays from 10 a.m. to 5 p.m. The properly Spartan interior contains a fine organ from 1687 as well as Rembrandt's tomb, although it is not known whether the artist is actually buried here. A carillon in the tower plays lovely tunes every half-hour, day and night. From here, a short stroll down Raadhuis Straat returns you to the Royal Palace (2) and Dam Square.

Busy, narrow, and completely pedestrianized, **Kalverstraat** is Amsterdam's most popular shopping street. Despite its crowds, it leads to one of the quietest and most unusual attractions in town. Turn right into a tiny alleyway at number 92 to reach the **Amsterdam Historical Museum** (7), located in the rambling rooms and corridors of the former municipal orphanage. Parts of this fascinating complex date from as far back as the 16th century. The number of interesting displays here is immense, as befits one of the world's major trading cities. To see even a decent sampling of them will require several hours, so you may want to return on another day. Holders of the economical Museum Card can, of course, just wander through for a quick look without having to invest in a admission charge. A floor plan in English, showing a suggested route, is available, and the museum is open daily from 11 a.m. to 5 p.m.

The south exit from the museum opens into the utterly delightful *Begijnhof (8), an anachronism in this busy metropolis. Founded in 1346 as a quiet residential courtyard for members of a lay sisterhood who cared for the poor and sick, but were not bound by religious vows, it is still lined with ancient houses, one of which (number 34) dates from 1470. The rest are from the 16th through the 18th centuries, and are occupied by elderly women who pay nominal rents. The church at the south end was turned over to the Scottish Presbyterian Church in 1607 and was used by the Pilgrim Fathers before leaving for the New World. It remains with that faith today. Opposite it is a small Catholic chapel where the *Begijns* continued to worship in secret after the Reformation. Don't miss exploring this little oasis of serenity in the middle of a bustling city.

A tiny passageway leads onto Spui. Turn right and walk past the Singel Canal to the Herengracht, the loveliest of Amsterdam's canals. Many of the 17th-century houses here feature elaborate gables and, of course, the ubiquitous hoisting beams still used to haul furniture to the upper floors. Cross the water and turn left to the **Bijbels Mu-**

Viewing the Night Watch *in the Rijksmuseum*

seum (9), located in a fine old house from 1662. This non-denominational museum is devoted to Judaeo-Christian exhibitions of Biblical subjects and of ancient life in the Holy Land. It is open Tuesdays through Saturdays, 10 a.m. to 5 p.m.; and on Sundays and holidays from 1–5 p.m.

Continue along the canal and turn right on Leidsestraat. This busy shopping street leads to the Leidseplein, a highly popular square lined with cafés, restaurants, and entertainments. You may want to return there in the evening, but for now make a left turn after crossing the Keizersgracht Canal and amble down to Nieuwe Spiegelstraat. A right turn on this attractive street will take you past a wonderful assortment of quality antique shops.

Directly ahead of you lies the world-famous ***Rijksmuseum** (10), surely one of the greatest art galleries in Europe. Now, there are many *Rijksmuseums* (the word simply means "national museum") throughout Holland, but this is *the* Rijksmuseum. Its strong resemblance to the Centraal Station is more than coincidental; they were both built by the same architect in the 1880s. Hordes of visitors come here each day to see Rembrandt's masterpiece, the **Night Watch,* whose name is a misnomer, as the large canvas actually depicts a daylight scene, long obscured by so much grime that it was thought to be at night.

In the Begijnhof

Located in its own gallery, the painting is very easy to find—just follow the crowds.

While there, you will of course want to see works by some of the other ***Dutch Masters**, such as Frans Hals, Vermeer, Jan Steen, and many more. The collection of Rembrandts is particularly rich, as would be expected. Non-Dutch artists represented include Bruegel, Rubens, Fra' Angelico, Tintoretto, Botticelli, El Greco, Goya, and Velázquez. With over 250 rooms, the museum displays more art and related objects than you could possibly digest in one visit, so you may want to plan on coming back at another time. This makes a good argument for purchasing the economical Museum Card *(Jaarkaart)*, available at the entrance and elsewhere. The Rijksmuseum is open Tuesdays through Saturdays, from 10 a.m. to 5 p.m.; and on Sundays and holidays from 1–5 p.m. It is closed on Mondays. While there, you might ask about getting permission to visit the Six Collection (14), a private mansion located farther along this walking tour. Filled with outstanding art, it allows only a small number of visitors, who must first obtain a note of introduction from the Rijksmuseum to be admitted.

There are two other outstanding art museums in the immediate neighborhood, both of which also accept the Museum Card. The first of these is the ***Van Gogh Museum** (11), devoted primarily to the life and works of the renowned Dutch-born painter Vincent van Gogh (1853–1890). There are also pieces by some of his contemporaries, as well as his own private collection of Oriental art. All of this is housed in a strikingly modern structure, and may be seen on Mondays through Saturdays, from 10 a.m. to 5 p.m.; and on Sundays and holidays from 1–5 p.m.

Next door to this is the **Stedelijk Museum** (12), Amsterdam's municipal museum of modern art. Founded in the 1890s to display contemporary works for which there was no room in the already-overflowing Rijksmuseum, it is especially noted for its excellent **temporary exhibitions** . The permanent collection includes works by the Dutch artists van Gogh, Mondriaan, Karel Appel, and de Kooning. Among the foreigners represented are Chagall, Picasso, Cézanne, Dubuffet, Manet, Monet, Matisse, and Vlaminck; as well as present-day Americans such as Warhol and Lichtenstein. The outdoor sculpture garden is embellished with works by Rodin, Moore, and others. Visits may be made on any day, from 11 a.m. to 5 p.m. There may be an extra charge for special exhibitions.

Now follow the map along the Singelgracht Canal (not to be confused with the Singel), passing many of the houseboats on which thousands of Amsterdammers live, either by choice or because they can't find apartments on dry land. The route will also take you past the Heineken Brewery, which has extremely popular tasting tours several times a day.

Make a left into Frederiksplein and continue along Sarphatistraat across the Amstel River, then turn left past the locks to the rather quaint **Magere Brug** (13), a hand-operated wooden drawbridge originally built in 1671 and faithfully reconstructed several times since. Stroll across this and turn right along the water's edge. The **Six Collection** (14) is located in a luxurious 17th-century house at Amstel 218. Jan Six, a former mayor of Amsterdam, was a friend and patron of Rembrandt's, whose paintings grace the house—along with works by other noted Dutch artists of the period. Because the house is still owned by descendants of *Burgemeester* Six, and because its contents are priceless, only a small number of visitors are allowed in, after first obtaining a card of introduction from the Rijksmuseum.

Continue along the Amstel River to the **Blauw Brug**, an ornate bridge obviously inspired by the Pont Alexandre III in Paris. Despite its name, it's not blue. From here, Amstelstraat leads into **Rembrandtsplein** (15), a large square with many attractive cafés and restaurants, an excellent place for a well-deserved rest stop. Along with the Leidseplein, this is a very popular spot for night life. The difference between the two is that the Rembrandtsplein appeals to a some-

The Muntplein

what more sedate crowd than the young people who dominate the Leidseplein.

Muntplein (16) is just a block away. Named for the 15th-century *Munttoren,* an elegant tower that once housed the mint and is now an Amsterdam landmark, this large square is actually a bridge over the junction of two canals. The 17th-century steeple atop the tower has a carillon that chimes out old Dutch tunes every half-hour. Right behind it, on the Singel Canal, is the colorful floating **flower market**, where you can buy flowers right off the barges on Mondays through Saturdays.

Cross the little extension of the Amstel River and turn left on Oude Turfmarkt past the **Allard Pierson Museum**, which houses the University of Amsterdam's archaeological collections. The route now threads its way through an old part of town, going through one of the university's buildings in a delightful passageway called the Oudemanhuis-poort, sheltering a variety of second-hand bookstalls. Crossing another drawbridge, it follows Staalstraat and turns left just before the modern City Hall *(Stadhuis)* and Opera House.

The **Rembrandt Huis** (17) at Jodenbreestraat 4 was, for about 20 years, the home of the renowned artist, whose full name is Rembrandt Harmenszoom van Rijn. Born in Leiden in 1606, he bought this rather comfortable house in 1639, after he was already famous and commanded lucrative commissions. Rembrandt lived luxuriously in those days, and after his popularity declined—due partly to his refusal to compromise his art by flattering patrons—his expensive tastes got him into financial trouble. He was declared bankrupt in 1656, and the house was sold to help pay the debts, although he continued to live in it until 1660. Despite these crushing burdens and the deaths of both his wife and son, Rembrandt's art became increasingly rich in spiritual values right up until his death in 1669. Purchased by the city in 1906, the interior of the house has been restored as nearly as possible to its original condition, with some of his personal possessions on display. It contains a fabulous collection of some 250 etchings by the master. The Rembrandt Huis is open Mondays through Saturdays, from 10 a.m. to 5 p.m.; and on Sundays and holidays from 1–5 p.m. Museum cards are accepted.

From here you might want to make a little side trip into the old Jewish quarter, just a few blocks to the southeast. Continue down Jodenbreestraat to Mr. Visserplein, near which is the famous **Mozes en Aaron Kerk** . An impressive neoclassical Catholic church built in 1840 whose name reflects the Jewish character of this area, it serves today primarily as a youth center. Close by, on Jonas Daniel Meijerplein, stands the beautiful **Portugees-Israelitische Synagoge** (18), built in the baroque style in 1675 by the local Sephardic community. These were descendants of refugees from Portugal and Spain, one of the many religious groups who have always found acceptance among the tolerant Dutch. Visitors are welcome to view the fine interior, said to be modeled after the Temple of Solomon, on Sundays through Fridays from 10 a.m. to 4 or 5 p.m.

Crossing the adjacent square, you will pass the **Dock Worker Statue**, a memorial to the brave Amsterdammers who went on a 24-hour strike in February, 1941, in protest against Nazi deportation of Jews. Near this is the **Joods Historisch Museum** (19), located in four adjoining former synagogues. Its exhibits are mostly concerned with the history of Jewish life in Holland, and may be seen daily except on Yom Kippur, from 11 a.m. to 5 p.m. Museum Cards are accepted.

Return on Jodenbreestraat and turn left on Nieuwe Hoogstraat. At this corner stands the **Zuiderkerk**, the first church to be built in Amsterdam after the Reformation. It served as a subject for some of Rembrandt's paintings, as well as an inspiration for Sir Christopher Wren in his designs for London church steeples. A right turn at the canal takes you past the 17th-century **Trippenhuis**, a magnificent mansion built by two wealthy munitions manufacturers. Note the gun-barrel motifs on the chimneys and on the pediment. From 1815 until 1885 this was the home of the Rijksmuseum. Opposite, at number 26, is the Little Trip House, built for one of the servants and reputed to be the narrowest house in the world.

Just a few more steps and you are in the Nieuw Markt, a large open square noted for its imposing **Waag**, or weighhouse. Originally a 15th-century gate in the old town walls, it has seen many other uses over the years. During the 17th century, the surgeon's guild held their weekly anatomy lessons here, as is commemorated by Rembrandt's two renowned paintings on the subject. You are now entering the notorious *Walletjes*, Amsterdam's famous **Red Light District**. It is perfectly safe for tourists to walk around here, but be sure to hang onto your wallet and be careful about taking pictures. True to its name, there actually are red lights illuminating the shop windows, behind which sit the available girls. Prostitution is legal here, and drugs—though technically forbidden—are sold in some of the bars. Zeedijk, actually a rather elegant old street, is lined with sleazy porno shops and cheap bars, as are many of the surrounding streets and alleyways.

Ironically, right in the middle of all this "sin" stands the venerable **Oude Kerk** (20), Amsterdam's oldest church. Built around 1306 and enlarged over the next few centuries, it is also the biggest church in town. Much of its pre-Reformation splendor has survived the Calvinist desecrations, making it among the most interesting churches in Holland to visit. Of particular interest are the three 16th-century stained-glass windows in the north aisle, opposite the choir, and the elaborately carved wooden choir stalls. The church is open to tourists on Mondays through Saturdays, from 11 a.m. to 5 p.m., and Sundays afternoons; with shorter hours in winter.

Now follow the canal to the last attraction on this walking tour. The **Museum Amstelkring** (21), otherwise known as *"Ons Lieve Heer op Solder"* ("Our Dear Lord in the Attic"), is a perfectly preserved example of the clandestine Catholic churches that thrived in Amsterdam during the Calvinist era. Actually, they were tolerated as long as they remained "invisible." As the name suggests, this one was in the attic of three adjoining houses. The rest of the building, which you pass through, is furnished as it was in the 17th and 18th centuries. Still used for occasional services, such as weddings, the secret church is open for visits Mondays through Saturdays, from 10 a.m. to 5 p.m.; and on Sundays and holidays from 1–5 p.m. Museum Cards are accepted. From here it's a short stroll back to Centraal Station.

ADDITIONAL SIGHTS:

Amsterdam has a great many other attractions, which could not be covered on this walking tour, but which you might want to visit between daytrips to other parts of Holland. Among the most interesting are:

The **Nederlands Historisch Scheepvaartsmuseum**, or Netherlands Maritime Museum, is located on Kattenburgerplein at the east end of Prins Hendrikkade, about a mile southeast of Centraal Station (bus number 22 or 28). A real treat for ship enthusiasts, this 17th-century arsenal has fabulous displays of Holland's maritime history, as well as a few actual vessels moored outside. It's open on Tuesdays through Saturdays, 10 a.m. to 5 p.m.; and also on Sundays and Mondays in summer.

The **Heineken Brewery** at Stadhouderskade 78, a short stroll east of the Rijksmuseum (trams 16, 24, or 25 from Centraal Station) offers free beer at the end of their tour, on Mondays through Fridays at 9:30 and 11 a.m., and also at 1 and 2:30 p.m. in summer. The nominal admission goes to charity.

The **Tropenmuseum** (Tropical Museum) is at the edge of the Oosterpark, about two miles southeast of Centraal Station. You can get there via tram numbers 9 or 14, or bus number 22. Formerly concerned with colonial affairs, it is now devoted to life in Third World countries. Visits may be made Mondays through Fridays from 10 a.m. to 5 p.m., and on weekends and holidays from noon to 5 p.m. Museum Cards accepted.

The **Aviodome** at Schiphol Airport is a fascinating place to examine the history of aviation, complete with old planes, while waiting for your flight. It's open daily, except on Mondays in winter.

Volendam, Marken, and Edam

Volendam is almost certainly the number one daytrip destination for tourists staying in Amsterdam. Most of its many visitors come on highly promoted guided tours, but you can have much more fun by doing it yourself. Not only will you see more worthwhile sights, but you'll travel at your own pace—and save money, too. This easy little excursion includes a boat trip to nearby Marken, and winds up in the delightful cheese town of Edam before returning to Amsterdam.

Sophisticated travelers may dismiss Volendam—and to some extent Marken—as tourist traps, which of course they are, but they're good ones if taken in the right spirit. Cute, quaint, and ever so commercialized, these two small towns can nevertheless be very enjoyable places to visit. Much less touristed, Edam offers genuine Old Dutch charm along with a refreshing interlude away from the hordes.

When the former Zuider Zee was cut off from the North Sea by the completion of the Afsluitdijk in 1932, it became the IJsselmeer, which is gradually being reclaimed by the creation of *polders,* areas of dry land lying below sea level and protected by dikes. Until then, both Volendam and Marken were fishing villages whose prosperity depended on access to the open sea. Now, surrounded by fresh water and under the threat of eventually becoming nearly landlocked, they have found a new source of employment in the tourist trade. Much of their charming, old-fashioned character has been preserved, even if some of it is more than a little commercialized. Despite this, and despite the pictures in travel brochures, exceedingly few of the local people continue to wear the traditional costumes they were once famous for. Edam, on the other hand, is the real thing. Lying slightly inland, its well-preserved atmosphere has made it a choice residential community for some of Amsterdam's commuters.

GETTING THERE:

This compact trio of small towns, just outside Amsterdam, is in one of the few areas of Holland that is not served by rail.

Buses operated by NZH depart central Amsterdam frequently for the 30-minute ride to Volendam. You can board one of these from the platforms to the left as you leave Centraal Station—just across the water beyond the tourist office (VVV). Routes number 110 and 112 go direct to Volendam; take number 111 if you prefer to start with Marken. Be careful not to confuse these with the NZH *"Marken Express"* bus, which is for package tours. As with all public buses in Holland, holders of the Rail Rover Pass with the Public Transport Link option travel free—otherwise you can pay the driver or use the national *Strippenkaart*.

By car, take the IJ Tunnel from central Amsterdam and continue on the N-10 and N-247 highways to Volendam, a distance of 13 miles. It is possible to drive to Marken by way of Monnickendam, but the boat is more fun.

WHEN TO GO:

This trip can be made on any fine day between early April and the end of October. Good weather is essential. A few sights are closed on Sunday mornings.

FOOD AND DRINK:

Some choice restaurants are:

In Volendam:

Van Diepen (Haven 35, at the north end of the harbor) A popular restaurant by the waterfront, with Old Dutch atmosphere. $$$

Spaander (Haven 15, just north of the harbor) A hotel with a dining room and outdoor café, *Neerlands Dis* menu. $$

De Witte Haven (Zuideinde 5, at the south end of the harbor) A *gezellig* fish restaurant with other dishes available, *Tourist Menu.* $

In Edam:

Damhotel (Keizersgracht 1, near Damplein) A small old hotel with a specialty restaurant. $$

TOURIST INFORMATION:

The tourist office (VVV) for Volendam, phone (02993) 63-747, is at Zeestraat 37, by the bus stop. In Edam, the local VVV is in the Town Hall on Damplein, phone (02993) 71-727.

The Harbor at Volendam

SUGGESTED TOUR:

Begin your walk in Volendam at the **bus stop** (1) on Zeestraat, next to the tourist office. Those coming by car will find several parking lots in the immediate area. Continue straight ahead to the harbor and turn left. The town is full of interesting little sights, best seen by just ambling around aimlessly. The shops, cafés, and restaurants along Haven are completely tourist oriented—at some of them you can even have your picture taken wearing the old traditional costumes. There is, of course, no shortage of wooden shoes for sale, should you actually want a pair. Be sure to get off the main street and stroll among the small houses to the north and west.

Return to the **harbor** (2) and board a **Marken Express boat** to Marken, first buying a round-trip (*retour*) ticket and making sure that the boat is going direct to Marken. These leave about every half-hour, from 10 a.m. until 5:30 p.m. daily, between March 1st and October 31st. There are outdoor seats on the top deck and a bar down below.

Marken was an island, isolated from the rest of Holland until 1957, when a causeway was built connecting it to nearby Monnickendam. This is eventually to become a part of the proposed Markerwaard *polder,* whose development has been held up (hopefully forever) by environmental considerations. Being Calvinist for many centuries, its traditions are quite different from those of Catholic Volendam. You will actually see older people here wearing the rather severe local costumes, and perhaps even wooden shoes. Although the island is

In the Marker Museum

often overrun with tourists, the natives pay little attention to them other than extracting a few guilders in the shops near the harbor.

The boat arrives at Marken's compact ***harbor** (3), which is lined with picturesque little wooden houses. One or two of these can even be visited for a small fee. The same style of building continues throughout the entire village, which is remarkably free of traffic, as only the local residents are allowed to drive there. Visitors must park in the huge lot at the end of the causeway. A walk through the village will reveal many interesting details, and should include a visit to the **main church**, from whose ceiling hang ship models and fishing nets. Close to this is the **Marker Museum** (4), located in four small adjoining smokehouses on the Kerkbuurt. Reconstructed room settings here tell the story of local life in former times, a treat not to be missed. The museum is open between Easter and the end of October, Mondays through Saturdays from 10 a.m. to 4:30 p.m.; and on Sundays from noon until 4 p.m.

Just beyond the village, particularly to the north, are small market gardens, where you might see older farmers working the land in their traditional costumes, including wooden shoes. Return to the harbor and board the boat back to Volendam. Ask to make certain that it is not going somewhere else, as some of them do.

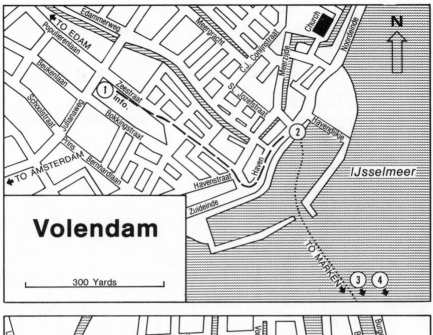

Volendam

300 Yards

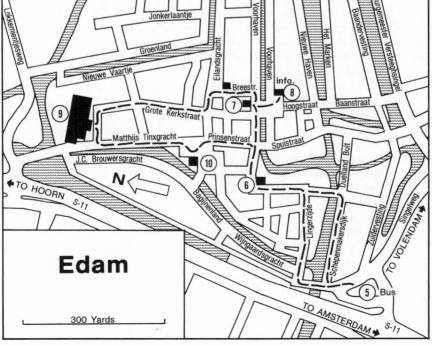

Edam

300 Yards

From the Volendam harbor (2), stroll back to the bus stop (1) and get on the next bus to Edam (routes 110 or 112), a trip of only two miles. Edam began in the 12th century as a little settlement on the Ee River, and received its charter as early as 1357. It was an important shipbuilding center until the 17th century, when flood control measures cut it off from the Zuider Zee. The surrounding land, formerly underwater, made excellent pasturage, thus paving the way for its world-famous cheese industry. Alas, precious little Edam cheese is still made in Edam itself, although the town continues to function as an aging and distribution center. You are probably familiar with Edam cheese in its export version, with the red skin; what is sold locally has a yellow skin and seems to have a stronger flavor. Try some!

From the **Edam bus stop** (5) it is only a short stroll into the heart of this lovely old town. Follow the map to the **Speeltoren** (6), a 15th-century tower to a church that was torn down in 1883. It has one of the oldest carillons in Holland, built in 1561, and it leans a bit to one side.

*Damplein, the picturesque main square of the town, is actually a broad humped bridge, from which there are delightful views in all directions. Next to it, in an unusually attractive 16th-century house, is the **Edams Museum** (7). Step inside to see the wonderful old furnishings, and don't miss the paintings of some of the local celebrities, including the 445-pound innkeeper from the 16th century, the over-8-foot-tall girl who died in 1633, and the 16th-century man with the 10-foot beard. The most unusual attraction in the museum is its floating cellar, made of brick and tiles, which still goes up and down as the groundwater level changes. The museum is open from the beginning of April until the end of October, Mondays through Saturdays from 10 a.m. to 4 p.m.; and on Sundays from 2–4 p.m.

Across the square from this is the 18th-century **Town Hall** (*Stadhuis*) (8) with its elegant façade and interesting council chamber decorated with biblical scenes. Now follow the map past the 15th-century *Houtenhuis*, the oldest wooden house in town, at the corner of Breestraat and Eilandsgracht. Grote Kerkstraat leads to the **Grote Kerk of St. Nicholaas** (9), an enormous Gothic church from the 15th century. It is famous for its early-17th-century stained-glass windows, 18th-century organ, and Gothic pews.

Return on Matthijs Tinxgracht to the 16th-century **Kaaswaag** (10), where cheese was once weighed before being sold. During the summer months demonstration cheese markets are held here, and local Edam cheese may be purchased. Now return to the bus stop (5), from which bus numbers 110 or 112 will take you back to Amsterdam in only half an hour.

*Haarlem

One of the oldest cities in Holland, Haarlem is also among the least changed. Its quiet streets exude an aura of refinement that makes it quite different from lively Amsterdam. During the 17th century it was a major art center, with many outstanding talents revolving around the singular genius of Frans Hals. Much of this era can still be felt today amid the narrow lanes and delightful old buildings of the town's historic center.

Haarlem's roots go back as far as the 10th century, when a feudal castle offered protection against marauding West Frisians. The counts of Holland soon established their seat in this strategic location and the town grew rapidly, receiving its charter in 1245. It bravely fought the Spaniards in 1573, surrendering only after a cutoff of the food supply had brought it to the brink of starvation. The reprisals were brutal, with many of Haarlem's citizens massacred and the town largely destroyed. Recaptured by the Dutch under William of Orange, it entered a period of prosperity that has lasted ever since.

Haarlem is most famous as the flower capital of Holland. Its horticultural industry had long been established, and grew to enormous size after the introduction of the tulip from Turkey to the ideal sandy soil just south of the city. Chance mutations there resulted in wild color variations, providing the base for a lucrative business in the export of bulbs. Short excursions to the growing fields by bus or car, described at the end of the chapter, can easily be added to this daytrip.

GETTING THERE:

Trains depart Amsterdam's Centraal Station at very frequent intervals for the 15-minute run to Haarlem. Return service operates until late evening.

By car, take the N-5/A-5 highway (*Haarlemmerweg*) from central Amsterdam due west to Haarlem, a distance of 15 miles. The most convenient parking there is between the Grote Markt and the Spaarne River.

WHEN TO GO:

Haarlem may be visited at any time, but note that the Grote Kerk is not open to tourists on Sundays, and that the Teylers Museum is closed on Mondays and some holidays. Short excursions to the flower growing area can be made, in the case of Keukenhof, daily between the end of March and the end of May; and in the case of Aalsmeer, Mondays through Fridays all year round, but before 11 a.m. only.

FOOD AND DRINK:

There are a great many restaurants along most of the walking route. Some good choices are:

Peter Cuyper (Klein Houtstraat 70, between the Grote Kerk and the Frans Hals Museum) French and Dutch cooking in a quaint atmosphere, outdoor terrace in summer. Phone (023) 32-08-85. X: Sat. lunch, Sun., Mon. $$$

Napoli (Houtplein 1, 2 blocks southwest of the Frans Hals Museum, across the canal) Italian cuisine. $$

Carillon (Grote Markt 27, facing the Grote Kerk) Both a tavern and a restaurant. $ and $$

Stationsrestauratie (on the platform in the train station) Good-value meals in a convenient location. $

TOURIST INFORMATION:

The local tourist office (VVV), phone (023) 31-90-59, is located just outside the train station. You might want to ask them about the various *hofjes* (almshouses) for which the town is noted. Most of these are not on this walking route, but may be interesting places to visit.

SUGGESTED TOUR:

Haarlem was the terminus of the first Dutch rail line, which was opened in 1839 and which ran to Amsterdam. The present **station** (1), built in the Art Nouveau style in 1908, is a fitting introduction to this historical city. From here it is a half-mile walk down Kruisweg, Kruisstraat, and the pedestrianized Barteljorisstraat to the **Grote Markt**, one of the more impressive town squares in Europe. The statue near its center honors Laurens Coster, born in Haarlem in 1370, who is locally believed to have invented printing from movable type, despite evidence that Germany's Gutenberg was first with the discovery. A colorful outdoor **flower market** is held in the square on Saturdays from 9 a.m. to 4 p.m.

The west side of the market square is bordered by the **Stadhuis** (Town Hall) (2), built on the site of the 13th-century hunting lodge of the counts of Holland. The oldest part of the present structure dates from the mid-14th century, while the rest of the building has been

In the Grote Kerk

enlarged and altered many times since. Visitors are usually allowed to see the Great Hall (*Gravenzaal*) and possibly other parts of the elegant interior. Ask at the reception desk, but only on weekdays.

Continuing around the square will bring you to the magnificent **Vleeshal** (3), a Renaissance meat market from 1603 that is now used as an extension of the Frans Hals Museum for temporary art exhibitions. Close to it and attached to the church is the **Vishal**, a fish market built in 1768. It is also used by the museum for temporary exhibitions. Just across the square is the **Hoofdwacht**, the former guardhouse of the police, whose façade dates from 1650.

Despite these interesting buildings, the market square is almost totally dominated by the huge ***Grote Kerk** (4), also known as the **Church of St. Bavo**. Begun around 1400 and largely completed by 1550, it was originally a Catholic cathedral and has fortunately retained some of its pre-Reformation decorations, although it now belongs to the Dutch Reformed Church. The entrance for visitors is around the corner, through the verger's house at Oude Groenmarkt 23. Inside, the most impressive feature is the splendid Müller **organ** of 1738, one of the largest and most famous in the world. Its 5,000 pipes have responded to the touch of such outstanding musicians as Mozart (then ten years of age), Handel, and Schweitzer. With luck, you might get here in time to enjoy one of the frequent recitals and hear what it must have sounded like to them. The artist Frans Hals is buried in the choir, under slab number 56. There is a plaque dedicated to Laurens Coster, the printing innovator, near the crossing, and he is buried somewhere in this church, but no one knows where. A pamphlet in English explaining many of the other features is available at the entrance. The church receives visitors Mondays through Saturdays, from 10 a.m. until 4 p.m., and there is a small admission charge.

Now follow the map through some interesting streets to the world-renowned ***Frans Hals Museum** (5), located in the former *Oudemannenhuis,* an almshouse for men, built in 1608. Even if you have little interest in art, a visit here will give you a chance to see the exceptionally well-preserved interior of an outstanding building. Frans Hals was probably born in Antwerp in 1580, but moved to Haarlem while still a child. He spent the rest of his long life in that city, and achieved great fame with his amazingly lively portraits. Several of his most famous works, particularly the eight group portraits, form the nucleus of the museum's collection, which includes quite a few other artists as well. A new wing displays a well-rounded selection of modern and contemporary Dutch art, with many temporary exhibitions. The museum is open Mondays through Saturdays, from 11 a.m. to 5 p.m.; and on Sundays and holidays from 1–5 p.m. Museum Cards are accepted.

The route now follows a canal and the Spaarne River to the **Gravenstenenbrug** (6), a picturesque lift bridge of traditional Dutch design. From here you might want to make a little side trip to Haarlem's only remaining town gate, the **Amsterdamse Poort** (7). Looking terribly medieval, this fortification dates from the late 14th century. To get there, just follow the map down Wijde Steeg and Spaarnwouderstraat.

Return and cross the bridge to the ***Teylers Museum** (8). Founded in 1778, this is the oldest museum in Holland—and it sure looks its age. Nothing ever seems to have changed here. The incredibly old-fashioned displays encompass a wide range of interests, from sketches by Rembrandt, Raphael, and Michelangelo, to ancient fossils, bones, and rocks. Perhaps the most interesting are the weird electrical apparatuses from the late 18th century, such as the enormous electrostatic generator that looks like something out of a Frankenstein movie. You will never forget this place, and you can see it Tuesdays through Saturdays, from 10 a.m. to 5 p.m.; and on Sundays from 1–5 p.m. Yes, the Museum Card is accepted.

Stroll along the river to Damstraat, at the corner of which is the **Waag**, a stone structure built in 1598 for the purpose of weighing goods arriving by ship. From here, the route returns you to the station via the 14th-century **Waalse Kerk** (9), the oldest church in Haarlem. It is surrounded by an especially attractive *Begijnhof,* formerly a con-

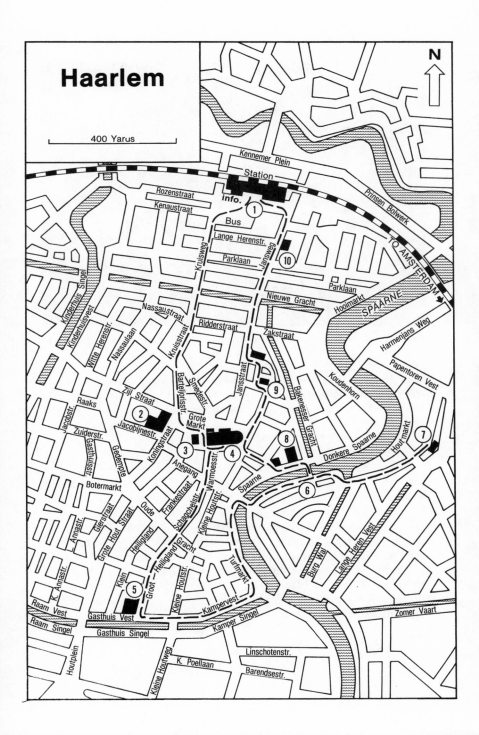

In the Frans Hals Museum

vent. Farther along you will come to the **Hofje van Staats** (10), one of the many *hofjes* that grace the city. This particular almshouse dates from 1730. Step in for a quick look, then continue on to the nearby station.

NEARBY SIGHTS:

If you happen to be in Haarlem between the end of March and the end of May, you may want to visit the world-famous **Keukenhof Gardens**. During that time the bulbs are in bloom, millions and millions of them, all spread out over a 70-acre site of astonishing beauty. They can be admired daily during that period, from 8 a.m. to 8 p.m. Buses, marked for Lisse, leave frequently from the front of Haarlem Station. Flower lovers may also want to visit the year-round international flower auction at **Aalsmeer**, near Schiphol Airport. It is held Mondays through Fridays, from 7:30–11 a.m. only. Be sure to get there early, and see the town later. Again, there is a bus from Haarlem Station, and others direct from Amsterdam.

Hoorn and the Historic Triangle

Here is an easy and thoroughly enjoyable daytrip that is just filled with sun and fun. You can travel by train or car to the historic port of Hoorn, then ride an ancient steam train through the lovely North Holland landscape to Medemblik, where you board an excursion boat to Enkhuizen. From there it's a short train ride back to Hoorn, a most delightful place to explore on foot.

Known as the "Historic Triangle," (*Historische Driehoek*), this rich agricultural area is loaded with memories of the former Zuider Zee, the arm of the North Sea that became the land-locked IJsselmeer. Many of its traditions may be probed at the Westfries Museum in Hoorn, while the magnificent and truly fascinating outdoor museum at Enkhuizen—described in the next chapter—brings the rural past to life. This latter attraction could be included on this trip instead, by cutting both walking tours short and eliminating the museum in Hoorn.

First settled in the early 14th century, Hoorn was a major port for international trade until the late 17th century. It gave its name to Cape Horn, the southernmost tip of South America, which was discovered in 1616 by the locally-born navigator, Willem Schouten. This was an important center of the Dutch East Indies Company, which brought about the prosperity so clearly seen in the town's many beautiful old buildings. Alas, as trade increased, so did the draught of the ships needed to carry the goods. The local waters are relatively shallow and subject to silting, and so the maritime trade gradually moved to deeper ports. One of the most attractive towns in Holland, Hoorn thrives today as a regional shopping and yachting center.

GETTING THERE:

Trains, marked for Enkhuizen, depart Amsterdam's Centraal Station at half-hour intervals for the 36-minute run to Hoorn. Return service operates until late evening.

By car, the most attractive route to follow from central Amsterdam is through the IJ Tunnel, then the N-10 and N-247 roads north by way of Edam to Hoorn. It may be slightly faster to take the A-7/E-22 motorway instead. In either case, the distance is about 25 miles.

WHEN TO GO:

This trip may be taken on any day during July and August; and Tuesdays through Saturdays during April–June and September–October. The "Historic Triangle" steam train and boat combination does not operate at other times. To avoid disappointment you should check first with the information office in Amsterdam's Centraal Station, or with the tourist office in Hoorn. Good weather is essential, as is an early start—around 8 a.m. at the latest.

FOOD AND DRINK:

Snacks and drinks are available on both the steam train and the boat. Restaurant choices for Enkhuizen are noted in the next chapter. Some good restaurants in Hoorn are:

Bontekoe Taverne (Nieuwendam 1, near the Binnenhaven) Upstairs, in a 17th-century warehouse, with indoor and outdoor tables. Phone (02290) 173-24. X: Mon. $$$

De Waag (Rode Steen 8, near the Westfries Museum) Meat and fish specialties. Phone (02290) 151-95. X: Tues. $$

Azië (Veemarkt 49, a block south of the train station) Superb Chinese cuisine. Phone (02290) 185-55. $$

Stationsrestauratie (in the train station) Inexpensive and convenient. $

The tourist office (VVV) in Hoorn, phone (06) 34-03-55, is at Veemarkt 4, three blocks south of the train station. Current schedules for the "Historic Triangle" combination can be had by phoning (02290) 14-862.

SUGGESTED TOUR:

Begin your tour at the **Hoorn Train Station** (1), where you cross a pedestrian bridge over the tracks to the **Steam Train Station** (2). There is a great deal of intriguing activity here, as locomotives and open-ended cars, some nearly a century old, are shunted about. Buy a combination ticket for the *steam train and boat* (combi stoomtram + boot) and study the printed schedule (in English) carefully. These rides are privately operated and are not covered by any railpass.

You will probably have time before departure to enjoy visiting the yards and special steam exhibitions. No one seems to mind your walk-

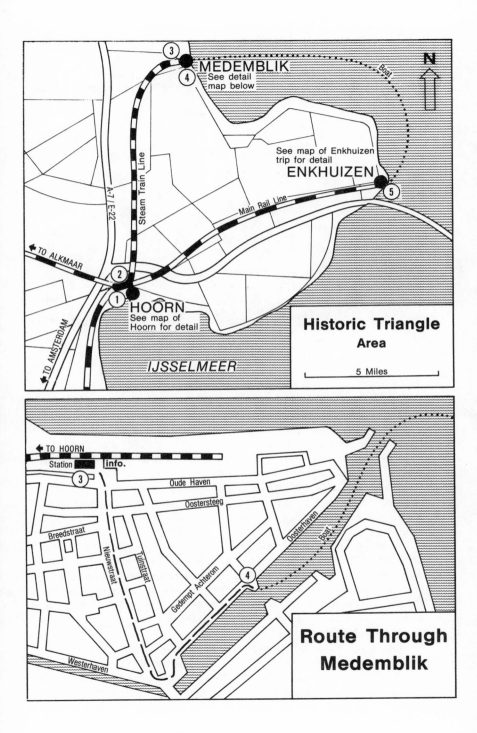

Historic Triangle
Area

N

TO ALKMAAR

TO AMSTERDAM

A-7/E-22

Steam Train Line

Main Rail Line

Boat

MEDEMBLIK
See detail
map below

See map of Enkhuizen
trip for detail
ENKHUIZEN

HOÔRN
See map of
Hoorn for detail

IJSSELMEER

5 Miles

Route Through
Medemblik

TO HOORN

Station   Info.

Oude Haven

Oostersteeg

Breedstraat

Nieuwstraat

Tuinstraat

Gedempt Achterom

Oosterhaven

Boat

Westerhaven

In the Steam Train Station at Hoorn

ing around on the tracks or even in the train sheds and machine shops. This is a *very* popular outing with Dutch families, so expect to run into hordes of little children.

Now board the ancient train and take delight in the passing coun-tryside. The ride to Medemblik takes about one hour, and there is a primitive bar car to help you pass the time. Upon arrival at **Medemblik Station** (3), walk straight ahead down the main street to the **harbor** (4), where you will find the large excursion boat (probably the *Stad Enkhuizen*) that will take you to Enkhuizen. This delightful cruise on the IJsselmeer takes about 75 minutes. Again, snacks and drinks are available.

From the **Enkhuizen Pier** (5) it is only a few steps to the train sta-tion, where there are frequent trains back to Hoorn. While here, how-ever, you might want to explore one or more of the outstanding at-tractions this town is famous for. You will find a full description of these, along with a map, in the next chapter. Remember that a stop here will most likely eliminate the possibility of a visit to the Westfries Museum in Hoorn.

Return to Hoorn by train and begin your walking tour of the old port town by following the map to the **Town Hall** *(Stadhuis)* (6), a lovely twin-gabled building from 1613. Continue down Nieuwstraat past the enormous **Grote Kerk**, a 19th-century church that has been

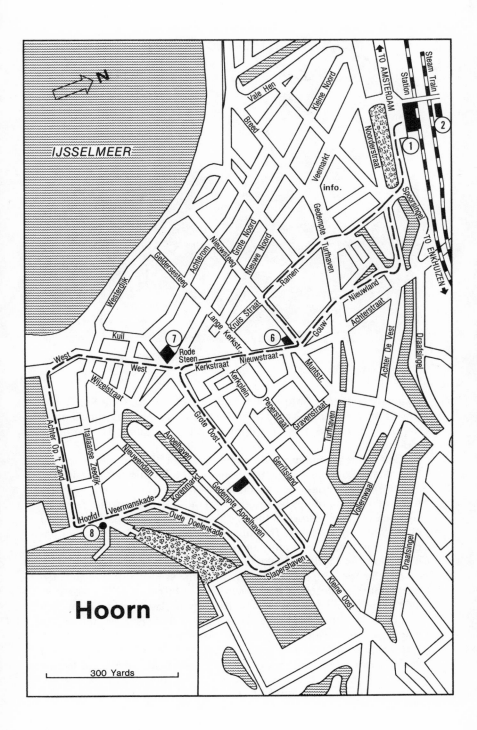

Hoorn

300 Yards

The Rode Steen in Hoorn

strangely converted into shops. Kerkstraat leads to Rode Steen, the town's main square. Named after the red stone that was once a place of public execution, this large open square is surrounded by exquisite old buildings.

One of these structures, the highly-ornate 17th-century Staten College (State Council) is now the home of the **Westfries Museum** (7). Step inside to witness the wealth this town once possessed. Sumptuous furniture, paintings, weapons, ship models, and anything else associated with the history of the region—they're all there, all displayed in elegant surroundings. The museum is open Mondays through Fridays, from 11 a.m. to 5 p.m.; and on Saturdays and Sundays from 2–5 p.m. Museum Cards, happily, are accepted.

On the opposite side of the square is the **Waag**, an especially nice weighhouse from 1609. Stroll down Grote Oost past the **Oosterkerk**, a Gothic church founded in 1450. Its stained-glass window from 1620 depicts a famous naval battle. Turn right at Slapershaven and amble along the picturesque harbor, busy with pleasure boats. The early-16th-century **Hoofdtoren** (8) was a part of the old fortifications, and sports a delicate belfry from 1651. From here you may want to just wander around and soak up the delicious atmosphere before returning to the train station and Amsterdam.

Enkhuizen

The way of life in northern Holland was dramatically changed in 1932 when the former Zuider Zee was sealed off from the sea to become the freshwater IJsselmeer. No longer were fishing and shipping of great importance; new industries appeared and brought with them a different kind of prosperity. As the old traditions began to die away, there was a very real danger that they would be forgotten forever. Fortunately, the Dutch government recognized this peril to the nation's heritage and began to gather artifacts to form the first Zuider Zee museum, established in the lovely old port of Enkhuizen in 1950.

In the meantime, old houses, churches, and other structures were saved and moved to a site just outside the town, where they were reassembled into villages. After decades of work, this was finally opened in 1983 as the Zuider Zee Outdoor Museum, one of the best and most enjoyable open-air museums in the world. Not only have the buildings been preserved, but also the crafts, trades, lifestyles, and traditions that went with them. This is surely one of the most fascinating attractions in all of Holland, something that really is not to be missed.

Enkhuizen itself is an unusually attractive old port. Founded in the 14th century, its economy peaked in the 17th, when many of its most impressive buildings were erected. After that it more or less went to sleep, only to be reawakened by tourists in search of a well-preserved past.

GETTING THERE:

Trains depart Amsterdam's Centraal Station at half-hour intervals for the one-hour ride to Enkhuizen. Return service operates until late evening. Those without railpasses or Museum Cards might want to use the economical Netherlands Railways day excursion package number 9, which includes the Zuider Zee museums.

By car, the most enjoyable route from central Amsterdam is to take the IJ Tunnel, followed by the N-10 and N-247 highways past Edam to Hoorn. You might get there faster via the A-7/E-22 motorway instead. From Hoorn take the local road to Enkhuizen and park in the Zuider Zee Museum lot, at the beginning of the dike road to Lelystad. The total distance from Amsterdam is 38 miles.

WHEN TO GO:

The Zuider Zee Museum is open daily from April through October, but closed the rest of the year. Good weather is essential for enjoyment of this trip.

FOOD AND DRINK:

You will find a restaurant and several inexpensive cafeterias and cafés within the outdoor museum area. Some choice restaurants in Enkhuizen itself are:

Die Drie Haringhe (Dijk 28, 4 blocks northeast of the station) Upstairs in an ancient warehouse. X: Tues. $$$
Markerwaard (Dijk 62, 3 blocks northeast of the station) A picturesque location on the old harbor. $$

TOURIST INFORMATION:

The local tourist office (VVV), phone (02280) 13-164, is on the harbor just east of the train station.

SUGGESTED TOUR:

Leave the **train station** (1) and follow the map a short distance to the tourist office, where you can purchase a museum ticket. Continue on to the **Zuider Zee Museum pier** (2), boarding a ferry to the main **parking lot** (3). Those coming by car should begin their tour here. The boat then takes you to the Outdoor Museum, which is open daily from April through October, from 10 a.m. until 5 p.m. Be sure to allow a minimum of at least two hours to see it, and don't forget to pick up a map and a guide pamphlet in English.

You'll have a lovely panoramic view of Enkhuizen as you approach the ***Outdoor Museum** (*Buitenmuseum*) (4). Once there, you can wander around some 130 buildings grouped into several villages. Quite a few of these are open for inspection, and many are staffed with people performing the old crafts and trades. Various events and activities are staged throughout the day. Everything is very well explained with signs, exhibitions, and even a video show. You won't go hungry or thirsty either, as there are several places to eat or drink along with an attractive crafts shop.

To continue into Enkhuizen, take the land exit marked for *Stad en Binnenmuseum*. Just beyond this is the **Zuider Zee Indoor Museum** (*Binnenmuseum*) (5), occupying several old warehouses of the Dutch East Indies Company. Opened in 1950, the museum displays a remarkably thorough collection of fishing boats, house furnishings, utensils, and just about everything else that pertains to life in this region prior to 1932. The most popular exhibits here are probably those of local costumes in period room settings. The Indoor Museum is open daily all year long, except on Christmas and New Year's days, from 10 a.m. to 5 p.m.

Continue across an old lift bridge to the **Town Hall** (*Stadhuis*) (6), a rather imposing structure from 1688. Behind it is the former jail (*Oude*

N

Groene Wierdijk

Noordergracht

Noorderweg

Handvastwater

Leger

Spaans

Visserdijk

Wegjes

Vizelstraat

Waagstraat ⑦

Westerstraat

⑧

Kaasmarkt

Nieuwstr.

ZUIDER ZEE
OUTDOOR
MUSEUM

④

⑥

Zwaanstr.

Zuider Havendijk

Breedstraat

Oosterhavenstr.

Kade

Wierdijk

⑤

St. Janstr.

Venedie

Dijk

Paktuinen

Parklaan

⑨ ⑩

info.

Station ①

← TO AMSTERDAM

②

Flevolaan

③

N-302

IJSSELMEER

Enkhuizen

500 Yards

TO LELYSTAD →

In the Zuider Zee Outdoor Museum

Gevangenis) of 1612. In about another block or so you will come to the **Waag** *(Weighhouse)* (7), an early Renaissance building from 1559. It is now used as the town museum, and has some interesting displays of early medical instruments along with the expected curiosities. Visits may usually be made on Tuesdays through Fridays, from 11 a.m. to 5 p.m., and on weekends from 2–5 p.m.

Stroll down the pedestrians-only Westerstraat, passing the 15th-century **Westerkerk** (8). You might want to step inside to see one of the nicest choir screens in the country, dating from 1542, as well as the 16th-century pulpit. Now follow the map to the picturesque **Old Harbor** . At the far end of this is the dramatically sited **Drommedaris Tower** (9) of 1540, a massive fortification with dungeons and one of the best carillons in Holland. Another attraction, just steps away, is the highly unusual **Bottle Ship Museum** (10), featuring the world's largest collection of model ships inside bottles. From here it's only a short stroll back to the train station, or the ferry back to the parking lot.

Zaanse Schans

You don't have to go far from Amsterdam to see working windmills in a setting of preserved quaintness. The Zaanse Schans is an extremely popular destination for visitors in search of a bit of *Oud Holland*, all neatly packaged and ready to be enjoyed. At first, this may seem like the ultimate Dutch tourist trap, but it can also be a lot of fun and should not be missed.

As the Zaan region, just northwest of Amsterdam, developed industrially, its traditional buildings were in danger of being lost forever. Fortunately, some of Holland's precious heritage was saved in the 1950s by the Zaanse Schans Foundation, which moved an assortment of old windmills, houses, and other interesting structures to a 20-acre site on the banks of the Zaan River. Restored to their 18th-century appearance, the houses are not just an outdoor museum— indeed, most of them are actually lived in today, bringing real life to what would otherwise be only another tourist attraction. Some of the working windmills as well as all of the craft shops and small museums may be visited.

This trip can easily be combined in the same day with one to Alkmaar, described in the next chapter. They are both on the same rail line.

GETTING THERE:

Trains, bound for Alkmaar, depart Amsterdam's Centraal Station at frequent intervals for the 16-minute ride to Koog-Zaandijk, which is just a short walk from the site. Be sure to get on a local train *(stoptrein)*. Return service operates until late evening. Those without railpasses may want to take advantage of the Netherlands Railways day excursion package, which includes museums, the river cruise, and a snack.

By car, leave Amsterdam via the Coen Tunnel and take the A-8/E-22 motorway past Zaandam in the direction of Purmerend, then follow signs to Zaandijk. The total distance from central Amsterdam is 10 miles.

WHEN TO GO:

The Zaanse Schans site is always open, and admission to it is free. Most of the attractions there are open daily between 10 a.m. and 5 p.m., from March through October, and also on winter weekends. A few are closed on Mondays. If you combine this daytrip with Alkmaar, you may prefer to go on a Friday, in which case you should see Alkmaar first.

FOOD AND DRINK:
Two good places to eat within the Zaanse Schans site are:

De Walvis (along Kalverringdijk, the main street) Superb French dining in an 18th-century house. Reservations preferred, phone (075) 16-56-29. X: Sun. $$$

De Kraai (at the east end of the site) All sorts of pancakes, some with meat or cheese, along with sandwiches and drinks. Self-service in a colorful old warehouse, outdoor tables available. X: winter. $

TOURIST INFORMATION:
For further information contact the Zaanse tourist office (VVV) in Zaandam by phoning (075) 16-22-21.

SUGGESTED TOUR:
Begin at the **Koog-Zaandijk Station** (1) and follow the signs to Zannse Schans, a walk of about ten minutes. Those coming by car should park at the eastern end of the site itself and adjust the walk accordingly.

Kalverringdijk is the main street of the village. On the left as you enter, there is an attractive French-style garden with a small tea pavilion, now a pewter shop. The house next to it was originally a workshop from the 17th century, and now houses a fascinating **Clock Museum** (2), where you can examine antique timepieces from around the world and particularly from this part of Holland. Standing next to it is a 19th-century **grocery store** (3), operated as a small museum. Step inside to see (and smell!) how food was sold in the days before supermarkets. Continue on past several other old houses and the noted restaurant "De Walvis," an 18th-century structure once used as an orphanage. Near the end of the row is **Het Noorderhuis** (4), a merchant's house built in 1670. Its interior is filled with antique roomsettings complete with figures in period costumes, and may be visited for a small fee.

Boat trips on the Zaan River, going past a nice variety of windmills and lasting about 50 minutes, may be taken from the **pier** (5). Close to this is an 18th-century windmill, **De Huisman**, first built to grind snuff and later used for making mustard. A shop inside sells the mustard in an assortment of lovely containers.

From here, a row of windmills stretches along the river. The first of these, **De Poelenburg**, was built in 1869 to saw wood. A much older

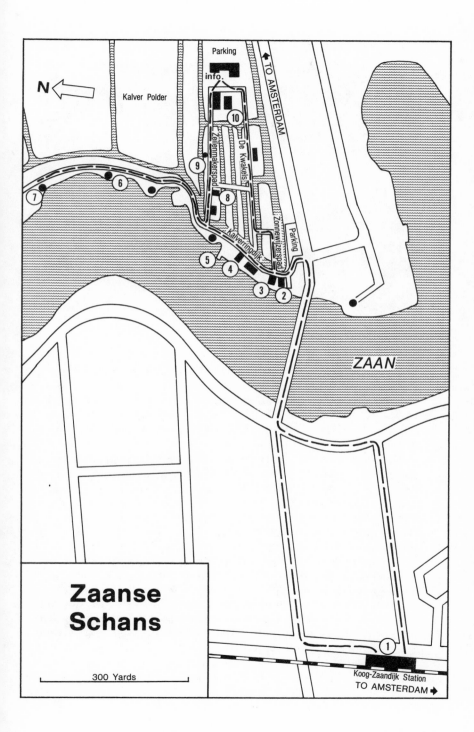

N

Kalver Polder

Parking

info.

TO AMSTERDAM

10

9

De Kwakels

8

6

7

Zeilenmakerspad

Zonnewijzerspad

Parking

5

4

Kalverringdijk

3

2

ZAAN

Zaanse Schans

300 Yards

Koog-Zaandijk Station
TO AMSTERDAM →

1

Windmills at Zaanse Schans

one, called ***De Kat** (6) and originally built elsewhere in the region in 1696, still grinds pigments for paints. You are welcome, for a small fee, to climb all over its interior and watch the process at work. Beyond it is a mill used to extract oil from grains. Known as **De Zoeker** (7), it is also open to visitors. The mills extending beyond this are in various states of reconstruction.

Return to the village and turn left on Zeilenmakerspad (Sailmaker's path). Passing the oldest house at Zaanse Schans, built for a Zaandam merchant in 1623 and now home to an antique shop, you will soon come to the **Bakery** (8). Beginning as a private house in 1658, it was converted to make bread in 1753 and is now restored as a small museum. Note the outdoor toilet over a ditch at its rear—those canal waters were not always so clean!

On your left is the **Cheese Farm** (9), where they sell good home-made cheese. Yes, you can taste some. Continue on past the small drainage windmill, which still functions, and cross a tiny lift bridge. You are now at the eastern end of the site, where a café and self-service restaurant occupies a complex of old structures, along with gift shops. The **Wooden Shoe Workshop** (10) is sure to have a pair of clogs in your size, should you feel so inclined. Return via a path called De Kwakels, along which is an old **shipyard**. It is now only a short walk back to the station or the parking lot.

Alkmaar

The world-famous Cheese Market at Alkmaar is a tradition going back to the early 17th century. Although more efficient distribution methods have been developed over the years, this colorful weekly wholesale auction is still held, partly as a tourist attraction and partly to preserve a worthwhile link with the past.

But there is much more to this lovely old town than cheese. The historic center, surrounded by moats and canals, still maintains its Old World character, with many fine buildings from the 15th through the 18th centuries remaining in use today.

Alkmaar was first mentioned in the 10th century and received its charter in 1254. It played a pivotal role in the Dutch struggle for independence when the town defeated the Spaniards in 1573 by opening the sluices, thus flooding the surrounding area. This marked the beginning of the end of Spanish domination in the Low Countries, and led eventually to self-rule.

You may prefer to combine this daytrip with one to Zaanse Schans, described in the previous chapter. If you do so on a Friday in season, be sure to visit Alkmaar first.

GETTING THERE:

Trains leave Amsterdam's Centraal Station frequently for the 30-to-45 minute ride to Alkmaar, with return service until late evening.

By car, the fastest route is the N-5/A-5 highway west in the direction of Haarlem, then the A-9 north to Alkmaar. The total distance from central Amsterdam is 25 miles. You might want to drive back by way of Zaandam, stopping at Zaanse Schans en route.

WHEN TO GO:

Tourists by the thousands flock to Alkmaar on Friday mornings between mid-April and mid-September to see the famous Cheese Market in action. If this spectacle does not excite you, consider coming on another day. The Municipal and Beer museums are closed on Mondays, while the Cheese Museum closes on Sundays and completely from November through March.

FOOD AND DRINK:

Being a favorite tourist attraction, Alkmaar has a wide variety of restaurants and cafés in all price ranges. Some good choices for lunch are:

Hof van Sonoy (Hof van Sonoy 1, 2 blocks northwest of the Waag) Luxury dining in an old almshouse just off Nieuwesloot. Phone (072) 12-40-33. $$$

Koekenbier (Kennemerstraatweg 16, 3 blocks south of the windmill) Scandinavian food. X: Mon. $$

't Pannekoekschip De Kajuit (at the Fries Bridge 3 blocks east of the Beer Museum) All kinds of pancakes served on a boat in the canal. X: Mon. $

Stationsrestauratie (in the train station) Good food at low prices. $

SUGGESTED TOUR:

Leave the **train station** (1) and follow the map into the historic center. On your left is the **Noord Hollands Kanaal**, opened in 1825 to link Amsterdam directly with the North Sea. Much too shallow for large ships, it was later superseded by the larger North Sea Canal. A right turn on Doelenstraat leads to the **Stedelijk Museum** (Municipal Museum) (2), located in an impressive building from 1520. Its exhibits, including a great deal of good art, artifacts, and historic objects, relate mainly to the town and surrounding areas; with a particular emphasis on the famous siege of 1573. If you come on a Friday morning in season you might want to return here after seeing the Cheese Market, which is all over by noon. The museum is open on Tuesdays through Saturdays, from 10 a.m. to 5 p.m.; and on Sundays and holidays from 1–5 p.m. Museum Cards are accepted.

Turn left on Nieuwesloot and follow it to Waagplein, where the famous *Cheese Market is held on Fridays from 10 a.m. to noon, between mid-April and mid-September. A delightful anachronism in an age of efficient distribution, this staged event carries on traditions begun in the early 17th century, primarily for the benefit of the thousands of tourists who come to witness the spectacle. The cheeses, sold by auction to wholesale dealers, are mostly of the Edam variety, although usually without the red export covering that you are probably familiar with. Brought to the large open square by truck, they are tested by prospective buyers, who accompany their bids with brisk

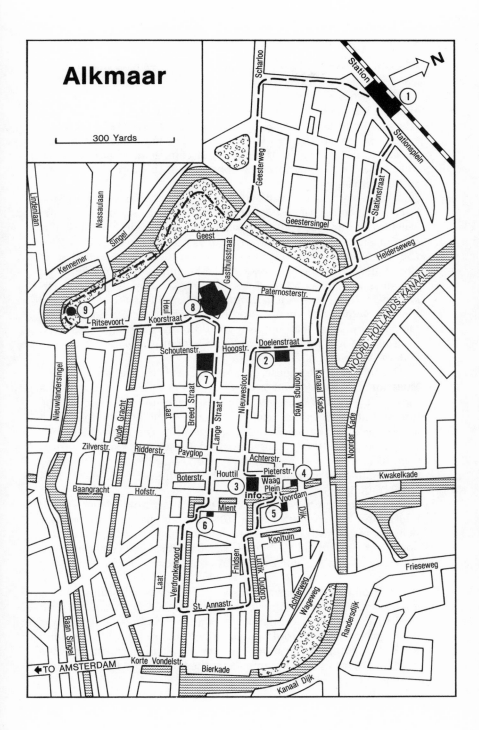

clapping of hands. Deals are consummated by handshakes, after which the real ceremony begins.

Cheese porters, wearing immaculate white uniforms and belonging to an ancient guild, carry heavy loads of the cheeses on traditional litters to the weighhouse (Waag), where the totals are tallied, then to the purchasers' trucks. Working in pairs, they jog along with a peculiar gait to prevent spills. There are four companies of porters, each with its own hat color, and each consisting of six porters, a weigher, and a foreman.

A good place to watch all of this activity is from the windows of the **Kaas Museum** (Cheese Museum), located upstairs in the weighhouse, or **Waag** (3). Originally built as a church in 1341, this magnificent structure was converted to its present use as early as 1582. The lovely Renaissance façade and ornate tower were added soon after that. A carillon plays between 11 a.m. and noon on market days, and jousting figures on horseback appear as a trumpeter blows a clarion call. Exhibits in the museum are concerned with both past and present methods of cheese production, with delicious samples on sale. The museum may be visited on Mondays through Saturdays, from 10 a.m. to 4 p.m., April through October. It opens at 9 a.m. on Fridays. Museum Cards are accepted.

Having tasted the cheese, you may be ready for the **National Beer Museum** (4), just a few steps beyond the Waagplein. Housed in the former "De Boom" brewery, it traces the history of beer making throughout the ages. You can enjoy some of the liquid refreshment in the bar or at the adjoining canal-side café. The Beer Museum is open from April through September on Tuesdays through Saturdays from 10 a.m. to 4 p.m., on Sundays from 1–4 p.m.; and on Thursdays through Sundays from 1–4 p.m. the rest of the year. Museum Cards are accepted.

Cross a bridge to Voordam and the **Hans Brinker Museum** (5), housed in five warehouses from 1635. The famous story of the silver skates is retold with period room sets, costumes, and artifacts. It is open from April until October, on Tuesdays through Fridays and Sundays, from 1–5 p.m.; and on Sundays only from 1–5 p.m. the rest of the year.

Now follow the map through some of the most colorful streets in town. Along the way you will pass the 16th-century **Vismarkt** (Fish Market) (6), which also operates on Friday mornings, and which is noted for its sculpted roof figures and old pump from 1785. Around the corner from this, at number 23 Mient, is a house whose gable displays Alkmaar's coat of arms—with the lions facing the wrong way as an insult to the town fathers.

Continue down Lange Straat, the main shopping street, to the

Cheese Porters in the Waagplein

Stadhuis (Town Hall) (7), a late Gothic structure begun in 1509. Some of its beautifully decorated rooms may usually be seen by asking at the reception desk, but only on Mondays through Fridays, from 9 a.m. to noon and 2–4 p.m.

Just a few more steps and you are at the **Grote Kerk** (8), a splendid Dutch Reform church dedicated to St. Laurens. Built between 1470 and 1516 in the Gothic style, it has a very impressive interior. The large organ in the nave dates from 1643, while the small one in the north ambulatory—from 1511—is the oldest still in use in Holland. Recitals are frequently held on Cheese Market days.

The route now wanders down to the old waterside ramparts, along which is the 18th-century **Molen van Piet** (9). Still grinding flour as it has for centuries, this ancient windmill may be visited. A stroll through the park and a left turn over the bridge onto Geesterweg will return you to the station.

Texel

Lying just two miles off the shores of North Holland, the delightfully peaceful island of Texel is a rather unusual but highly enjoyable destination for a daytrip from Amsterdam. Much of it is devoted to nature reserves, especially for birds, and to raising the famous Texel sheep. There are, however, a few villages, of which the most interesting is Den Burg. You won't be alone there since its cafés and shops are popular with Dutch, German, and British vacationers, who mostly stay at the seaside resort of De Koog.

This is an especially nice place to explore by rented bicycle or by a combination of buses and walking. One day of its rural tranquillity makes a perfect breather in the middle of a hectic sightseeing schedule. There are absolutely no mandatory cultural sights, although the attractions do include a preserved old-time dwelling, a collection of antique farm implements, and a maritime and beachcombers' museum.

Texel is the largest and southernmost of the West Frisian (or *Wadden*) islands, which stretch across the north coast of Holland all the way to Germany. Most of it is *polder* land, whose reclamation from the sea began as early as the 11th century. Visits to the wildlife sanctuaries must be arranged in advance. Information about this is available from the Texel tourist office in Den Burg. The name, incidentally, is pronounced as *Tessel*.

GETTING THERE:

Trains to Den Helder depart Amsterdam's Centraal Station at half-hour intervals, with the ride taking 75 minutes. From the station at Den Helder take an NZH bus number 3 to the ferry terminal and board the boat for the 20-minute ride to Texel. Return trains run until late evening, but note that the last boat is usually around 9 p.m. If you don't have a railpass, you should consider using the Netherlands Railways day excursion package, which includes the boat, all buses, and other items.

By car, the best route from Amsterdam is via the A-7 (E-22) motorway past Hoorn. Take the exit for Den Oever/Den Helder, follow-

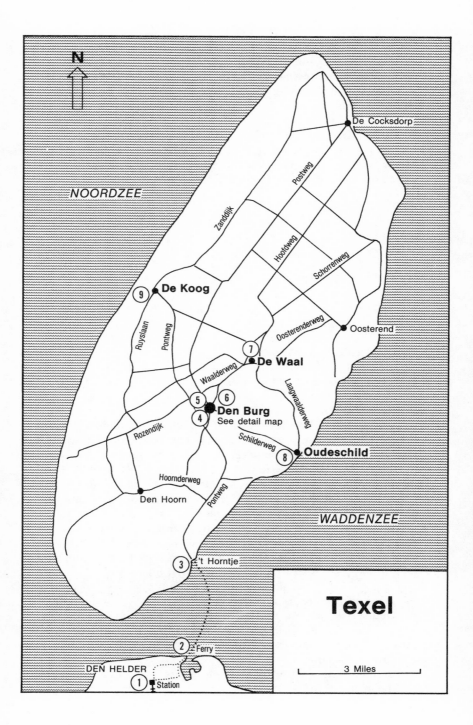

ing this to the ferry terminal *(veerhaven)* at Den Helder, about 50 miles north of Amsterdam. Your car can be taken on the boat without delay, although you might prefer to park here and use buses or rental bicycles on the island.

WHEN TO GO:

Fine weather is essential for this trip, which should be made between mid-May and mid-September. Most of the attractions are closed on Sundays, one on Saturdays, and one on Mondays.

FOOD AND DRINK:

Snacks and drinks are available on the ferryboat. Besides several outdoor cafés, some places to eat in Den Burg are:

Herbergh De Smulpot (Binnenburg 5, in the center of town) Specializes in Texel dishes, meat, and fish. $$

De Lindeboom (Groeneplaats 14, 2 blocks north of the bus stop) A small hotel with a restaurant. $$

De Kelder (Vismarkt 6, in the center of town) A grand café with traditional Dutch food. $

TOURIST INFORMATION:

The Texel tourist office (VVV), phone (02220) 31-47-41, is at Emmalaan 66, 3 blocks south of the bus stop.

SUGGESTED TOUR:

Arriving at the **Den Helder Train Station** (1), immediately board the NZH bus number 3, which is marked for "Texelse Boot." This will take you to the **ferry terminal** (2). Buy a round-trip ticket and board the ferry for the 20-minute ride to the Texel pier at **'t Horntje** (3). From there you can either board an AOT bus marked for Den Burg or rent a bicycle and pedal your way, a level distance of four miles. Bikes are also available in Den Burg and elsewhere on the island.

*****Den Burg** is the main village on Texel and has neatly accommodated itself to the summer tourists with shops and outdoor cafés. On Mondays it is busy with a colorful open-air market. From its **bus stop** (4) it is only a short stroll south to the **tourist office** (VVV) (5), where you might want to ask about visiting a wildlife sanctuary or some of the other attractions not described here. Otherwise, continue on to the **Oudheidskamer** (6), an old 17th-century village house filled with folkloric antiquities. Well worth a quick visit, it is open from April through October, Mondays through Fridays, from 10 a.m. to 12:30 p.m. and 1:30–3 p.m.

An interesting walk or bicycle ride of less than a mile and a half can be made through the countryside to the farming hamlet of

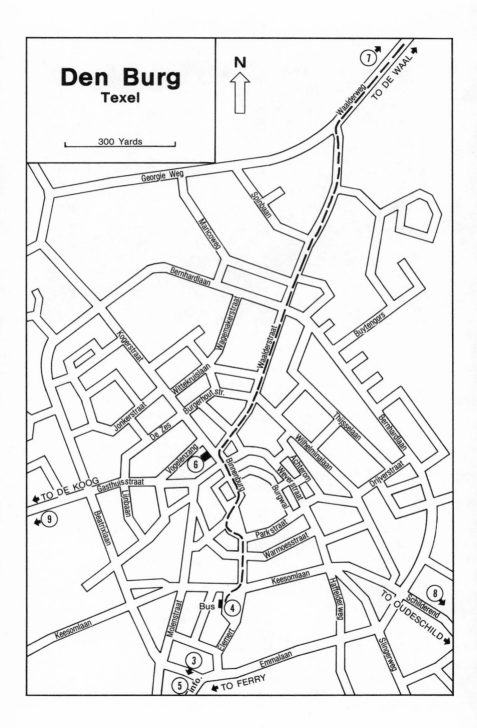

Outdoor Cafés at Den Burg

De Waal (7). Here, in a converted barn, you will find the **Wagen Museum**. All sorts of farm implements and wagons, from as far back as 1700, are displayed along with a rustic slide show narrating more than you ever wanted to know about Texel agriculture. A bucolic delight for some, it is open from Easter through mid-October; Mondays through Fridays from 2–5 p.m.; and on weekends from 2–4 p.m. Museum cards are accepted.

You may want to explore more of the island, especially if you've rented a bicycle or brought a car. Some nice destinations are:

Oudeschild (8), reached by bus from Den Burg, is a picturesque old fishing harbor. Be sure to visit its **Maritime and Beachcomber Museum**, a fascinating collection of junk washed up on the beach or salvaged from nearby wrecks. You can see it all on Mondays through Saturdays, from 9 a.m. to 5 p.m.

De Koog (9) is Texel's seaside resort, where you'll find the usual amenities. It can be reached by bus from Den Burg or the ferry port, or by bike or car. Just south of this is **EcoMare**, a nature recreation center with live seals and displays of Texel's natural history, next to a pretty area for dune walks. It is open daily from 9 a.m. to 5 p.m., but closed on Sundays in winter.

Be sure to begin your return journey before the last ferryboat departs, usually around 9 p.m.

Leiden

Holland's first university was established at Leiden in 1575 and is still going strong. Especially renowned for its faculties of medicine and law, it remains the nation's most prestigious center of higher learning. With such a scholarly background, it is perhaps not surprising that the city possesses an exceptionally broad range of museums. These are, in fact, its major attraction to tourists. If you enjoy visiting museums, you will love Leiden.

Although thought by some to have Roman origins, Leiden was probably founded in the 12th century. Its prosperity dates from the 14th-century immigration of Flemish weavers who fled north to escape the plague. Another form of pestilence came in the form of the Spanish army, which besieged the city in 1574. Refusing to surrender, the population suffered terribly from hunger and disease before finally being rescued by William the Silent's naval forces sailing over a landscape flooded by cutting the dikes. The Spaniards retreated in such a hurry that, according to legend, they left behind an uneaten pot of beet stew. Quickly consumed by the starving citizens, this became the basis for the traditional Dutch dish of *hutspot*. The day of their salvation, October 3rd, is still celebrated with city-wide festivities. As a reward for their steadfast courage, William allegedly offered them a choice of tax relief or a university. Tax rates probably being lower in those days, they opted for the school.

Leiden is also noted as the birthplace of Rembrandt, Jan Steen, and several other famous painters. The Pilgrim Fathers, having fled England for Amsterdam, moved to the university town in 1609, where they lived until departing for the New World in 1620.

Holders of the economical Museum Card will be delighted to know that it is accepted at virtually all of Leiden's many great museums. This trip could easily be combined in the same day with one to Delft, described in a later chapter. There is direct train service between the two towns.

GETTING THERE:

Trains leave Amsterdam's Centraal Station very frequently for the 35-minute ride to Leiden. Return service operates until late evening, after which hourly trains run all night long.

By car, take the A-4 highway past Schiphol Airport. Leiden is 25 miles southwest of central Amsterdam.

WHEN TO GO:

Avoid coming to Leiden on a Monday, when practically everything is closed. Most museums are open on Sundays and holidays after 1 p.m., although the Pilgrim Fathers Documents Center is closed on weekends. October 3rd is the local festival day—expect all attractions to be closed.

FOOD AND DRINK:

Some good restaurant choices in the old part of town are:

Rôtisserie Oudt Leyden (Steenstraat 51, 4 blocks south of the station) Fine dining in an Old Dutch atmosphere, possibly the best in town. Phone (071) 13-31-44. X: Sun. $$$

't Pannekoekenhuis (Steenstraat 51, 4 blocks south of the station) Pancakes and the like, not to be confused with its expensive neighbor. $

Bernsen (Breestraat 157, near the Town Hall) Features the Tourist Menu. $

Surakarta (Noordeinde 51, 3 blocks northwest of the Oudheden Museum) Indonesian cuisine, with a Tourist Menu. $

TOURIST INFORMATION:

The local tourist office (VVV), phone (071) 14-68-46, is just across from the train station at Stationsplein 210.

SUGGESTED TOUR:

From the **train station** (1) walk straight ahead on Stationsweg until you get to a canal. On the right stands the first of Leiden's many museums. At this point you'll have to decide which of these interest you most, since you can't possibly see them all in one day without suffering a terminal case of cultural burnout. The **Rijksmuseum voor Volkenkunde** (Ethnology Museum) (2) presents a sweeping survey of civilizations from outside the European world. Of particular interest here are the marvelous Buddhas from Japan; religious artifacts from Indonesia, Tibet, China, and elsewhere; houses and boats from the South Pacific; and displays on Native American, Mexican, and South American cultures. The main focus is, naturally, on the former Dutch colo-

The Temple of Taffeh at the Oudheden Museum

nies. Visits can be made on Tuesdays through Fridays from 10 a.m. to 5 p.m., and on weekends from noon–5 p.m. Museum Cards are accepted.

Continue down Steenstraat and follow the map across the canalized waters of the Rijn *(Rhine)* river, whose main flow is now to the south through Rotterdam. The lovely Rapenburg canal leads to what is perhaps Leiden's most outstanding museum, the ***Oudheden** *Rijksmuseum van Oudheden)* (3). Housing one of the major archaeological collections in Europe, it gets off to an impressive start right in the entry hall with the entire ***Temple of Taffeh**, donated in 1969 in recognition of Holland's role in the rescue of Nubian treasures threatened by the construction of the Aswan dam. Originally built in the 1st century A.D., it was converted during the 4th century for the worship of Isis and later used as a Christian church. Other displays here are of equal calibre, covering Egyptian, Greek, Roman, and other eras of classical antiquity. The top floor is devoted to archaeology in the Netherlands, from prehistoric times through the Middle Ages. All of this may be seen on Tuesdays through Saturdays, from 10 a.m. to 5 p.m.; and on Sundays and holidays from noon–5 p.m. The Museum Card will get you in free.

Now cross the canal and wander down to the **Academie** (4), the main building of the university since 1581. Originally built as a church, it has a fine bell turret and now houses, among other things, the small **Academisch Historisch Museum**. Displays here all relate to the long history of the university, and may be seen on Wednesdays through Fridays, from 1–5 p.m. Behind the building is one of the oldest botanical gardens in Europe, the **Hortus Botanicus**. A perfect place to relax, it was laid out in 1590 and features an extraordinary assemblage of plants and trees from all over the world, both outdoors and in greenhouses. Don't miss the historic Clusiusgarden, a re-creation of the original 16th-century garden. You can enter the gates at Rapenburg 73 on Mondays through Saturdays, from 9 a.m. to 5 p.m.; and on Sundays from 10 a.m. to 5 p.m. The Museum Card is accepted.

A short stroll down Kaiserstraat and a left at the next canal brings you to the **Pilgrim Fathers Documents Center** (5), whose displays concern the life of the Pilgrims in Leiden before they left for America in 1620. It is open on Mondays through Fridays, from 9:30 a.m. to 4:30 p.m., and admission is free.

Now follow the map to the **Pieterskerk** (6), a large 15th-century church with a fine interior. Next to it is the **Jan Pesijnshofje**, a 17th-century almshouse built on the site of the home of John Robinson, the leader of the Pilgrims. A plaque in English explains all.

The route continues past the **Stadhuis**, or Town Hall, with an impressive restored façade of 1600 in the Dutch Renaissance style. Behind this, along the Nieuwe Rijn canal, a lively outdoor market is held on Wednesdays and Saturdays. Cross the unusual bridge and wander through some narrow streets to the **Burcht** (7), a 12th-century fortress atop a mound of Saxon or possibly Roman origin. It once guarded the confluence of the Old and New Rhine *(Rijn)* rivers, both of which have long since been turned into canals with most of the water diverted to the south. You can climb to the top of the citadel for a superb view of Leiden.

Return to Nieuwstraat and take a look at the **Hooglandse Kerk**, an imposing church from the 15th century. It contains the tomb of the heroic Mayor Van der Werff, who led the citizens during the terrible siege of 1574. According to legend, at one point the starvation became so bad that many wanted to surrender, but the mayor set an example by offering his own body as feed. This was rejected, and relief came soon after.

Continue on through the old town, following the map to the **Boerhaave Museum** (8). Specializing in the history of science from a Dutch point of view, it displays a formidable collection of antique instruments and medical devices. Among the treasures are some wonderful skeletons in the Anatomical Theatre, scary electrostatic generators, and ancient microscopes. These may be seen on Tuesdays through Saturdays, from 10 a.m. to 5 p.m.; and on Sundays from noon–5 p.m. Museum Cards are accepted.

Cross another canal and stroll over to Leiden's superb art gallery,

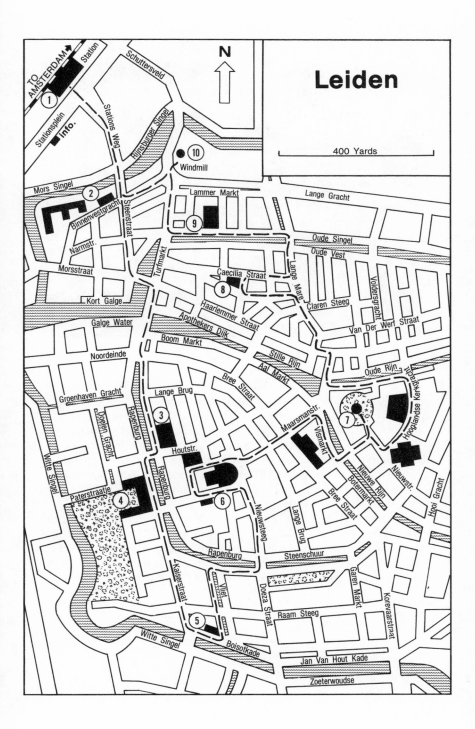

The Market on the Nieuwe Rijn Canal

the ***Stedelijk Museum "De Lakenhal"** (9). Erected in 1640, this former cloth weavers' guildhall now exhibits 16th- and 17th-century paintings by such local artists as Jan Steen and Lucas van Leyden. Native-son Rembrandt is represented by an early work. There are also period room settings, sculptures, decorative art works, armor, tiles, and historical artifacts on display. The museum is open on Tuesdays through Fridays, from 10 a.m. to 5 p.m.; and on Sundays from noon–5 p.m. Yes, they accept the Museum Card.

On the way back to the station you'll pass a windmill used as the **Molenmuseum "De Valk"** (10). Built in the mid-18th century, it has been restored to its condition of about 1900, and may be visited on Tuesdays through Saturdays, from 10 a.m. to 5 p.m.; and on Sundays from 1–5 p.m. The Museum Card will get you in free.

The Hague

(Den Haag or 's-Gravenhage)

Amsterdam is officially the capital of the Netherlands, but the government and all that goes with it sits at The Hague, making this in fact the real capital. With more than 60 foreign embassies, three royal palaces, and the parliament, The Hague has an air of international sophistication that sets it apart from every other Dutch city. Actually, "Europe's largest village" did not become a city at all until as late as the 19th century, when King Louis Bonaparte granted it a charter. Don't look for canals here—there are precious few—or typical Dutch charm, for this is first and foremost a place of stately elegance.

The Hague began as a hunting preserve for the counts of Holland. During the mid-13th century a proper castle was built, around which the town developed. Since then it has always been a favored venue for diplomatic negotiations, and as such, naturally developed a sense of luxurious living and recreation. This character remains with it today and is enhanced by a multitude of excellent museums, cultural institutions, exclusive shops, and fine restaurants.

By limiting the number of museums and other attractions you visit, it is quite easy to combine this trip in the same day with one to Scheveningen. This is actually a part of The Hague although it lies a few miles to the northwest. Described in the next chapter, the Scheveningen trip includes a famous seaside resort, several superb museums, and the ever-popular Madurodam "Holland in a Nutshell."

GETTING THERE:

Trains depart Amsterdam's Centraal Station very frequently for the 45-minute ride to Den Haag HS *(Hollands Spoor Station)*, the mainline station for The Hague. Here you transfer to another frequently running train for Den Haag Centraal *(CS)* Station, a quick 2-minute ride. Return service operates until late evening, after which hourly trains run all night long.

By car, take the A-4 highway past Schiphol Airport and Leiden. The Hague (*Den Haag* or 's-Gravenhage) is 34 miles southwest of Amsterdam.

GETTING AROUND:

You may want to use the trams or buses for part of this trip, especially if you combine it with the trip to Scheveningen in the next chapter. Public transit maps, information, and day passes are available at the HTM office on the west side of Den Haag Centraal Station, or at the tourist office.

WHEN TO GO:

Some of the best sights in The Hague are closed on Mondays. Check the descriptions of the attractions you'd like to visit to determine which day of the week to come on. Good weather is important if you intend to combine this trip with the one to Scheveningen.

FOOD AND DRINK:

The Hague is well endowed with restaurants and cafés, especially in the expensive category. Some outstanding choices are:

Saur (Lange Voorhout 47, 2 blocks north of the Mauritshuis Museum) An upstairs restaurant, very famous for its seafood. Reservations preferred, phone (070) 346-2565. X: Sun. $$$

Da Roberto (Noordeinde 196, 2 blocks south of the Panorama Mesdag) Italian cuisine. Phone (070) 346-4977. X: Sat. lunch, Sun. lunch. $$$

Le Bistroquet Lange Voorhout 98, 4 blocks west of Centraal Station) A small and very popular French restaurant. Phone (070) 360-1170. X: Sat. lunch, Sun., holidays. $$$

The Ajoe Lange Poten 31, 1 block south of the Binnenhof) Indonesian food. Phone (070) 364-5613. X: Mon. $$

't Goude Hooft (Groenmarkt 13, 3 blocks west of the Binnenhof) Noted for its Old World atmosphere. Phone (070) 346-9713. $$

Stationsrestauratie (Kon. Julianaplein 10, by Centraal Station) Convenient for an inexpensive meal. $

De Dageraad (Hooikade 4, 5 blocks north of the Mauritshuis Museum, beyond Lange Voorhout) Vegetarian meals by a canal. $

TOURIST INFORMATION:

The local tourist office (VVV) is next to Den Haag Centraal Station. You can phone them at (06) 3403-5051 (toll call).

The Ridderzaal in the Binnenhof

SUGGESTED TOUR:

Begin at The Hague's modern **Centraal Station** (1) and follow the map a short distance to the 17th-century ***Mauritshuis** (2), a Dutch Renaissance mansion that today houses one of the best small art museums in the world. Officially known as the Royal Picture Gallery *(Koninklijk Kabinet van Schilderijen)*, its collection includes quite a few of Rembrandt's most notable works such as the **Anatomy Lesson of Dr. Tulp*, along with world-famous masterpieces by Frans Hals, Jan Steen, Vermeer, Van Dyck, Hans Memling, both Cranachs, and many others. Be on the lookout for the unusual *Adam and Eve in Paradise*, a joint collaboration of the talents of both Rubens and Bruegel. The museum is open Tuesdays through Saturdays, from 10 a.m. to 5 p.m.; and on Sundays and holidays from 11 a.m. to 5 p.m. Museum Cards are accepted.

From here it is only a few steps into the **Binnenhof** (3), the courtyard of the former castle and now the seat of the Dutch parliament. Long the center of political life in the Netherlands, it may be seen on guided tours that begin in the basement of the 13th-century **Ridder-**

zaal (Knights' Hall), a stunning medieval structure with conical towers, in the center of the courtyard. The tour, given in English and other languages, begins with an audio-visual show and a visit to the Ridderzaal upstairs, where joint sessions of the parliament are held, and where its members are addressed by the Queen. It then moves on to one of the two chambers of the States General, as the parliament is called. The workings of Dutch democracy are explained as you sit in one of the representatives' seats. Tours are held all year round, Mondays through Saturdays, from 10 a.m. to 4 p.m., but not on holidays. This is a very popular attraction, so it may be wise to make reservations in advance by phoning (070) 364-6144 in order to avoid a wait. The tours are sometimes modified to meet the needs of government functions.

Exit from the west end of the Binnenhof and turn right to the 14th-century **Gevangenpoort** (Prison Gate) (4), which once guarded the entrance to the counts' castle. Used as a prison until the 19th century, it now houses an interesting museum of torture instruments. You can visit its dark cells on conducted tours that depart frequently from the small entrance to the left. The Gevangenpoort is open Mondays through Fridays, from 10 a.m. to 4 p.m.; and on Sundays from 1 to 4 p.m. The tours are held at least hourly, and admission is free to holders of the Museum Card.

Stroll through the Buitenhof, originally the outer courtyard of the castle and now a lovely square. A few steps beyond this is the **Grote Kerk** (5), also known as Sint Jacobskerk. Dating from the 14th century, and later modified, this is the most interesting church in The Hague. Its 320-foot tower was first built in 1423 and has long been a major landmark. Step inside to see the remarkable stained-glass windows, the pre-Reformation pulpit, and the coat-of-arms of the Knights of the Golden Fleece.

The route now leads up the pedestrians-only Noordeinde to an equestrian statue of William the Silent. Opposite this is the **Paleis Noordeinde** (6), an old royal palace erected in 1553 as a private mansion. Recently renovated, it is presently used as Queen Beatrix's office and so cannot be visited. You can, however, enjoy the garden behind it and take a look at the royal stables, which remain in use.

Continue up Noordeinde, here lined with expensive shops, and cross a section of the old town moat, now used as a canal. Zeestraat leads to the **Panorama Mesdag** (7). Billed as the world's largest panoramic painting, this huge circular canvas is among the few survivors of a once-popular genre. It was created in 1881 by the local artist H. W. Mesdag and depicts the nearby seaside town of Scheveningen (see next chapter) as it looked at that time. The illusion of reality is so startling that it makes you feel you have stepped back in time to an-

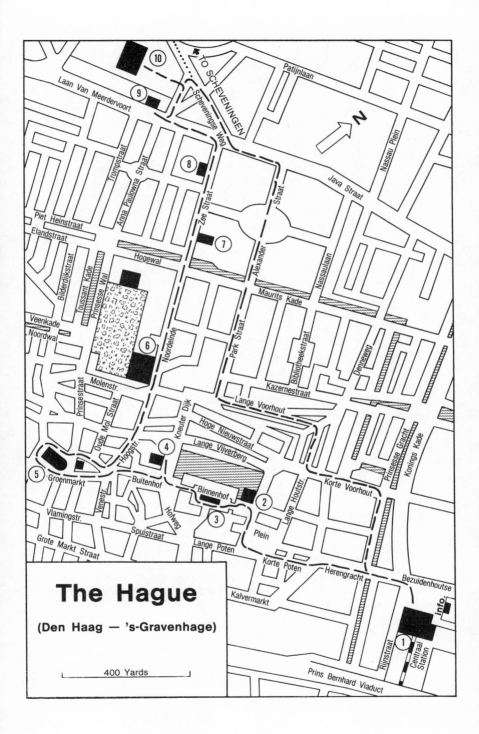

other era. Visits may be made Mondays through Saturdays, from 10 a.m. to 5 p.m.; and on Sundays and holidays from noon until 5 p.m.

Just up the street is the **Post Museum** (8), where you can explore the history of communications in the Netherlands. It is also noted for its large collection of stamps from all over the world. The museum is open Mondays through Fridays, from 10 a.m. to 5 p.m.; and on weekends from noon until 5 p.m.

The same artist who created the *Panorama Mesdag,* a man of independent means, lived in a mansion just around the corner. This is now the **Rijksmuseum H. W. Mesdag** (9), which specializes in works of The Hague School and the French Barbizon School of the 19th century. Although the museum is more than a little run down and the manner of display terribly old fashioned, the art itself is superb and offers an unusual opportunity to see minor works by such famous artists as Delacroix, Corot, Millet, Courbet, Rousseau, and Daubigny. There are, of course, quite a few paintings by Mesdag himself. This rather strange museum is open Tuesdays through Saturdays, from 10 a.m. to 5 p.m.; and on Sundays and holidays from 1–5 p.m.. Museum Cards are accepted.

The enormous **Peace Palace** *(Vredespaleis)* (10) is only a few steps away. Built as a headquarters for international agencies that promote world peace, it was financed by a donation from Andrew Carnegie. Ironically, its completion date of 1913 nearly coincides with the outbreak of World War I. Since the 1920s it has been occupied by the International Court of Justice (a UN agency) and the Academy of International Law, as well as by the Permanent Court of Arbitration. Its pompous interior is heavily decorated with gifts from nations all over the world, and is worth seeing for the rich diversity it offers. The Peace Palace is open Mondays through Fridays, from 10 a.m. to noon and 2–4 p.m., with hourly guided tours. Phone (070) 346-9680 for reservations. There are no tours when court is in session.

From here you may want to continue with the **Scheveningen** daytrip described in the next chapter, as you are practically there. To do this, just board northbound tram number 7 or 8 at the stop opposite the Peace Palace. Otherwise, you can return to the center of The Hague by following the route on the map, or by taking southbound tram number 7 to Den Haag Centraal Station or tram number 8 direct to Den Haag HS Station.

Scheveningen

The popular seaside resort of Scheveningen is actually a part of The Hague, but is located a few miles from the city center and has enough sights of its own to keep you busy for an entire day. Its name is so difficult to pronounce correctly that during World War II it was used as a test to separate the genuine Dutch from German infiltrators.

Scheveningen began as a small fishing village in the 14th century, although only a little of that atmosphere survives today. It became popular as a resort in the early 1800s and by the end of the century it was a favored meeting place for European society. Today, its restored ambiance, and its casino and pier, are once again attracting crowds of vacationers. To round things out, this trip includes several attractions in the northern part of The Hague as well as the world-famous Madurodam, a miniature slice of Holland that delights young and old alike.

This trip can easily be combined in the same day with one to The Hague, described in the last chapter. Doing this will cut down the amount of time that can be spent seeing the sights, but will still be very enjoyable.

GETTING THERE:

Trains leave Amsterdam's Centraal Station very frequently for the 45-minute ride to Den Haag HS *(Hollands Spoor Station)*, the mainline station for The Hague. From the front of the station take tram number 9 in the direction of Scheveningen. Return service operates until late evening. If you combine this trip with one to The Hague you should follow the directions at the end of the previous chapter.

By car, follow the directions to The Hague in the previous chapter and park near Centraal Station, from which you can take tram number 1, 7, or 9 to Scheveningen.

GETTING AROUND:

Unless you drive to each attraction, you will need to use the trams for parts of this trip. Information, maps, and day passes are available from the HTM offices at the train stations or at the tourist office. You can, of course, just ask the conductor and pay as you board.

WHEN TO GO:
 This trip should really be made in the summer, and only on a fine warm day at that. Some of the museums are closed on Mondays, while Madurodam is open daily from late March until early January. The casino is open daily and requires proper dress, including jacket and tie for men.

FOOD AND DRINK:
 Some good choice restaurants are:

> **Ducdalf** (Dr. Lelykade 5, on the inner harbor) Exclusively sea-food. Phone (070) 355-7692. $$$
>
> **Raden Mas** (Gevers Deynootplein 125, near the casino) Indonesian specialties. Phone (070) 354-5432. X: weekend lunches. $$$
>
> **Golden Duck** (Dr. Lelykade 29, on the inner harbor) Chinese cuisine. Phone (070) 354-1095. X: Tues. $$
>
> **De Goede Reede** (Dr. Lelykade 236, on the inner harbor. A good value in seafood. Phone (070) 354-8820. $$
>
> **La Galleria** (Gevers Deynootplein 105, near the casino) A full range of Italian dishes. Phone (070) 352-1156. $$

In addition, there are plenty of inexpensive snack bars and fast-food outlets along the waterfront and near the casino.

TOURIST INFORMATION:
 The tourist office (VVV) in Scheveningen is located at Gevers Deynootweg 1134, near the casino, or you can inquire at the office next to Den Haag Centraal Station. The phone number for either is (06) 3403-5051 (toll call).

SUGGESTED TOUR:
 Begin your tour by boarding tram number 9 from the front of **Den Haag HS** *(Hollands Spoor)* **Station**, the mainline station for The Hague, in the direction of Scheveningen. If you are starting from downtown The Hague you should board tram number 7 from Centraal Station instead, and if you are continuing from the Peace Palace at the end of the last trip you can take number 7 from the stop opposite the palace.
 Get off the tram at the Congresgebouw stop at the intersection of Johan de Wittlaan. From here it's a short walk to the museum complex on Stadhouderslaan. The **Haags Gemeentemuseum** (1) is the city's municipal museum and specializes in modern art, the applied arts, musical instruments, and costumes. It has the world's largest collec-

tion of works by Piet Mondriaan as well as paintings by such 19th- and 20th-century luminaries as Monet, Jongkind, Millet, Sisley, Courbet, Van Gogh, Picasso, and Léger. The musical instruments are from all over the world and date from as far back as the 15th century. Among the applied arts exhibits are period room settings and objects from every corner of the planet, from the prehistoric to the present. Allow plenty of time for a visit, which can be made on Tuesdays through Sundays, from 11 a.m. to 5 p.m. Museum Cards are accepted, but there may be an extra charge for special temporary exhibits.

Adjacent to this, and sharing a common entrance, is the **Museon** (2). This thoroughly contemporary museum uses the latest techniques to cover no less a subject than man's life on earth and beyond. Its dazzling displays and audiovisual shows are great fun to experience, especially for children, but they can also exhaust you. The Museon is open on Tuesdays through Fridays from 10 a.m. to 5 p.m.; and on weekends and holidays from noon to 5 p.m. A Museum Card will get you in free.

Just around the corner is the spectacular **Omniversum** (3), a "space theater" in which the audience sits under a dome, almost completely surrounded by multiple film projections. The shows vary, but their theme is always one of science and discovery. This is a very popular attraction and fills up quickly, so it is best to make reservations by phoning (070) 354-5454, or by stopping in before visiting the previous two museums. It is open daily except on Mondays.

From the front of the municipal museum you can board tram number 10 to the **Scheveningen Harbor** (Haven) (4), the end of the line. This is where the original fishing village began in the 14th century. Although the harbor is still busy with fishing and shipping activities, very little of its old-time atmosphere survives today. The waterfront along Dr. Lelykade is noted for its fine seafood restaurants. You might want to visit the **Marine Biological Museum** (Zeebiologisch Museum) (5), with its specimens of marine life from all the seven seas. It is open Mondays through Saturdays, from 10 a.m. to 5 p.m.; and on Sundays from 1–5 p.m.

Now follow the map to the Strandweg, a promenade along the edge of the beach, and continue towards the pier. Along the way there are many snack bars and other seaside diversions, including the **Scheveningen Sea Life Centre** where you can walk through a transparent tunnel under a huge aquarium filled with exotic creatures. The **Casino** (6) is housed in the historic Kurhaus, an enormous heap of fanciful architecture dating from 1885. Along with the other resort facilities, this has been renovated after a long period of slow decline. The crowds are back now, and many of them head for the gambling tables and slot machines, which are open daily from 1:30 p.m. until

The Kurhaus

2 a.m. There is an admission charge and proper attire is required. The Casino is scheduled to move into new quarters across the street at the end of 1995.

The **Pier** (7) juts out into the North Sea just beyond this. Equipped with the usual fun and games as well as an observation tower, it is open daily with a small admission charge. Heading back inland, you might want to visit the **Scheveningen Museum** (8) at Neptunusstraat 92. Life in the old fishing village is re-created here with room sets, costumes, model ships, and fishing artifacts. It is open Mondays through Saturdays, from 10 a.m. to 5 p.m., but is closed on Mondays during the off season.

From the front of the casino at Gevers Deynootplein you can take tram number 1 or 9 to what is undoubtedly one of Holland's greatest tourist attractions. Whatever you do, don't miss a visit to the magical ***Madurodam** (9). About 150 of Holland's most outstanding buildings have been reproduced as 1/25th scale models and laid out as a miniature city over a five-acre site. Not only are they amazingly well detailed, but many of them provide action as well. Trains run along two miles of track, tiny cars speed down highways, boats move through the harbor, airliners taxi on the tarmac, and windmills turn in the breeze. There are sound effects, too, with music coming from within the churches, the barrel organs, and the street fairs. At night it be-

A Small Corner of Madurodam

comes a different world when over 50,000 lights come on. Now, you may think that this is just for kids, but in fact most of the people who come to Madurodam are adults—and even the most skeptical of them love it! Visits to this diminutive wonderland may be made between late March and early January, daily from 9 a.m. until 6, 9:30, 10:30, or 11 p.m. depending on the season. Madurodam operates under the royal patronage of Queen Beatrix, with profits going to charity.

From here you can take tram number 9 back to either Den Haag Centraal or Den Haag HS (mainline) station.

*Delft

Long famous for its distinctive blue porcelain, historic Delft is among the best preserved and most picturesque places in Holland. Its lovely old buildings and tree-shaded canals make it everything a Dutch town should be, a scene right out of a painting by Vermeer. That renowned 17th-century artist was in fact born in Delft, and lived and died there. Another celebrated resident was William the Silent, in some ways the father of modern Holland, who was murdered there in 1584.

Settled since at least the 11th century, Delft received its charter in 1246. Trade grew with the development of a harbor on the Maas river, a short distance away in what is now Rotterdam. A great fire in 1536 almost totally destroyed the town, but it was soon rebuilt. The manufacture of porcelain brought about a great prosperity that lasted until the late 18th century. Later revived, this industry today plays only a minor role in the town's economy.

As you will quickly discover, Delft is very popular with tourists. Fortunately, most of them never get beyond the pottery shops in the market place, leaving the tranquil streets and narrow canals there for you to enjoy in peace. This trip could be combined in the same day with one to Leiden, described in an earlier chapter. There is direct train service between the two towns.

GETTING THERE:

Trains depart Amsterdam's Centraal Station frequently for the 55-minute ride to Delft. A local *(stoptrein)* runs at half-hour intervals and goes directly there, while the express *(IC)* trains require a change at Den Haag HS Station. Return service operates until late evening, followed by hourly departures all night long.

By car, take the A-4 highway southeast to Den Haag, followed by the A-13 into Delft. The total distance from Amsterdam is 36 miles.

WHEN TO GO:

Most of the museums are closed on Mondays, and the main churches are not open to tourists on Sundays. A colorful **outdoor market** is held on the Markt every Thursday from 9 a.m. until 5 p.m., and there is a fascinating **flea market** along the canals on Saturdays from May through September.

FOOD AND DRINK:

Delft has an unusually broad range of restaurants and cafés, mostly geared to the tourist trade. Among the better choices are:

> **Prinsenkelder** (Schoolstraat 11, by the Prinsenhof Museum) El-egant French-inspired dining. Reservations preferred, phone (015) 12-18-60. X: Sat. lunch, Sun. $$$

> **Redjeki** (Choorstraat 50, 3 blocks northwest of the Nieuwe Kerk) Superb Indonesian dishes. Phone (015) 12-50-22. $$

> **Le Vieux Jean** (Heilige Geest Kerkhof 3, by the Oude Kerk) Classic French cuisine. Phone (015) 13-04-33. X: Sun., Mon. $$

> **Monopole** (Markt 48, on the market square) Light meals and drinks, Tourist Menu. $

> **Locus Publicus** (Brabantse Turfmarkt, 3 blocks south of Nieuwe Kerk) All kinds of sandwiches and beer. $

> **Stationsrestauratie** (in the station) Convenient and inexpen-sive dining. $

TOURIST INFORMATION:

The local tourist office (VVV), phone (015) 12-61-00, is in the market square at Markt 85.

SUGGESTED TOUR:

It is an easy and rather pretty walk from the **train station** (1) to the market square *(Markt),* a busy place lined with outdoor cafés and shops. Just follow the map. At its west end stands the imposing **Town Hall** *(Stadhuis)* (2), a Renaissance structure built in 1618. The tower dates from the 14th century and was part of the original building that was destroyed in the great fire of 1536. It may be possible to step inside to view the richly decorated council chamber and wedding hall. Horse carriage rides depart from the outside of the building during the tourist season, every day except Thursdays—when the traditional outdoor market fills up the square.

The east end of the square is dominated by the ***Nieuwe Kerk** (3), a Gothic church which, despite its name, is not all that new, having been built between 1384 and 1496. Its tower—all 365 feet of it—may be climbed for a fine view, and contains a noted 17th-century carillon

The Bridge behind the Nieuwe Kerk

that serenades the square below. Step inside to see the magnificent mausoleum of Holland's greatest hero, William the Silent, who was assassinated in Delft in 1584. In the vaults below (not open to the public) lie the remains of more than 40 other members of the royal House of Orange, including Queen Wilhelmina, who died in 1962. Other features of the church include some fine stained-glass windows and an exhibition on royal funerals. Visits may be made Mondays through Saturdays, from 9 a.m. to 5 p.m.; with shorter hours off season. There is an admission charge.

The walk now leads around the rear of the church, passing a small canal, a remarkably picturesque little bridge, and some gorgeous houses. Turn left on Voldersgracht, a narrow lane alongside an equally narrow canal. On Saturdays in summer a flea market is held here, where you can have fun bargaining for all kinds of junk and perhaps a few treasures. Some of the 17th-century façades along the street are interesting, notably that at number 6, as is the former meat market *(Vleeshal)*, decorated with animal heads, at the west end. The **Waag** (4), a former weighhouse built in 1770, was once the guildhall of the gold and silversmiths, and today serves as a small theater.

Continue on, following the map, to the ***Oude Kerk** (5). The tower of this 13th-century Gothic church leans precariously, but since it

Flea Market along the Voldersgracht

hasn't toppled over yet it is presumably safe to enter for a look at the tombs of several national heroes. Among these are memorials to the great artist Johannes (Jan) Vermeer (1632–1675) and the scientist Anton van Leeuwenhoek, who is reputed to have invented the microscope. While inside, be sure to take a look at the strangely carved 16th-century pulpit and the modern stained-glass windows depicting recent Dutch history. The church doors are open for tourists from the beginning of April until the end of October, Mondays through Saturdays, from noon until 5 p.m. There is an admission charge.

Now stroll over to the ***Prinsenhof Museum** (6), housed in a 15th-century convent that was once the residence of William the Silent. It was also the scene of his assassination, and the bullet marks are still there on the wall at the foot of the stairs. The museum that now occupies the premises is mostly devoted to the struggle for Dutch independence from Spain and also has exhibits relating to the royal House of Orange-Nassau, which has supplied Holland with its monarchs down to the present. It is well worth a visit for its elegantly decorated interior, as well as for its splendid paintings, tapestries, silverware, and porcelain. The museum is open on Tuesdays through Saturdays, from 10 a.m. to 5 p.m., and on Sundays and holidays from 1–5 p.m. The same admission is also valid for the Nusantara and Huis Lambert van Meerten museums, below.

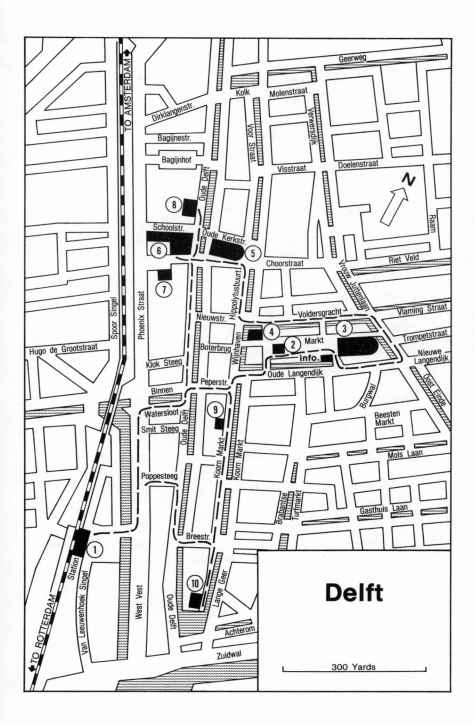

Delft

300 Yards

TO AMSTERDAM

TO ROTTERDAM

Geerweg

Kolk

Molenstraat

Dirklangenstr.

Bagijnestr.

Bagijnhof

Verwersdijk

Visstraat

Doelenstraat

Oude Delft

Schoolstr.

Oude Kerkstr.

Choorstraat

Riet Veld

Raam

N

Phoenix Straat

Spoor Singel

Hippolytusbuurt

Voldersgracht

Vlaming Straat

Vrouw Juttenland

Nieuwstr.

Boterbrug

Markt

Trompetstraat

Hugo de Grootstraat

Klok Steeg

Wijnhaven

info.

Nieuwe
Langendijk

Binnen

Peperstr.

Oude Langendijk

Burgwal

Oost Einde

Watersloot

Smit Steeg

Oude Delft

Beesten
Markt

Poppesteeg

Koorn Markt

Koorn Markt

Mols Laan

Breestr.

Brabantse Turfmarkt

Gasthuis Laan

Station

Van Leeuwenhoek Singel

West Vest

Oude Delft

Lange Geer

Achterom

Zuidwal

Just across the square from this is the **Nusantara Museum** (7), which specializes in ethnology with an emphasis on Indonesian artifacts. It is open during the same times as the Prinsenhof Museum (above) and shares a common entrance ticket.

Another nearby museum is the **Huis Lambert van Meerten** (8). This is of great interest for its collection of antique Delft tiles, beautiful room settings, and lovely old furniture. Again, it is open at the same time as the Prinsenhof Museum (above), and the same ticket will get you in.

Before heading back to the train station, you might want to visit the small **Museum Tétar van Elven** (9). Named after a very obscure 19th-century painter who lived here, it is noted more for its stylish atmosphere than for the art it contains. The museum is open from May through mid-October, on Tuesdays through Saturdays, from 1– 5 p.m.

Continuing down the same street will bring you to the **Armamentarium** (10), a 17th-century warehouse that now houses the Dutch Army Museum. Military buffs will enjoy the weapons on display here, ranging from ancient times to the present. They may all be seen Tuesdays through Saturdays, from 10 a.m. to 5 p.m.; and on Sundays from 1–5 p.m.; but not on major holidays. From here it is only a short stroll back to the station.

NEARBY SIGHTS:

Delft is world-famous for its traditional porcelain objects, many of which are sold—at rather steep prices—in the shops on and around the Markt. If you'd like to watch porcelain being hand-crafted in the old manner, you can do so at two factories just outside the town center, both of which also make sales. They are:

Royal Delftware De Porceleyne Fles at Rotterdamseweg 196, just south of the town. Founded in 1653, this is the most famous of the makers. Ask at the tourist office for current times and travel information.

De Delftse Pauw at Delftweg 133, just north of the town. Again, inquire at the tourist office for more details.

Rotterdam

On May 14th, 1940, Rotterdam was practically bombed out of existence in an unprovoked attack on a neutral nation by Hitler's *Luftwaffe*. What rose from the smoldering ashes after the war was an aggressively modern city totally unlike anything else in Holland. Located at the mouth of the Rijn *(Rhine)* and Maas *(Meuse)* rivers, it is now the world's largest port, with harbor facilities extending some 20 miles west to the open sea. Having a population of over a half-million, it is also the second-largest city in the Netherlands.

Like Amsterdam, Rotterdam began in the late 13th century when a dam was erected across one of its rivers, in this case the Rotte. Full recognition as a city came in 1340, and soon after that a canal was dug, attracting commercial traffic away from nearby Delft—whose ancient harbor is now a part of Rotterdam. The war with Spain ultimately resulted in the transfer of overseas trade from Antwerp to the Dutch port. Since then, industrial development along the entire length of the Rhine has assured Rotterdam's position as the main transit point for Europe.

This intriguing daytrip covers an unusually wide variety of attractions, ranging from a cruise through the busy harbor to a look at one of the world's best art museums, and from a climb to the top of a soaring "space tower" to a stroll through the delightfully quaint village of Delfshaven.

GETTING THERE:

Trains depart Amsterdam's Centraal Station very frequently for Rotterdam's Centraal Station (CS), a ride of about one hour. Some of these go by way of Haarlem and others via Schiphol Airport. Return service operates until late evening, followed by hourly departures all night long. Those without a railpass should consider using the Netherlands Railways day excursion package number 5 or number 71.

By car, take the A-4 highway southwest past Schiphol Airport to Den Haag, then the A-13 into Rotterdam. The total distance is 47 miles.

GETTING AROUND:

You may want to use public transportation for part of this trip, especially if you go all the way out to Delftshaven. Maps and information are available at the tourist office.

WHEN TO GO:

Nearly all of the museums are closed on Mondays and on April 30th (Queen's Day). The harbor cruise operates frequently from April through September, but only a few times a day during the rest of the year. Good weather is essential for enjoyment of this trip, as much of it is out of doors.

FOOD AND DRINK:

Rotterdam has an enormous range of restaurants in all price ranges, with the majority concentrated between Centraal Station, the Maritime Museum, and the Boymans–Van Beuningen Museum. You will also find many snack shops and fast-food outlets in the center of town. Some good restaurant choices are:

La Vilette (Westblaak 160, 3 blocks northeast of the Boymans–Van Beuningen Museum) Superb French cuisine. Phone (010) 414-8692. X: Sat. lunch, Sun., holidays. $$$

Old Dutch (Rochussenstraat 20, 1 block north of the Boymans–Van Beuningen Museum) A luxurious Dutch restaurant with atmosphere. Phone (010) 436-0344. X: Sat., Sun. $$$

Coq d'Or (Van Vollenhovenstraat 25, 3 blocks southeast of the Boymans–Van Beuningen Museum) Regarded as Rotterdam's leading French restaurant. Phone (010) 436-6405. X: Sat., Sun. $$$

Napoli (Meent 81, 5 blocks northeast of the Maritime Museum) Fine Italian dining. $$

Indonesia (Rode Zand 34, 3 blocks north of the Maritime Museum) Genuine Indonesian food, with *rijsttafel* specialties. $$

Engels Restaurants (Stationsplein 45, by the Centraal Station) Six restaurants of different nationalities all combined together—French, Spanish, Scandinavian, Hungarian, English, and Dutch. $$ and $

Euromast (340 feet up in the Euromast tower) A self-service cafeteria with a fabulous view. There is also an expensive ($$$) French restaurant at the same level. $

Bongers (Meent 20, 5 blocks north of the Maritime Museum) Pancakes of all sorts. $

TOURIST INFORMATION:

The city tourist office (VVV), phone (06) 3403-4065 (toll call), is at Coolsingel 67, a few blocks southeast of Centraal Station. There is also a convenient branch at the station.

SUGGESTED TOUR:
Leave the **Centraal Station** (1) and follow the map through the heart of modern Rotterdam to the first attraction. You could also get there by taking the subway *(Metro)* to the Beurs stop. Some of the streets along the way are reserved for pedestrians and form an attractive shopping area, while the broad Coolsingel is a major tree-lined boulevard with cafés. Along the way you will pass the City Hall *(Stadhuis)*, a pre-war building that survived the bombing, as well as the World Trade Center and the Stock Exchange *(Beurs)*. Streets on either side of these lead into modern shopping malls.

The **Schielandshuis** (2) is the only 17th-century structure in central Rotterdam to have made it through the war intact. Today its elegant interior houses the city's **Historical Museum**, with exquisite period room settings, displays of the fine and applied arts, porcelain, costumes, toys, household equipment, and many other interesting subjects. There is also an audio-visual show on the bombardment of Rotterdam, plus a shop and a rather good restaurant. Visits can be made Tuesdays through Saturdays, from 10 a.m. to 5 p.m.; and on Sundays and holidays from 11 a.m. to 5 p.m. They accept the Museum Card.

From here it is only a short stroll to the stunning new **Maritime Museum Prins Hendrik** (3) on the edge of Rotterdam's original man-made harbor. Changing exhibitions here cover the entire history of Holland's maritime exploits, with many models, artifacts, and a real periscope you can peer through. Part of the museum is outdoors on the waterfront and consists of floating ships, cranes, a lighthouse, and so on. A special treat here is to board the 19th-century warship *Buffel* and explore its fascinating interior. All of this may be seen Tuesdays through Saturdays, from 10 a.m. to 5 p.m.; and on Sundays and holidays from 11 a.m. to 5 p.m. Admission is less for Museum Card holders. In the open area next to the museum is the famous *City Destroyed* monument of 1953, expressing the anguish of the 1940 bombing.

Now follow the map to one of the finest art museums in all of Europe. The ***Boymans-van Beuningen Museum** (4) is unusual in that it covers a vast sweep of art over a long period of time, from medieval paintings to the most modern industrial design. You can't possibly see it all in a day, but a quick tour of the highlights can be done in an hour or so. The older part of the museum houses, naturally, the older art, while the modern section is devoted to contemporary works. A very few of the artists represented are Rembrandt, Jan Steen, Memling, Bruegel, Dürer, Titian, Rubens, Van Dyck, Van Gogh, Picasso, Ernst, Dali, Magritte, Warhol, and Stella. The museum is open Tuesdays through Saturdays, from 10 a.m. to 5 p.m.; and on Sundays and holidays from 11 a.m. to 5 p.m. The Museum Card gets you in free, but some special shows have an extra charge. Don't miss this.

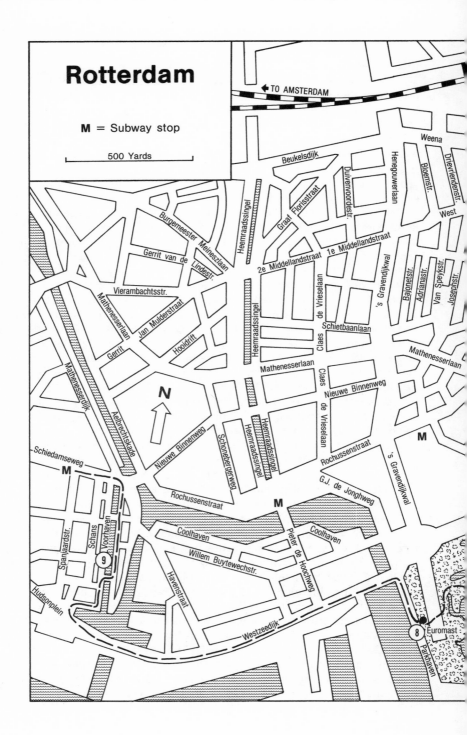

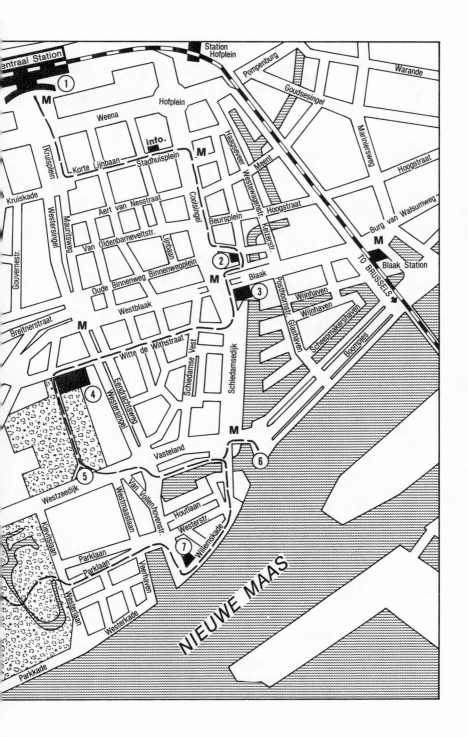

In the Space Cabin of the Euromast

The route leads through Museum Park to the new **Kunsthal Rotterdam** (5), a superb contemporary venue for changing exhibitions covering all of the main art forms and cultural/historical themes, both intimate and monumental. It's open on Tuesdays through Saturdays, from 10 a.m. to 5 p.m.; and on Sundays from 11 a.m. to 5 p.m.

Now wander over to the **SPIDO landing stage** (6), where you can board a boat for a delightful ***harbor cruise** . Several tours are offered, ranging from 75 minutes to over two hours in length. All of them are exciting and give you close-up views of ships from all over the world, along with oil refineries and other harbor installations. A running commentary is made in English, and explanatory brochures are available. Snacks and drinks are sold on each of the boats. The 75-minute cruise departs at least every 45 minutes between 9:30 a.m. and 5 p.m., daily from April through September. During the rest of the year the service is less frequent, but still runs every day.

Back on dry land, follow the map along the harbor to the **Museum voor Volkenkunde** (7), Rotterdam's noted museum of ethnology. Using the latest methods of presentation, the museum specializes in non-Western cultures, especially those of the former Dutch colonies. Its restaurant features exotic Third World dishes. The museum is open on Tuesdays through Saturdays, from 10 a.m. to 5 p.m.; and on Sundays and holidays from 11 a.m. to 5 p.m.

Now follow the map through a lovely park to Rotterdam's great landmark, the *Euromast (8). Built in 1960 and later made even higher, this tower offers spectacular panoramic views of the harbor and city. An elevator takes you up to the 340-foot level, where you will find an observation platform and two restaurants. If that isn't high enough, you can board the revolving Space Cabin and blast off on a slightly unnerving ride spiraling up the Space Tower to the 600-foot level, after which a retro-rocket returns you to the platform. The ups and downs can be experienced on any day from 10 a.m. to 7 p.m., but not after 5 p.m. from October through March. During January and February it operates on weekends only, and in July and August it remains open until 10:30 p.m. on Tuesdays through Saturdays.

So far, nearly everything in Rotterdam has been modern. If you'd like to see a picturesque old corner of town that survived the war, you should head on to **Delfshaven** (9). Once the port for Delft, it was connected to that town by a canal dug as early as 1389. This is where the Pilgrim Fathers departed for the New World in 1620, making stops in England en route. You can get there either by walking the somewhat dreary one-mile distance, or by taking a tram from the corner near the Euromast. The tiny harbor with its restored windmill has been preserved for posterity and still looks much as it did in centuries past. A branch of the Rotterdam Historical Museum called **De Dubbelde Palmboom**, located at Voorhaven 12, is devoted to regional life in times past. Its interesting and atmospheric displays can be seen on Tuesdays through Saturdays, from 10 a.m. to 5 p.m.; and on Sundays and holidays from 1–5 p.m. Close to and facing the water is the **Oude Kerk**, a 15th-century church where the Pilgrim Fathers held their last service before departing on the *Speedwell*, which they left for the *Mayflower* in Plymouth. A plaque in English recalls the story.

The quickest way back to Rotterdam's Centraal Station is to take the subway *(Metro)* from the Delfshaven stop, changing to the northbound line at Churchillplein-Beurs.

Dordrecht

Historically one of the most important places in Holland, Dordrecht survives as a pleasant seafaring town with a strong sense of the past. Not many foreign tourists come this way, but those who do are in for a special treat as they wander through its ancient streets.

Dordrecht, or *Dordt,* as it is often called, is strategically located at what is possibly the busiest river junction in Europe. Continuous boat traffic from both the Rijn *(Rhine)* and the Maas *(Meuse)* passes by its atmospheric old harbor on the way to the North Sea. At one time this made it the major shipping center of the Netherlands, but that commerce declined as the port of Rotterdam grew.

No one knows for certain just how old Dordrecht really is, although records suggest that it was destroyed by Norsemen in 837. A castle was built here in the 11th century and the town received its charter in 1220. The disastrous flood of 1421, in which over 10,000 people drowned, took a heavy toll on Dordrecht and forever changed its landscape. Rebuilt, it was again devastated, this time by fire, in 1457. Holland's independence had its earliest beginnings here in 1572 when a meeting of the provinces declared their freedom from the king of Spain and elected William the Silent as their leader.

GETTING THERE:

Trains leave Amsterdam's Centraal Station quite frequently for Dordrecht, a run of between 80 and 95 minutes. The slower ones go by way of Haarlem, while the faster IC expresses run via Schiphol Airport. Return service operates until late evening.

By car, take the A-4 southwest past Schiphol Airport to Den Haag, then the A-13 to Rotterdam, followed by the A-20 and the A-16 into Dordrecht. The total distance is 59 miles.

WHEN TO GO:

Avoid going to Dordrecht on a Monday, when its attractions are closed. On Sundays and holidays they do not open until 1 p.m.

FOOD AND DRINK:

Au Bon Coin (Groenmarkt 1, 2 blocks northwest of Statenplein) Excellent French cuisine. Phone (078) 13-82-30. X: Sat. lunch, Sun. lunch, Mon. $$$

Marktzicht (Varkenmarkt 17, near the foot of the old harbor) Noted for its seafood. Phone (078) 13-25-84. X: Sun., Mon. $$$

Jongepier (Groothoofd 8, near the Groothoofdspoort) Café dining with a view. $$

Crimpert Salm Visstraat 5, just south of the Town Hall and Visbrug) A good value in French-inspired meals. $

Stationsrestauratie (in the train station) Basic food at a minimal price. $

TOURIST INFORMATION:

The local tourist office (VVV), phone (078) 13-28-00, is just north of the train station. You might want to ask them about boat trips and about getting to Kinderdijk, an outlying area noted for its many working windmills.

SUGGESTED TOUR:

Leave the **train station** (1) and follow the map past the tourist office, across a canal, and through the Statenplein shopping area to the **Dordrecht Museum** (2). Located in a former asylum, this is an unusually good local art museum, whose collections focus mainly on paintings by Dordrecht artists from the 17th century to the present and include works by Albert Cuyp, Ferdinand Bol, and Ary Scheffer. It is also well known for its temporary exhibitions, particularly of recent art. The museum is open Tuesdays through Saturdays, from 10 a.m. to 5 p.m.; and on Sundays and holidays from 1–5 p.m. Museum Cards are accepted, but there may be an extra charge for special shows.

Now return to Statenplein and turn right on Hofstraat. This leads to a quiet and rather picturesque little courtyard called **De Hof** (3), where Holland's independence began in 1572 when a meeting of the provinces was held in the *Statenzaal* on the southeast side.

From here, take the narrow passageway through to Voorstraat and turn right. The *Muntpoortje,* at number 188, dates from 1555 and is all that remains of the one-time Dutch mint. Make the next left to a bridge, but don't cross it. Instead, go down the steps to a path on the Wijnhaven harbor and continue along the water's edge to the Boombrug, a small drawbridge.

Just beyond this is the **Groothoofdspoort** (4), a domed structure rebuilt in 1618 that was once the main gate to the town. Pass through it for a marvelous view of the confluence of the Oude Maas (which

Along the Kuipershaven

carries the waters of the Rhine), the Beneden Merwede, and the Noord rivers. Well over a thousand ships a day pass this point, and you can sit down and leisurely watch their progress from one of the outdoor café tables. Boat trips are also available here.

Now follow the map along Kuipershaven, a waterfront street lined with some strangely attractive old warehouses. Cross a bridge separating the two harbors and stroll over to the * **Museum Mr. Simon van Gijn** (5). This is truly a gem of a provincial museum, one that should not be missed by any visitor to Dordrecht. Housed in an 18th-century mansion owned by a banker and art collector named van Gijn, its period rooms contain a fabulous collection of furnishings, tapestries, musical instruments, paintings, and the like. Be certain to visit the Toy Pavilion in the attic, where a huge assortment of children's toys are on display. The museum is open Tuesdays through Saturdays, from 10 a.m. to 5 p.m.; and on Sundays and holidays from 1–5 p.m. You get in free if you have a Museum Card.

Continue along the inner harbor past the unusual Lange IJzeren-brug pedestrian bridge to the **Grote Kerk** (6). One of the largest and finest churches in Holland, it was begun in the 13th century but mostly dates from the 15th. Its 230-foot tower, leaning slightly to one side, is topped off with some oddly incongruous clocks and may be climbed for a magnificent view of the countryside. Step inside to see

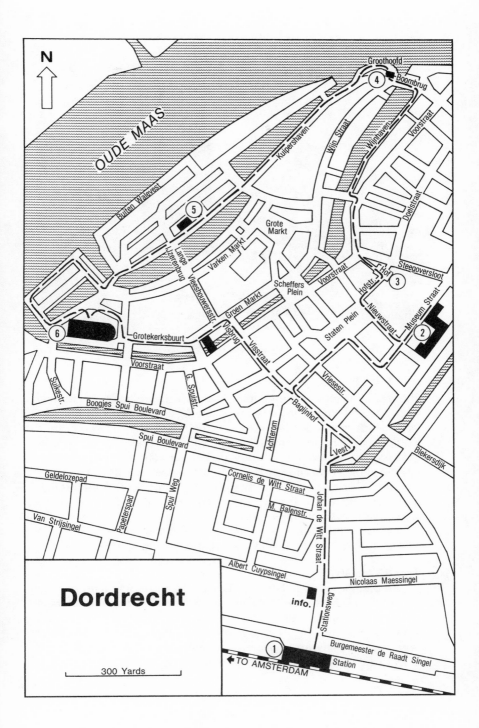

N

OUDE MAAS

Groothoofd
Boombrug
④
Voorstraat

Kuipershaven

Wijnstraat

Wijnhaven

Doelstraat

⑤

Grote
Markt

Buiten Walevest

Lange IJzerenbrug

Varken Markt

Voorstraat

Steegoversloot

Hof
③

Hofstr.

Scheffers
Plein

Nieuwstraat

Museum Straat

②

Groen Markt

Vleeshouwersstr.

Visbrug

Staten Plein

⑥

Grotekerksbuurt

Visstraat

Vriesestr.

Voorstraat

G. Spuistr.

Baginhof

Suikestr.

Boogjes Spui Boulevard

Achterom

Vest

Blekersdijk

Spui Boulevard

Geldelozepad

Papeterspad

Spui Weg

Cornelis de Witt Straat

M. Balenstr.

Johan de Witt Straat

Van Strijsingel

Albert Cuypsingel

Nicolaas Maessingel

info.

Dordrecht

Stationsweg

①
← TO AMSTERDAM   Station

Burgemeester de Raadt Singel

300 Yards

The Grote Kerk

the beautiful 16th-century **choir stalls**, which predate the Reformation. Other features include the stained-glass windows at the east end, which depict the flood of 1421, the fire of 1457, and an historic battle scene. The white marble pulpit with its wooden canopy is outstanding, as is the 17th-century organ. An 18th-century memorial plaque in the north choir aisle is dedicated to a British officer and tells his story in English. The church is open to visitors from April through October, on Tuesdays through Saturdays, from 10:30 a.m. to 4 p.m.; and on Sundays from noon–4 p.m.

Return to the station via the route on the map, passing the Town Hall *(Stadhuis)* and the quaint Visbrug (bridge) along the way.

NEARBY SIGHT:

Kinderdijk, midway between Dordrecht and Rotterdam, has the greatest concentration of working windmills in Holland. Most of them are operated on Saturday afternoons in July and August, but at least one is open to tourists every day from April through September. Boat trips past the mills are available. Ask at the tourist office for details on how to get there, or phone the mills at (01859) 15-179.

Middelburg

Middelburg is an exceptionally pleasant and beautifully restored old town that offers its many visitors a chance to enjoy a different aspect of Holland. Throughout the centuries its low-lying, isolated location near the North Sea has exposed it to catastrophic flooding, but this has finally been checked by the recent completion of the Delta Project.

As its name suggests, Middelburg is in the middle of something. That something is Walcheren, a one-time island now connected to the mainland as a result of land reclamation projects. Much of it lies at or below sea level and is protected by dikes. It is the most historic and certainly the most interesting part of Zeeland, a watery province of which Middelburg is the capital. The island lies at the mouth of the Schelde estuary and therefore controls shipping into the Belgian port of Antwerp. This fact has always made it strategically important, especially during World War II when Middelburg was practically destroyed by the invading Germans. To flush them out, the Allies, in 1944, resorted to bombing the dikes, thus flooding the island for over a year. Tragedy struck again during the great floods of 1953, but since then all of the damage has been repaired and effective measures taken to prevent the sea from ever again claiming victory over the land.

Although this is a rather long daytrip, it is a thoroughly enjoyable one and should be particularly attractive to those traveling with a railpass.

GETTING THERE:

Trains depart Amsterdam's Centraal Station at half-hour intervals for the approximately 2½-hour run to Middelburg. A change at Roosendaal is necessary for some of these trains. Return service operates until mid-evening.

By car, take the A-4 southwest past Schiphol Airport to Den Haag, then the A-13 into Rotterdam. Crossing the river via the Maas Tunnel, take the A-29 south almost to Willemstad. From there, the N-59 and N-256 leap between the islands on long bridges to Goes, after which you follow the A-58 into Middelburg. The total distance from Amsterdam is about 120 miles.

WHEN TO GO:

Most of the attractions are open daily between the beginning of June and late September. During other months you should check the times given for each sight to determine which day is best. A colorful outdoor market is held on Thursdays. Good weather will make this trip much more enjoyable.

FOOD AND DRINK:

A popular tourist destination, Middelburg abounds in places to eat and drink. Some choices are:

Het Groot Paradijs (Damplein 13, 1 block east of the Abbey) French-inspired food in a classic old house. Phone (01180) 26-764. X: Sat. lunch, Sun., Mon. $$$

Visrestaurant Bij Het Stadhuis (lange Noordstraat 8, by the Town Hall) All kinds of seafood. Phone (01180) 27-058. X; Mon. $$

Rôtisserie Michel (Korte Geere 19, 3 blocks south of the Markt) A small rustic restaurant with local specialties. Phone (01180) 11-596. X: Sat. lunch, Sun., Mon. $$

De Huifkar (Markt 19, on the square) Both a café and a restaurant. Phone (01180) 12-998. X: Sun. $ and $$

De Kabouterhut (Oosterkerkplein 8, by the East Church) A large variety of pancakes and simple Dutch fare. $

Stationsrestauratie (in the train station) Good, inexpensive food. $

TOURIST INFORMATION:

The local tourist office (VVV), phone (01180) 16-851, is on the market square facing the Town Hall.

SUGGESTED TOUR:

Leave the **train station** (1) and follow the map past a canal and a small harbor to the **Markt** (Marketplace) (2). Lined with outdoor cafés and restaurants, this busy square is a delightful place to sit down for lunch or at least a drink. Rides through the town in a horse-drawn coach are available here at modest cost.

Completely dominating the north side of the square is the fantastically ornate **Town Hall** *(Stadhuis),* an almost magical vision of Gothic splendor. Begun in 1452, its façade is decorated with statues of the counts and countesses of Zeeland. The soaring clock tower with its needlelike pinnacles was added in the 16th century, and later additions include the wings to the rear. What is truly interesting about this magnificent structure is that it exists at all, as it was almost totally destroyed by German bombing in 1940. This is in fact a meticulous

The Town Hall in the Market

reconstruction started immediately after the last war. Conducted tours of its interior are held Mondays through Fridays in season, at times posted on the sign outside.

Now continue down Nieuwe Burg, a pedestrians-only shopping street, to Middelburg's landmark **Abbey Tower** (3). Affectionately known as *Lange Jan* (Long John), this 280-foot octagonal belfry was originally built in the early 14th century. After a long history of fires, it collapsed during the German air raid of 1940 and wrecked the three churches at its base. Rebuilt after the war, it may be climbed between April and the end of September, Mondays through Saturdays, from 10 a.m. to 5 p.m. The stunning view from its summit takes in virtually all of Walcheren.

The tower is part of an **Abbey** *(Abdij)* founded in the early 12th century. Rebuilt several times after that, it was secularized in 1574 and thereafter used as government offices, although the now-Protestant churches remained. The entire complex has been reconstructed after being destroyed in World War II. Its three adjacent churches *(Abdij-kerken)* are internally connected and are definitely worth visiting. Enter the 16th-century **Nieuwe Kerk** to see its splendid 17th-century organ, then continue through to the *Wandel Kerk*, which miraculously survived the bombs. Beyond an enormous arch is the base of the tower, and near this a doorway leads into the 14th-century *Koor Kerk,* where you can take a look at the famous 15th-century organ.

A passageway just outside the Koor Kerk opens into the Abbey Courtyard *(Abdijplein).* Guided tours of the entire abbey complex are available here at 2:30 p.m. on Tuesdays through Thursdays in season, or you can just explore them on your own. Near the cloister is the **Roosevelt Study Center,** which commemorates the ancestral link between Zeeland Province and the two American presidents. Its exhibits are open to tourists on Mondays through Fridays, from 10 a.m. to 12:30 p.m and 1:30–4:30 p.m.

Also within the Abbey Courtyard is the fascinating ***Zeeland Museum** *(Zeeuws Museum)* (4), where you can probe the history and folklore of the Zeeland district from prehistoric to modern times. Some of its more interesting displays include the skeleton of a mammoth, tapestries depicting the war with Spain, and local costumes in authentic room settings. The museum is open all year round on Tuesdays through Fridays, from 10 a.m. to 5 p.m.; and on Mondays and weekends from 1:30–5 p.m. From November through March it is closed on Mondays. Museum Cards are accepted, and a brochure in English explains everything.

Now follow the map to the **Miniatuur Walcheren** (5), a huge outdoor model where the features and buildings of Walcheren have been reduced to a scale of 1:20. The concept is similar to that of the much larger Madurodam near Scheveningen, but here the subject is limited to the immediate region rather than encompassing all of Holland. Visits may be made from April through October, daily from 9:30 a.m. to 5 p.m. It remains open until 7:30 p.m. during July and August.

Continue on to the **Oostkerk** (East Church) (6), an octagonal domed church finished in 1667. This is one of the first churches in Holland to have been built specifically for the Protestant faith. A short stroll brings you to the small harbor, on whose south side is the atmospheric **Kuiperspoort** (7), once the headquarters of the Coopers' Guild. Amble through the narrow alleyway behind it to examine the picturesque 16th-century warehouses.

From here, you can return to the station via the route on the map, or head back to the marketplace for some well-deserved refreshments. If you do this, you may also want to see a bit of the west end of Middelburg by following the map to the **Kloveniersdoelen** (8). This early-17th-century structure was built as a meeting place for the Arquebus civic guard and later used by the East India Company. It is now occupied by a center for new music. The return route, by way of Lange Viele and Pottenmarkt, features a number of inviting bars and outdoor cafés.

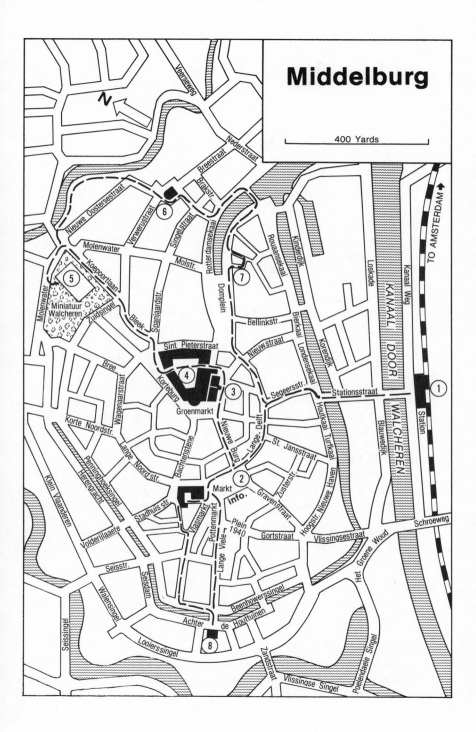

*Utrecht

One of the easiest and most satisfying daytrips you can take from Amsterdam is to Utrecht, a fair-sized city noted for its engaging combination of the past and the present. The area near its train station is as contemporary as any place on earth, yet step beyond this and you enter a world of preserved charm. Its picturesque sunken canals are unique, while some of its museums are among the most enjoyable in the nation. Home to Holland's largest university, Utrecht is alive with a youthful spirit.

The Romans built a fortification here around A.D. 47 to guard their crossing point on what was then the Rhine River. A town developed around this, and a church was built as early as A.D. 500, from which Christianity spread throughout the Netherlands. During the Middle Ages, Utrecht was frequently the residence of the Holy Roman emperors. In 1589, it was the setting for the *Union of Utrecht*, a pact that united the northern provinces against Spain. The troubled times that followed were finally resolved by the signing of the *Treaty of Utrecht* in 1713, ending the War of the Spanish Succession.

GETTING THERE:

Trains depart Amsterdam's Centraal Station at very frequent intervals for the 30-minute run to Utrecht's Centraal Station (CS). Return service operates until late evening, with reduced service all night long.

By car, Utrecht is 22 miles southeast of Amsterdam via the A-2 highway to the Utrecht-West exit. Convenient parking is available around the Hoog Catharijne complex.

WHEN TO GO:

Avoid going to Utrecht on a Monday, when nearly all of its attractions are closed.

FOOD AND DRINK:

The city offers a wide choice of restaurants and cafés, especially around the Hoog Catharijne and the Oude Gracht Canal. Some choices are:

The Domtoren from the Town Hall Area

Bistro Chez Jacqueline (Korte Koestraat 4, a block north of the tourist office) Dutch and Continental cuisine. Phone (030) 31-10-89. X: Sun., holidays. $$

Polman's Huis (Keistraat 2, 2 blocks northeast of the Domkerk) French-inspired fare in an old-fashioned setting. Phone (030) 31-33-68. $ and $$

Oude Muntkelder (Oude Gracht 112, on the canal near the Town Hall) A large, popular spot for Dutch-style pancakes. $

De Werfkring (Oude Gracht 123, on the canal near the Town Hall) Noted for its vegetarian food and young crowd. X: Sun., holidays. $

TOURIST INFORMATION:

The local tourist office (VVV), phone (06) 3403-4085 (toll call), is at the northern end of the Hoog Catharijne shopping center, adjoining the station.

SUGGESTED TOUR:

Utrecht's **Centraal Station** (1), one of the busiest in Europe, is connected to the immense **Hoog Catharijne** complex. This climate-controlled indoor city-within-a-city, embracing some 180 shops plus theaters, restaurants, cafés, offices, a hotel, and even apartment houses, was built in the late 1970s. Spanning the streets below, it can be somewhat confusing to negotiate although there are floor plans everywhere. Just follow the signs through it to Clarenburg, descend the escalators, and exit onto Lange Elisabeth Straat.

Make a right on Mariastraat and follow the map to the fascinating ***Nationaal Museum van Speelklok tot Pierement** (National Museum from Musical Clock to Street Organ) (2). Located in the Buurkerk, a former church dating in part from the 13th century, this is one of the most utterly joyful museums anywhere—and a favorite with children. Its displays of mechanical musical instruments from the 18th to the 20th centuries, some of which are quite huge, don't just sit there to be admired. They make music, lots of very loud barrel-organ music, much to the delight of everyone present. You can join the fun on Tuesdays through Saturdays, from 10 a.m. to 5 p.m.; and on Sundays from 1–5 p.m., but not on some major holidays. Guided tours with demonstrations begin every hour on the hour, or you can just walk through. Museum Cards are accepted.

Now continue around to the **Vismarkt** (3), a market place on the Oude Gracht canal, where fishermen have been selling their catch since the 12th century. Note how the canals of Utrecht are sunk well below the level of the streets, with old warehouse entrances opening directly onto them. Many of these have been turned into restaurants, with outdoor café tables facing the water.

A left on Servetstraat brings you to the **Domtoren** (4), at 367 feet the tallest church tower in Holland. It was completed in 1382 and stands apart from the cathedral of which it was a part. The nave of the cathedral collapsed during a storm in 1674 and was never replaced, although the rest of the church is still there. The tower, luckily, can be climbed for a wonderful ***view**. Ascents, accompanied by a guide, are made from April through October, on Mondays through Fridays from 10 a.m. to 4 p.m.; and all year round on weekends, from noon to 4 p.m.

As you stroll across Domplein you can see the outline of the former nave, indicated by colored paving stones. The present **Domkerk** occupies the choir and transepts of the one-time cathedral, built between 1254 and 1517 on the site of a Roman settlement.

Adjoining the church is the 15th-century **Kloostergang** (Cloister) (5), a spot of unusual beauty and tranquility. Amble through it to a picturesque old lane behind the church, named Achter de Dom. The route on the map now takes you down some interesting streets, along the Oude Gracht canal, and through a park to Utrecht's famous ***Centraal Museum** (6). Housed in a former convent, its displays cover a wide scope of interests, ranging from 20th-century Dutch art to period

In the Nationaal Museum van Speelklok tot Pierement

room settings to an unearthed 12th-century Viking ship. Upstairs, there is an excellent collection of Utrecht Old Master paintings, applied arts, and historical artifacts. The museum is open on Tuesdays through Saturdays from 10 a.m. to 5 p.m.; and on Sundays and holidays from noon to 5 p.m. A Museum Card will get you in free.

Return toward the center of town on Lange Nieuwstraat and turn right on Zuilenstraat. The ***Rijksmuseum het Catharijneconvent** (7) is located in a former 16th-century convent, whose entrance is at Nieuwe Gracht 63. Its modern interior contains nothing less than the largest collection of medieval art in Holland, along with a vast amount of religious artifacts and a sweeping survey of Christianity in the Netherlands. This renowned museum is open on Tuesdays through Fridays, from 10 a.m. to 5 p.m.; and on weekends and holidays from 11 a.m. to 5 p.m. Museum Cards, again, are accepted.

Continue across the town moat to the thoroughly enjoyable and very popular **Nederlands Spoorwegmuseum** (Railway Museum) (8), appropriately located in a former train station from the 19th century. Along its platforms and in its yards is a magnificent collection of locomotives, cars, and trams. Model trains speed along miniature tracks in the station itself, much to the delight of railfans young and old. Indoors, there is also a collection of railroading artifacts, and you can get refreshments in the old dining car outside. The museum is open

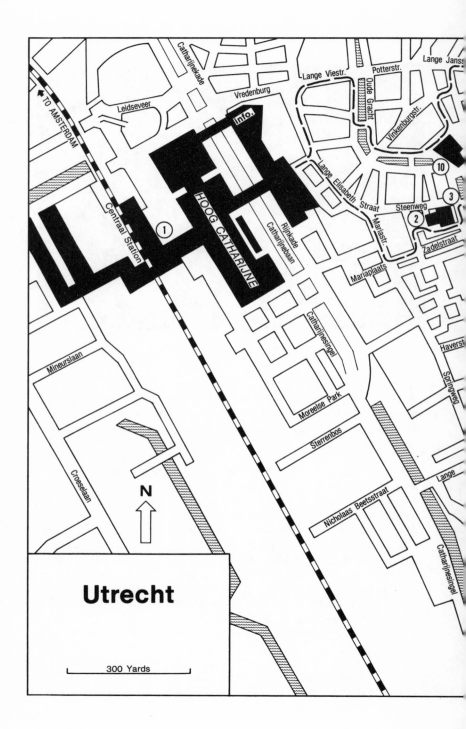

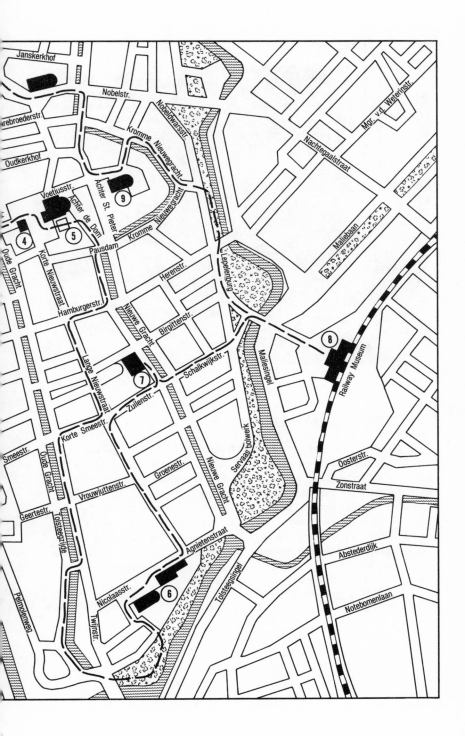

In the Railway Museum

on Tuesdays through Saturdays, from 10 a.m. to 5 p.m.; and on Sundays from 1–5 p.m.

A rather interesting route back to the center is to follow the canal and turn left into Kromme Nieuwe Gracht, a narrow street with a tiny canal. Another left brings you to **St. Pieterskerk** (9), an 11th-century Romanesque church that hasn't changed very much over the ages. Continue on Achter St. Pieter and Keistraat to Janskerkhof, then follow the map to the **Town Hall** *(Stadhuis)* (10) on the Oude Gracht canal. This area is particularly rich in outdoor cafés, mostly on the water's edge. ***Boat trips** through the canals are offered nearby, at the corner of Potterstraat and the canal, and make a fine way to finish off your trip to Utrecht before returning to the station.

Gouda

Few towns are more typically "Dutch" than Gouda, whose cheese is renowned throughout the world but whose name is usually mispronounced. Correctly said, the word is *How-dah*. Surprisingly, its marketplace is the largest in Holland, and its Gothic Town Hall is easily among the most impressive anywhere. Although a weekly market attracts huge crowds, most of these come from the local area and the event is not in any sense staged for tourists. What does bring visitors is the splendid St. Janskerk and the delightful *Het Catharina Gasthuis* museum, as well as the picturesque canal-lined streets.

Gouda began in the 12th century and received its charter in 1272. Early prosperity came with the development of a cloth industry and was later expanded by the manufacture of clay tobacco pipes, candles, pottery, and cheese. These later trades continue to play an important role in the economy today, and add a touch of Old World charm to a venerable town.

GETTING THERE:

Trains depart Amsterdam's Centraal Station at one-hour intervals for the 50-minute ride to Gouda. These are locals *(stoptrein)* marked for Rotterdam CS, but travel a strange route via the original Breukelen. Return service operates until late evening.

By car, leave Amsterdam on the A-4 highway past Schiphol Airport, then turn south on the N-207 into Gouda. The total distance is 33 miles.

WHEN TO GO:

The famous Cheese Market is held on Thursday mornings from mid-June through mid-August. There are also general outdoor markets all year round on Thursday mornings and all day on Saturdays. The church is closed to tourists on Sundays.

FOOD AND DRINK:

Gouda has a nice selection of restaurants and cafés, especially on and around the marketplace. Some choices are:

Rôtisserie l' Etoile (Blekerssingel 1, on the canal near the station) Noted for its fine French cuisine. Phone (01820) 12-253. X: Sun., Mon. $$$

De Zes Sterren (Achter de Kerk 14, in the Stedelijk Museum) Dutch food in a lovely setting. Phone (01820) 16-095. X: Sun., Mon. $$$

't Goudsewinkelje (Achter de Kerk 9a, by St. Janskerk) Dutch-style pancakes. $

Stationsrestauratie (in the train station) Convenient for a quick, inexpensive meal. $

TOURIST INFORMATION:

The local tourist office (VVV), phone (01820) 13-666, is on the Market Square.

SUGGESTED TOUR:

Leave the **train station** (1) and follow the map across a canal and down Kleiweg, a pedestrians-only shopping street. This will bring you to the **Markt**, the largest marketplace in Holland. At its north end is the **Waag** (2), a handsome 17th-century weighhouse for cheese that is open during the weekly market in summer, from 9:30 a.m. until noon. Its function is clearly depicted by the interesting carved relief above the doorway.

In the center of the square stands the magnificent **Town Hall** *(Stadhuis)* (3), a late Gothic structure that was once surrounded by a moat. Built around 1450, it has an unusually fine southern façade embellished with statues of the counts and countesses of Burgundy. A carillon along its east side plays every half-hour, accompanied by moving figures acting out the granting of the town's charter. You can visit the interesting interior and step out onto the stone scaffold at the north end for a good view of the market. The doors are open Mondays through Fridays, from 9 a.m. to noon and 2–4 p.m.

Stroll down to **St. Janskerk** (4), which has the curious distinction of being the longest church in Holland. It was begun in the 13th century but was almost totally destroyed by fire in 1552. What you see today is primarily a 16th-century reconstruction, famed for its extraordinary **stained-glass windows**. With a total surface area of about half an acre, all but 3 of the 70 windows were installed between 1555 and 1603, and so represent both the Roman Catholic and Protestant periods. The last three are from the 20th century, of which the *Liberation Window* of 1947—graphically recalling the horrors of World War II— is truly striking. An illustrated brochure that describes the windows and suggests a sequence for viewing them is available in English. The

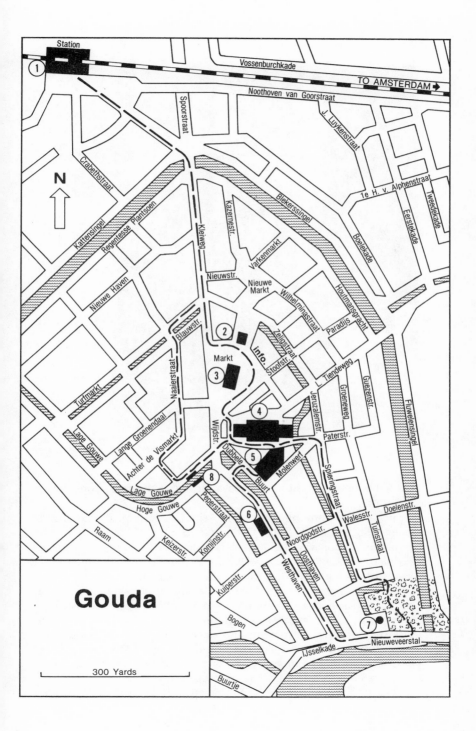

Gouda

300 Yards

The Town Hall

church is open to visitors Mondays through Saturdays, from 10 a.m. to 5 p.m.

Just across from the church, on Achter de Kerk, is the fascinating ***Stedelijk Museum "Het Catharina Gasthuis"** (Municipal Museum)(5). Occupying the 14th-to-17th-century buildings of a former hospice, its displays cover a wide scope of local history shown in a series of authentic room settings. There is, of course, a great deal of religious art as well as an excellent collection of 19th- and 20th-century paintings. An entire 18th-century dispensary has been reconstructed along with a kitchen and various domestic rooms. Don't miss the gruesome torture instruments and cells in the dark basement, or the room full of toys and dolls. The museum is open Mondays through Saturdays, from 10 a.m. to 5 p.m.; and on Sundays and holidays from noon to 5 p.m. Museum Cards are accepted.

Leave via the entrance on Oosthaven and cross the canal. In a few

Selling Cheese in the Markt

yards you will come to the **De Moriaan Museum** (6), where an unusual collection of tobacco pipes, tiles, and ceramics is displayed in a merchant's home of 1617. The building alone is worth a visit, and as a bonus there is a restored antique tobacco shop complete with inventory. The entrance ticket from the Municipal Museum (above) is valid here, as is the Museum Card. Visits may be made Mondays through Saturdays, from 10 a.m. to 12:30 p.m. and 1:30–5 p.m.; and on Sundays and holidays from noon to 5 p.m.

Continue along the canal to the river and turn left until you get to the 18th-century **'t Slot Windmill** (7). This is private and cannot be visited, but it makes a pretty sight as you turn left into a small park. From here, follow Spieringstraat back to Achter de Kerk and exit onto Wijdstraat.

Lage Gouwe leads along a canal to the 17th-century **Corn Exchange and Fish Market** *(Korenbeurs en Visbank)* (8), two colonnaded areas on either side of the water. Turn right into a narrow lane called Vissteeg, along which is a small artisan's shop where you can watch the traditional clay pipes being made and perhaps purchase one. From here you can follow the map back to the station.

Het Loo Palace

For nearly three centuries, the magnificent Palace of Het Loo was a favorite country seat of the House of Orange-Nassau, the family that continues to provide Holland with its sovereigns to this day. In the grand tradition of France's Versailles, Bavaria's Nymphenburg, and Austria's Schönbrunn, it is set on the edge of a large estate and is bordered by fabulous gardens. Until 1975, it was still occupied by members of the royal family, but after that it was transformed into a national museum and opened to the public in 1984.

The Het Loo Palace was begun in 1685 by William III, a descendant of William the Silent and later *stadhouder* of the Netherlands—the title "king" was not used by the House of Orange-Nassau until 1814. In 1689, William III and his wife, Mary Stuart, became joint sovereigns of England and ruled that country as William III and Mary II. William continued his position of leadership in Holland, however, and used Het Loo until his death in 1702. The palace remained in the family and has been used by all of the sovereigns of the Netherlands through the reign of Queen Wilhelmina, who abdicated in 1948 and died in 1962. Her granddaughter, Princess Margriet, lived there until 1975.

Seven years of expensive restoration work have returned the palace and its grounds to their original 17th-century appearance, with some of the interior rooms representing the centuries since then. A visit here, while very enjoyable in itself, will also leave you with some insight into the relationship between the House of Orange-Nassau and the nation as a whole.

GETTING THERE:

Trains leave Amsterdam's Centraal Station at half-hour intervals for the 65-minute ride to Apeldoorn, where the palace is located. Some of these require a change at Amersfoort and at least one does not run on Sundays and certain holidays. Return service operates until late evening. Those without a railpass or Museum Card may want to use the appropriate Netherlands Railways day excursion package.

By car, take the A-1 highway east from Amsterdam to Apeldoorn, a distance of 56 miles, and then follow local signs to Het Loo.

The Royal Palace from the Gardens

WHEN TO GO:

Avoid going on a Monday, when everything is closed. Fine weather will make this trip much more enjoyable. Buses to the palace run less frequently on Sundays and holidays.

FOOD AND DRINK:

There are a few good restaurants near the palace and a couple of cafeterias within its grounds. The town of Apeldoorn has several fine restaurants. Some suggestions are:

Le Petit Prince (Konigstraat 7, in the Keizerskroon Hotel near the palace) Luxurious French dining, phone (055) 21-77-44 for reservations. X: Sun. $$$

Poppe (Paslaan 7, 7 blocks northwest of the Apeldoorn train station) French-inspired food in the center of town. Phone (055) 22-32-86. X: Mon. $$

New Orient (Staionsplein 7, near the Apeldoorn station) Chinese and Indian cuisine. $$

Het Loo Palace Restaurants (in the palace grounds) Light meals and snacks in two self-serve cafeterias, with outdoor tables in good weather. $

Pannekoek Restaurant Loolaan (Loolaan 42, near the palace) Dutch pancakes and special lunches. $

TOURIST INFORMATION:

The local tourist office (VVV), phone (055) 78-84-21, is next to the train station in Apeldoorn.

SUGGESTED TOUR:

From the **Apeldoorn Train Station** (1) you have a choice of taking a bus, a taxi, or walking to the Het Loo Palace. The distance is a bit less than two miles via the route shown on the map. Buses number 102 and 104 leave from the square in front of the station and go directly to Het Loo (2), while the number 11 goes to a bus stop (3) within walking distance of it. The palace is open daily except Mondays and Christmas, from 10 a.m. to 5 p.m. The Museum Card will get you in free, and an illustrated guide booklet in English is sold at the entrance.

A visit to the ***Rijksmuseum Paleis Het Loo** begins at the **Royal Stables** (4), opposite which there is a cafeteria with outdoor café tables. Built around 1910, the stables hold an interesting collection of carriages, coaches, and even sleighs used by the royal family. Their automobiles, ranging from some real old-timers to relatively recent models, are especially fascinating.

From here, a path leads to the **Royal Palace** (5) itself. In a wing to the left of the courtyard, you can watch an introductory **video show** that lasts under 30 minutes and is given—on different screens—in English, Dutch, German, and French. Just beyond this, in a small courtyard, is another cafeteria where you can get light lunches or drinks. Again, outdoor café tables are available.

The **East Wing**, across the main courtyard, houses a collection of paintings, costumes, medals, and personal effects relating to the royal family.

Enter the **palace** proper and follow a well-marked route through its many rooms. This usually begins with the Entrance Hall, the old and new Dining Rooms, and the Chapel. It then goes upstairs to the Library, the Long Gallery, several apartments of various kings and queens, the Grand Staircase, and the Great Hall. Returning to the ground floor, the route leads through the Sitting Room and Workroom of Queen Wilhelmina, the last sovereign to reside at Het Loo.

A basement door at the rear of the palace brings you into the fabulous ***Gardens** (6), now restored to their 17th-century appearance. With over 200 varieties of plants, several working fountains, and colonnaded pavilions at its north end, there is enough here to delight your senses for quite a while before you return to the station in Apeldoorn.

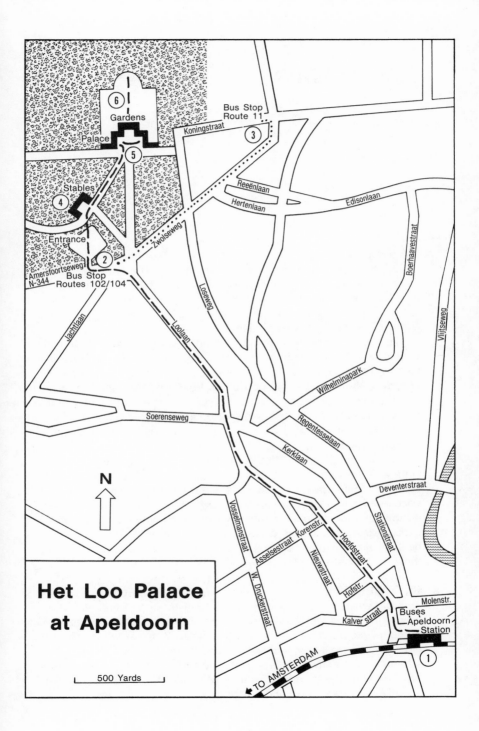

Bus Stop
Route 11

⑥
Gardens

Palace

⑤

Koningstraat

③

Reeënlaan

Hertenlaan

Edisonlaan

Stables

④

Entrance

Zwolseweg

②

Boerhaavestraat

Amersfoortseweg
N-344

Bus Stop
Routes 102/104

Loseweg

Vlijtseweg

Jachtlaan

Loolaan

Wilhelminapark

Soerenseweg

Regentesselaan

Kerklaan

Deventerstraat

N

Vosselmanstraat

Asselsestraat

Korenstr.

Nieuwstraat

Hoofdstraat

Stationstraat

W. Druckerstraat

Hofstr.

Molenstr.

Het Loo Palace
at Apeldoorn

Kalver straat

Buses
Apeldoorn
Station

①

TO AMSTERDAM

500 Yards

Giethoorn

Water, water everywhere—that's Giethoorn, an improbable Dutch village that calls itself the "Venice of Holland." The only way to get around this strange and wonderful place is by boat, on foot, or by bicycle. There are no roads at all, just narrow tree-shaded canals, paths, and tiny wooden bridges connecting the quaint thatched-roof cottages and lovely flower gardens.

Giethoorn has not exactly gone unnoticed by Dutch and German vacationers, but it is still an unusual destination for North American visitors. Fortunately, its charms are spread over a fairly large area, so crowding should never be a problem. Boat trips through its dreamy canals and on its lake are offered everywhere, or you can rent a hand-propelled *punter* or electric "whisper boat" and explore on your own. The entire area can also be seen on foot by following the walking tour described.

This unique place was first settled around 1230 by a sect of flagellants who came to escape religious persecution. They earned their living by digging peat in what was then bog country, and in so doing uncovered countless horns of goats who had presumably drowned during some of the periodic floods. Thus the name *Geytenhoren*, or goats' horns, which was eventually corrupted into Giethoorn. The peat digging, in time, caused many ponds and lakes to form, and these were connected by canals to facilitate transport.

GETTING THERE:

Trains marked for Groningen depart Amsterdam's Centraal Station hourly for the direct 92-minute ride to Meppel, where you get bus number 79 to Blauwe Hand, then bus number 72 to Giethoorn. Return train service operates until late evening, but check the local bus schedule. Alternatively, you can take a train to Steenwijk instead. This involves a change at either Zwolle or Amersfoort, but it's a bit quicker and the bus ride is short and direct.

Along the Canals of Giethoorn

By car, leave Amsterdam on the A-1 highway, heading east toward Amersfoort, then take the A-28 northeast to the first Zwolle exit. From there, follow local roads via Hasselt and Zwartsluis to Giethoorn. The total distance is 84 miles.

WHEN TO GO:

Those coming by train should avoid Sundays, when there is no connecting bus service. This is strictly an outdoor trip, so good weather is absolutely essential. You will encounter fewer tourists during the spring and fall, and in winter the canals may freeze over to produce an ice-skater's paradise. The Monday-to-Saturday bus service is reduced during the off season.

FOOD AND DRINK:

Being a popular vacation spot for the Dutch and the Germans, Giethoorn has a wide selection of restaurants and cafés in the moderate-to-low price range. A few choices are:

Hotel Giethoorn (Beulakerweg 128, on the main road, just south of the tourist office) A modern motel with lake-fish specialties among other dishes. $$

Hollands Venetië (Beulakerweg 167, near Petersteeg) Dutch and German food, popular with tourists. $$

De Rietstulp (Ds. T.O. Hylkemaweg 15, near the church) Dutch food, with a *Neerlands Dis* menu and a *Tourist Menu*. $ and $$

Smit's Paviljoen (Binnenpad 29, on the lake) A nice pavilion restaurant with a great view. $

TOURIST INFORMATION:

The local tourist office (VVV), phone (05216) 12-48, is on the Beulakerweg, near the bus stop at the south end of the village. After November, 1995, the phone number becomes (0521) 36-12-48.

SUGGESTED TOUR:

Leave the **Meppel Train Station** and turn left into the bus departure area. Here you can board the hourly NWH bus number 79 for a 20-minute ride through lovely countryside to Giethoorn, making an easy change en route at Blauwe Hand. If you came via **Steenwijk** instead, take bus number 72 for a very short ride direct to Giethoorn. Note that the buses do not run on Sundays.

Get off at the **bus stop** (1) near the **Giethoorn Tourist Office** (VVV) on Beulakerweg. Those with cars will find plenty of parking nearby. Enter the village on Frensensteeg and turn left at the canal onto a footpath called Zuiderpad. This crosses the water several times on tiny bridges, passing delightful country houses as it heads north. All along the way there are places that offer boat rides or rentals.

The simple **Village Church** (2) overlooks an especially picturesque junction of three canals. Close to it, in a thatched house, is the small ***Museum de Speelman** (3), where antique street organs and other musical instruments entertain visitors. It is open daily from March to November, 10 a.m. to 6 p.m.

Continue north on Binnenpad, passing the tiny ***Museum de Oude Aarde** (4). Exhibits here include crystals, semiprecious stones, and various minerals glowing under special illumination. There are also displays of local fauna. Visits can be made daily from March through October, from 10 a.m. to 6 p.m.; and on weekends in winter.

Now head out to **Smit's Paviljoen** (5) on the Bovenwijde lake. Various boating activities are offered here, along with light lunches and drinks in a beautiful setting.

Return to the church and follow Ds. T.O. Hylkemaweg past several shops and restaurants to the north **bus stop** (6) on Beulakerweg. From here you can get bus number 72 directly back to Steenwijk, or to Meppel with a change to number 79 at Blauwe Hand.

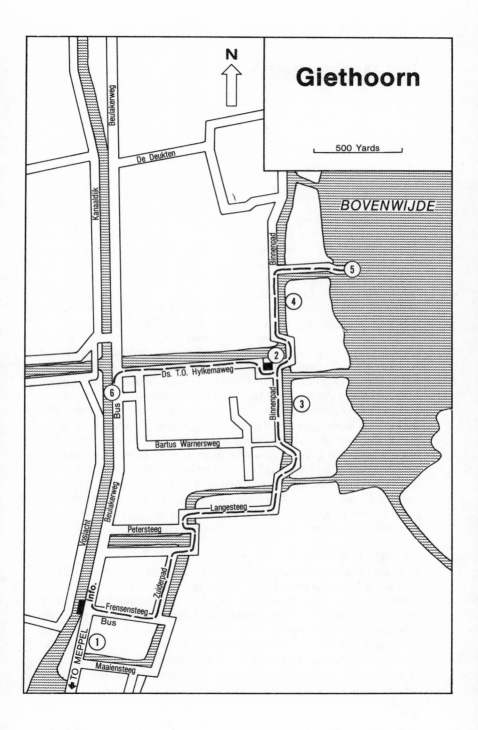

Leeuwarden
(Ljouwert)

Throughout history, Frisia has been a world apart—speaking its own language, waving its own flag, singing its own anthem, and stubbornly clinging to its fierce sense of individuality. These traditions live on in the ancient city of Leeuwarden, or *Ljouwert* as it is called in Frisian. Today the capital of Friesland Province, Leeuwarden offers its visitors the chance to experience a very different side of the Netherlands.

The economy of Frisia revolves around dairy farming, so it is perhaps not surprising that Leeuwarden's most striking public monument is a statue of a fat cow. The city's favorite daughter is remembered by a statue, too. Born here in 1876 as Margaretha Zelle, she was known to the world as the spy Mata Hari, and is depicted as an exotic dancer.

Frisian is regarded as the language most akin to English, and it is thought by some scholars that the "Anglo-Saxons" who invaded England after the fall of the Roman Empire were in fact Frisian adventurers. Leeuwarden has strong connections to the United States as well, for it was here, in 1782, that the first official recognition of the new American nation was declared, leading to a much-needed loan from the Dutch government. The local ties go back further than that, however, as this area also produced Peter Stuyvesant, an early governor of New York when it was still called New Amsterdam.

GETTING THERE:

Trains depart Amsterdam's Centraal Station at hourly intervals for Leeuwarden, a direct ride of just under 2½ hours. Be sure to get on the correct set of cars, as these trains split at Zwolle. In addition, there are other trains that require a change at Amersfoort. Return service operates until mid-evening.

By car, head north from Amsterdam on the A-7/E-22 highway and cross the IJsselmeer on the famous enclosing dike *(Afsluitdijk)*. When you reach the mainland, take the A-31 into Leeuwarden. The total distance is 86 miles.

The Waag

WHEN TO GO:
Leeuwarden may be visited at any time, but note that some of the attractions are closed on Mondays, and some on weekends.

FOOD AND DRINK:
Some good choices of places to eat in Leeuwarden are:

L'Orangerie (Stationsweg 4, across from the station) Excellent dining in the Hotel Oranje, with a less expensive tavern for lunch. Phone (058) 12-62-41. $$

Onder de Luifel (Stationsweg 6, across from the station) Dutch food, with a *Neerlands Dis* menu and a *Tourist Menu*. X: Sun. $$

De Stadhouder (Nieuwestad 75, near the Waag) Dutch food, *Neerlands Dis* menu, *Tourist Menu*. $

Kota Radja (Groot Schavernek 5, 2 blocks south of the Oldehove) Asian cuisines. Phone (058) 13-35-64. $$

Pannekoekschip (Willemskade, 2 blocks north of the station) A huge variety of pancakes served on a boat in the harbor. $

TOURIST INFORMATION:
The local tourist office (VVV), phone (06) 3202-4060 (toll call), is at the train station.

SUGGESTED TOUR:

Leave the **train station** (1) and walk straight ahead down Sophia Laan, crossing a canal. Just beyond this is the Wilhelminaplein, where an outdoor market is held on Fridays. Continue on and turn right at the next canal to a busy open square called Waagplein. In the center of this stands the **Waag** (2), an attractive 16th-century weighhouse in the Frisian Renaissance style. Once used as a cheese market, it is now home to a restaurant and a bank.

From here follow a narrow canal to the small **Mata Hari Statue** (3). Curiously, this depicts the famous World War I spy as an exotic dancer. A native of Leeuwarden, she was shot by a French firing squad in 1917 for giving secrets to the Germans, although she may actually have been a double agent working for the Allies.

Stroll down Korfmakersstraat and turn left to the ***Fries Museum** (4), one of the very best provincial museums in Holland. Housed in an 18th-century mansion, it is devoted to a sweeping survey of Frisian culture from prehistoric to modern times. Among the highlights are period room settings, 19th-century shops, costumes, and the famous painted furniture from Hindeloopen. There is a painting by Rembrandt of his wife, Saskia, who was born in Leeuwarden. Other treasures include ancient pottery, Roman coins dating from their occupation of the area, medieval sculptures, and a room full of old printing presses. All of these may be seen Tuesdays through Saturdays, from 10 a.m. to 5 p.m.; and on Sundays from 1–5 p.m. Museum Cards are accepted.

Now follow the map to the **Grote Kerk** (5), also known as the Jacobijnerkerk. The most important church in Leeuwarden, it was originally erected in the 13th century and was largely rebuilt in the 15th. Its simple but rather elegant interior houses some splendid tombs of the Frisian branch of the House of Orange-Nassau. Visits may be made during June through August, Tuesdays through Fridays, from 10–11 a.m. and 2–4 p.m.

Grote Kerkstraat leads to the **Mata Hari House** (6), home of the renowned spy from 1883 until 1890. This is now occupied by the **Frisian Literary Museum**, which promotes the use of Frisian in literature and everyday speech. You are most welcome to step inside and learn all you wanted to know about the Frisian language. The door is open on Mondays through Fridays, from 10 a.m. to noon and 2-5 p.m., and entry is free.

Continue down the street to the ***Museum Het Princessehof** (7). Devoted primarily to ceramics from all over the earth, the displays in this marvelous museum are so fascinating that you will surely enjoy a visit—even if you have no burning passion for pottery. Among the many features are the world's largest collection of tiles; Chinese ware

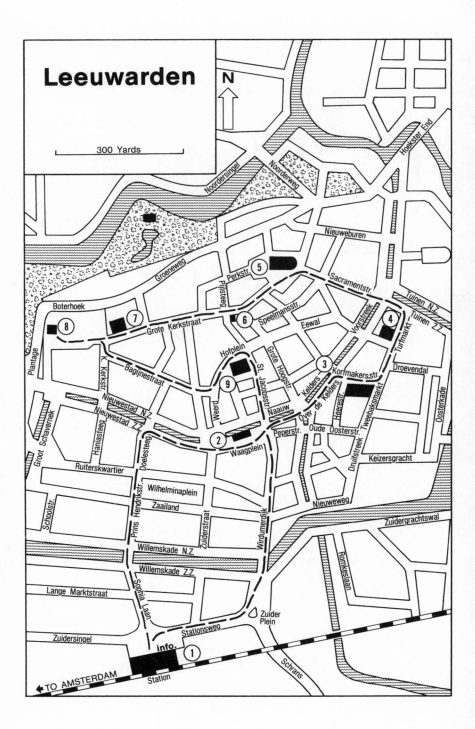

The Statue of Us Mem

from prehistoric to modern times; Art Nouveau and contemporary ceramics; and Indonesian puppets, weapons, and fabrics. The museum is open Mondays through Saturdays, from 10 a.m. to 5 p.m.; and on Sundays from 2–5 p.m. The Museum Card will get you in free. Don't miss this special treat.

In just a few more steps you will come to the **Oldehove** (8), the famed leaning tower of Leeuwarden. Rising rather forlornly at the end of a parking lot, this lopsided pile is 130 feet high and was begun in 1529 as part of a cathedral that never got built. Alas, the soil sank, the Reformation intervened, and the project ran out of money. You can climb to the top for an aerial view of the town, but only from mid-May through September, Tuesdays through Saturdays, from 9:30 a.m. to 12:30 p.m. and 1:30–4:30 p.m.

The park to the immediate north of this is a nice place to relax before carrying on. Looking across the canal, you'll see a strange statue of a cow called **Us Mem** (Our Mother), the symbol of Frisian prosperity. Now follow the map past the **Stadhuis** (9), a town hall built in 1715, then turn down St. Jacobsstraat and Wirdumerdijk to the Zuiderplein. From here it's only a short stroll back to the station.

Netherlands Open-Air Museum at Arnhem

Outdoor folk museums have become increasingly popular in Europe and throughout the world as more of the countryside succumbs to modern development and the traditional ways of life disappear. In many cases they are the only realistic way of saving a nation's domestic heritage from being paved over to make way for yet more shopping malls. Typically, threatened structures ranging from thatched farm cottages to early industrial buildings are moved into a protected park setting and reassembled in village groupings according to the region they represent. Trained personnel, often in folk costumes, carry on the old crafts and farm the fields in the traditional way, while reconstructed country inns continue to serve age-old recipes. A visit to one of the better open-air museums can be a lot of fun, and may be the only chance you'll ever get to experience some aspects of the Old World.

There are several open-air museums in Holland, notably at Zaanse Schans and Enkhuizen, but this one, at Arnhem, is by far the largest and most complete. Spread over an area of about 75 acres, it was begun in 1912 and now contains roughly 100 structures. All of these have been restored to their original appearance, and many are filled with period furnishings. Besides the farmhouses and barns, there are workshops, windmills, bridges, inns, a school, a church, and even some urban buildings.

The museum suggests two routes: a red one taking under two hours and sticking to easy paths, and a blue one that is hilly in spots and takes about three hours to complete. An illustrated guide booklet in English describing these in detail is available at the entrance. The tour outlined in this book is a modification of the blue route, and covers all of the interesting highlights. Food and drinks are offered at several places along the way, as are rest rooms.

By getting off to an early start, it is entirely possible to combine this trip in the same day with one to the Hoge Veluwe National Park with its famous Kröller-Müller Museum. This is described in the next chapter. To do this by public transportation, you must first return to the bus stop in front of the Arnhem train station. Those with cars can drive directly there.

GETTING THERE:

Trains leave Amsterdam's Centraal Station frequently for the 68-minute ride to Arnhem. In addition to the regular IC expresses, there are EuroCity trains that require a supplementary fare unless you are using a Eurailpass. Return service operates until late evening. Those without a railpass would do well to use the appropriate Netherlands Railways day excursion package, which includes the bus, museum, and refreshments.

By car, head south from Amsterdam on the A-2 highway past Utrecht, then take the A-12 east to the Arnhem-Apeldoorn exit and follow local signs to the Openlucht Museum. The total distance is 62 miles.

WHEN TO GO:

The museum is open daily from April through October. Good weather is essential for enjoyment of this trip.

FOOD AND DRINK:

There are several places to eat and drink at the outdoor museum as well as restaurants and cafés in Arnhem. Some choices are:

At the museum:

De Kasteelboerderij (in the museum grounds) Complete Dutch meals along with refreshments. Phone (085) 42-06-57. $$

De Hanekamp (near the far end) Pancakes and snacks. $

In Arnhem:

Da Zilli (Marienburgstraat 1, 5 blocks southeast of the station) Italian cuisine. Phone (085) 42-02-88. $$$

Haarhuis (Stationsplein 1, across from the station) Good-value meals in a small hotel. $$

TOURIST INFORMATION:

The tourist office in Arnhem (VVV), phone (085) 42-03-30, is at Stationsplein 45, across from the station. You can call the open-air museum at (085) 57-61-23.

SUGGESTED TOUR:

The easiest way to get from the **Arnhem Train Station** to the open-air museum is to take bus number 3 in the direction of Alteveer. This departs frequently from the square in front of the station, and the ride takes 10 minutes. Otherwise, it's a 2½-mile taxi ride or walk.

The ***Netherlands Open-Air Museum** *(Nederlands Openlucht Mu-*

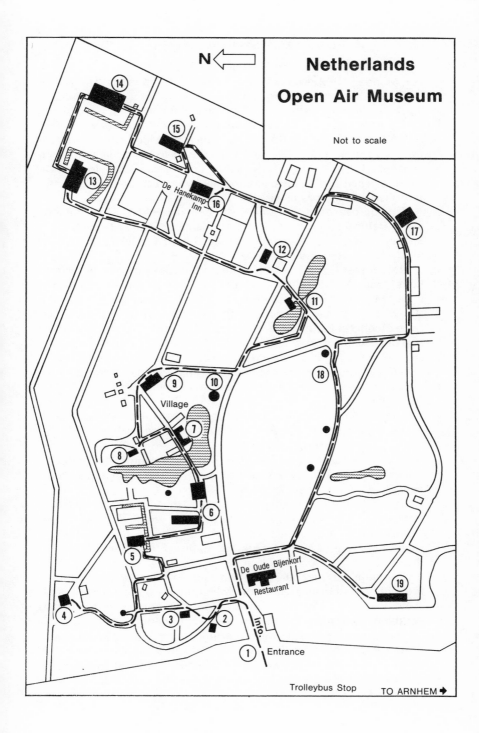

N

**Netherlands
Open Air Museum**

Not to scale

De Hanekamp Inn

Village

De Oude Bijenkorf
Restaurant

Info.

Entrance

Trolleybus Stop   TO ARNHEM ➔

seum) (1) is open from the beginning of April until the end of October, Mondays through Fridays from 9:30 a.m. to 5 p.m.; and on Saturdays, Sundays, and public holidays from 10 a.m. to 5 p.m. An illustrated guide booklet in English is sold at the gate.

Turn left just past the information booth and stroll down to the **Horse-Drawn Oil Mill** (2) from the province of Gelderland. Converted from a farmhouse around 1830, it was used to extract lighting and cooking oils by crushing seeds such as rape or flax. Close to this is a small thatched-roof **Veluwe Farmhouse** (3) from around 1850, whose furnished interior may be visited.

The route now passes a small exhibition of beekeeping on the way to the **Betuwe Farmhouse** (4), a rather large structure originally built in 1646. Also from Gelderland Province, it has an attached barn and a nicely-furnished interior.

Return past the bees and turn left to the romantically sited **Farmhouse from Giethoorn** (5), which of course is partially surrounded by water. Built in 1832, much of it was used for the storage of hay, with attractive living quarters at one end. Down the road from it stands the large **Staphorst Farmhouse** (6), a type still found in that conservative part of Holland. Most of this is devoted to the storage of hay, but the small living quarters are beautifully decorated with tiles and painted furniture. Behind it is the **Farmhouse with a Pyramid Roof**, erected in 1745 in North Holland province, and associated with the making of Edam cheeses.

The route now enters a small village over a typical wooden drawbridge from around 1800. The **Merchant's House** (7) from Koog on the Zaan (near Zaanse Schans) partially dates from 1686 and has the sort of comfortable interior favored by the 19th-century bourgeoisie. Adjacent to this is a tradesman's house from the same area, which now serves as a souvenir shop.

Turn left and stroll through the village to the **Fisherman's Cottage from Marken** (8), which is similar to the ones you find today on the island in the IJsselmeer just north of Amsterdam. Its tiny interior has excellent examples of the traditional cupboard beds then popular in the north.

Continue on past an early-19th-century **Laundry** (9) that was brought here from an area near Haarlem. Close to it is a refreshment stand, where you can take a break before admiring the unusual **Post Windmill** (10). This was once used to grind grain in North Holland, and parts of it are over 300 years old.

The **Paper Mill from the Veluwe** (11) is in a beautifully wooded location between two ponds. Powered by an overshot waterwheel, its mechanisms still work and are used to give demonstrations of hand paper-making.

The Drawbridge to the Village

Although it is a re-creation and not an original, the **Parlor from Hindeloopen** (12) is quite interesting for the stylized painted furniture that has come to be associated with that former Zuider Zee town.

Now follow the map past the lovely **Herb Garden** to the **Frisian Farmstead** (13), whose rather elegant living quarters reflect the prosperity of that dairy region. Near this is the **Farmhouse from Beerta** (14), an area in Groningen province. Its living section has been restored to the state it was in around 1935, after electrification provided such luxuries as lighting, kitchen appliances, and a radio. In contrast, the **Drenthe Farmhouse** (15) is a large but rather primitive affair dating from around 1700.

Continue on to the **De Hanekamp Inn** (16), an 18th-century country inn from Zwolle. It now functions as a delightful café for museum visitors, with both indoor and outdoor tables.

Limburg province, in the south and much hillier than the rest of Holland, is represented by the **Krawinkel Farmstead** (17) and other nearby structures. From here the route passes a grouping of various **Windmills** (18) on the way back to the entrance. Before leaving, you might want to make a little side trip to the **Exhibition of Costumes** (19) to see what they wore in times past.

Hoge Veluwe National Park and the Kröller-Müller Museum

You may be surprised to discover a genuine wilderness area in a country as jam-packed as Holland, but this 22 square miles of nature preserve is only part of the attraction. The other is the magnificent Kröller-Müller Museum located right in its heart. Easily counted as one of the very best modern art museums in the world, it is certainly worth a daytrip in itself. The park has other features as well, which can be explored by car, by bus, on foot, or on one of the 800 bicycles that are available free for your use.

Both the park and the museum were a gift to the nation, made in 1935 by a wealthy businessman named Anton Kröller and his art-collecting wife, Helene Müller. The museum's collections are absolutely first-rate, with no less than 278 paintings by van Gogh alone. Adjacent to it is a sculpture garden where over 60 contemporary pieces adorn some 26 acres of gorgeous landscape.

It is possible—by getting off to an early start—to combine this daytrip with one to the Netherlands Open-Air Museum at Arnhem, described in the previous chapter.

GETTING THERE:

Trains depart Amsterdam's Centraal Station frequently for the 68-minute ride to Arnhem, from which you take a bus into the Hoge Veluwe. In addition to the regular IC expresses, there are EuroCity trains that require a supplementary fare unless you are using a Eurailpass. Return service operates until late evening. If you don't have a railpass, you should consider using the appropriate Netherlands Railways day excursion package, which includes the bus, park, museum, and refreshments.

By car, take the A-2 highway south from Amsterdam to a point just beyond Utrecht, then the A-12 east to the Hoge Veluwe exit just before Arnhem. From there follow local signs to the entrance at Schaarsbergen. The total distance is about 60 miles.

WHEN TO GO:

The Kröller-Müller Museum is open every day except on Mondays, but note that its enormous sculpture garden is closed from November through March. The direct bus service from Arnhem runs from early July until late August, plus some holiday periods during the rest of the year. Good weather is essential unless you plan to spend the entire time in the museum.

FOOD AND DRINK:

Some places to eat and drink in the Hoge Veluwe National Park are:

Rijzenburg (at the south entrance to the park) Superb dining in an old farmhouse. Phone (085) 43-67-33. X: Mon. $$$

De Koperen Kop (near the Visitor Center) Pancakes and other light meals. $

Museum Restaurant (in the museum) Self-service with light meals, snacks, and drinks. $

Recommendations for Arnhem are shown in the previous chapter.

TOURIST INFORMATION:

The tourist office in Arnhem (VVV), phone (085) 42-03-30, is just across from the station. You can call the museum at (08382) 10–41, and the park Visitors' Center at (08382) 16–27.

SUGGESTED TOUR:

Those coming by rail will begin at the **Arnhem Train Station** and take a bus to the Hoge Veluwe park. Between early July and late August there is a direct hourly bus (route 12), which takes 30 minutes to reach the Kröller-Müller Museum. An admission ticket to the park, including the museum and all other attractions, is sold by the driver, along with a round-trip bus ticket that allows unlimited use of the bus within the park. Holders of the Rail Rover pass with the Public Transport Link option need only pay the park admission. This same bus also operates on a reduced schedule during school holidays throughout the rest of the year. At other times you can take bus number 107 to the Otterlo entrance and walk about two miles to the museum.

If you came by car you should enter the park via the **Rijzenburg Gate** (1) at Schaarsbergen, which is where bus number 12 enters. The museum is about 8 miles northwest of central Arnhem.

In the Kröller-Müller Museum

The **Hoge Veluwe National Park** covers an area of some 13,500 acres. A vast variety of wildlife lives in these woods and heathlands, including deer, mouflons, wild boars, foxes, badgers, hawks, and buzzards. During the rutting season (early September to mid-October), visitors are not allowed to leave the road in the game preserve area.

Begin your visit at the ***Kröller-Müller Museum** (2), where an extraordinary collection of art from the late 19th and 20th centuries is displayed in 2 adjoining structures. The first of these was built in 1938 and the second in 1977. The nucleus of the museum is a collection of 278 works by **Vincent van Gogh**, several of which are among the finest and most famous ever done by that renowned Dutch painter. Among the other artists represented are Picasso, Mondriaan, Léger, Redon, Seurat, and Ensor. To emphasize the universality of all art, the displays are interspersed with paintings from the 16th and 17th centuries, notably by Gerard David and both Cranachs; and with pottery from China and ancient Greece. Not everything is on view at any one time, as the collections are far larger than the size of the galleries allows, and space must be made for temporary shows. The museum is open Tuesdays through Sundays, from 10 a.m. to 5 p.m.. It is closed on Mondays and New Year's Day.

From the south wing of the museum you can step out into the fabulous ***Sculpture Garden** (3), the largest in Europe. More than 60

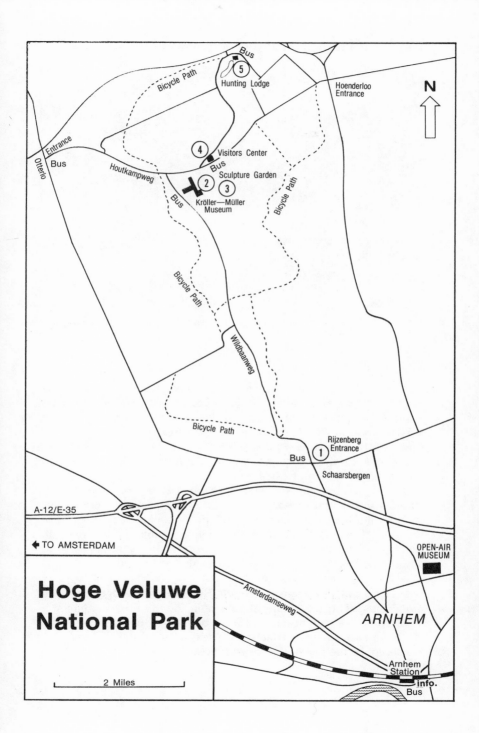

N

Bus
⑤
Hunting Lodge

Hoenderloo
Entrance

Bicycle Path

Entrance

Otterlo
Bus

Houtkampweg

Bus

④ Visitors Center
Bus
Sculpture Garden
② ③
Kröller—Müller
Museum

Bicycle Path

Bicycle Path

Bicycle Path

Wildbaanweg

Bicycle Path

Rijzenberg
Entrance
Bus ①

Schaarsbergen

A-12/E-35

← TO AMSTERDAM

OPEN-AIR
MUSEUM

Amsterdamseweg

ARNHEM

Arnhem
Station
info.
Bus

Hoge Veluwe
National Park

2 Miles

Atop the Jardin d'Email *Sculpture*

works are spread over a lovely area of some 26 acres. A few of the sculptors represented are Rodin, Moore, Lipchitz, Marini, and Oldenburg. The most spectacular piece, by far, is the enormous ***Jardin d'Email** by Jean Dubuffet—an abstract landscape so huge that hundreds of people can crawl over it at the same time. Climb the steps into it and join the fun! The Sculpture Garden is open April through October, from 10 a.m. to 4:30 p.m.

Now stroll over to the **Visitor Center** *(Bezoekers Centrum)* (4), where you can learn all about the rest of the park. It is open daily from April through October, and on Sundays and holidays the rest of the year. Nearby is the **Museonder**, offering a glimpse of life beneath the earth's surface. Some 800 bicycles are available without charge to all park visitors. You can borrow one of these and pedal over nearly 25 miles of special bicycle paths.

The best place to head for is the **St. Hubertus Lodge** *(Jachtslot Sint Hubertus)* (5), a country home built for the Kröller-Müllers in 1920. You can also get there by car, by bus, or on foot.

Buses back to Arnhem depart (in season) from the Koperen Kop restaurant by the Visitor Center and the museum.

Getting Around Belgium

Yes, there really is a magical kingdom of Belgium, and it lies just outside Brussels. You won't find much of the national character in this modern all-European headquarters city, but venture a few miles beyond and you step back in time to a world filled with art treasures; a land imbued with a lusty zest for life. So compact is this kingdom that nearly all of its wonders can easily be explored on daytrips from Brussels. Thirteen of the most fascinating destinations are described in the next section, preceded by a "get acquainted" walking tour of Brussels itself. The Flemish towns come first, followed by the French-speaking towns.

BY WAY OF BACKGROUND:

An imaginary line running from east to west just south of Brussels divides Belgium into two distinctly different worlds. To the north, but excluding the capital, lies the land of the Flemings, famous for its medieval art cities as well as for its seacoast. Here the Germanic influences are strong, and the culture somewhat related to that of Holland. Take one step south of the line, however, and you have entered the Latin-based world of the Walloons, where a more French way of life dominates the ancient towns and forests.

This division results from a tumultuous history extending over two millennia, beginning with the Roman conquest of the *Belgae* tribes by Julius Caesar in 57 B.C. Almost five centuries of peace as an imperial province ensued, until the fall of the empire brought on an invasion by Germanic tribes of Franks. A kingdom was established that eventually led to the 9th-century empire headed by Charlemagne, an empire later partitioned among his grandsons.

By the 12th century, the great Flemish towns had risen to positions of nearly unrivaled importance and were usually able to avoid domination by the French. The Hundred Years War between England and

France made a battleground of Flanders, relieved in 1384 by the transfer of power to the dukes of Burgundy, whose lands eventually extended to cover most of the Low Countries. Nearly a century later, these were turned over to the Austrian Hapsburgs, and through them to the king of Spain.

The Low Countries prospered greatly under Spanish rule, but the rise of Protestantism in the north soon brought on repression. A long period of conflict followed, with the south remaining loyal to Catholic Spain. In time, the Dutch won. What is now Belgium reverted to Austrian rule, and later to France. Napoleon's final defeat at Waterloo, in 1814, led to amalgamation with Holland. In 1830 the Belgians, by now tired of foreign domination, declared their independence. After a brief struggle, the Dutch bowed to the inevitable and let the troublesome Belgians go their own way.

The new kingdom prospered with the Industrial Revolution of the 19th century, particularly in the French-speaking south, which had most of the natural resources. An invasion by Germany in 1914 helped bring about a feeling of national unity, and in the aftermath of World War I the Flemish north began to gain its share of political power. In 1940 the Germans struck again, this time under Hitler. The Belgian king, Leopold III, surrendered, and the country suffered under Nazi tyranny until being relieved by Allied forces in 1944. Post-war reconstruction led to great prosperity, with Brussels emerging as the "capital" of Europe.

TRANSPORTATION:

All of the daytrips in Belgium described in this book can be made by rail, and all by car. Your choice depends on purely personal factors, but you may want to consider some of the following information before deciding.

BY RAIL:

Belgium was the first country in continental Europe to have passenger-train service, inaugurated in 1835 between Brussels and Mechelen. Today it boasts the densest rail network in Europe, with tracks radiating out from a Brussels hub to just about everywhere in the country. Service is so frequent that reference to a schedule is rarely necessary. With the short distances involved, trains are almost invariably the fastest way of getting around.

Much improved in recent years, the **Belgian National Railways** (*Société Nationale des Chemins der Fer Belges* or *SNCB/Nationale Maatschappij der Belgische Spoorwegen* or *NMBS)* has introduced an IC/IR system of departures at repeating intervals, which greatly simplifies knowing what time the train leaves. Fares are reasonable and can be considerably reduced by using one of the economical railpasses described later on.

There are very few places of tourist interest in Belgium that cannot be reached directly by train. Stations are usually located right in the heart of town, so close to the major attractions that all of the Belgian walking tours outlined in this book start right at the station.

Seasoned travelers often consider riding trains to be one of the very best ways of meeting the local people and making new friends. It is not at all unusual to strike up an engaging conversation that makes your trip all the more enjoyable. You will also get a marvelous view of the passing countryside from the large windows, and you will have time to catch up on your reading.

All trains operated by the Belgian National Railways belong to one of the following categories, as indicated on schedules and departure platforms:

EC — *EuroCity.* A new category of international expresses with special comforts, replacing the former TEE trains. Both first- and second-class seating is offered, and there is a supplementary fare that is covered by the Eurailpass. These trains really are not intended for trips solely within Belgium.

INT — *International Express,* an older category of long-distance trains intended for travel to other countries. Both first- and second-class seating is available.

EXT — Special relief trains run on busy days.

IC — *InterCity.* These comfortable expresses are usually your best bet for travel within Belgium. Most of them are made up of very modern cars and operate on frequently recurring schedules. Those on the Brussels-Mechelen-Antwerp-Rotterdam-The Hague-Amsterdam route use the latest *Beneluxtrein* equipment, featuring such niceties as on-board pay phones. There is no supplementary fare, and both classes are provided for.

IR — *InterRegion.* Connecting the smaller towns and other localities with large cities and the IC network, these modern trains have their schedules coordinated with the InterCity expresses. Both classes are available.

L — Locals making many stops, often used in commuter service.

Brussels has quite a few **train stations.** Only the three shown on the map are of interest to tourists, and it doesn't matter which of these you use as virtually all trains, except for a few international expresses, stop at all three. They are *Nord/Noord, Central/Centraal,* and *Midi/Zuid.* Pick the one closest to your hotel.

Most **destinations** in Belgium have both a French and a Flemish name, which might at first confuse you. This book uses the name most familiar to English-speaking people, followed by the alternative name(s) in parentheses. Thus, Antwerp can be *Antwerpen* or *Anvers; Bruges, Brugge;* Mechelen, *Malines;* and Tournai, *Doornik!* Schedules and signs in Brussels are bilingual, but those in the provinces often use only the local spellings. Be sure you know each of the possible variations before beginning any rail trip, or you just might stay on the train past a station marked *Brugge* when you wanted to get off at *Bruges.* All of the different names are shown on the heading to each daytrip.

Schedules are really not necessary, as you will seldom have more than a half-hour wait for a train going your way. Tables of departure are posted on yellow boards in each station, and times are expressed in terms of the 24-hour clock; thus a train at 4:52 p.m. would be marked as 16.52. A condensed schedule booklet listing most services of interest to tourists is available free at the information counters. The booklets are in either French or Flemish, but not both. The information personnel almost invariable speak English and will be only too pleased to help you. Real railfans will, of course, want to add the complete schedule book, called an *Indicateur/Spoorboekje,* to their collection. There is a modest charge for this. The **Thomas Cook European Timetable**, mentioned on page 12, is very useful to those whose train journeys will take them beyond the Benelux countries.

Reservations are neither necessary nor possible for travel within Belgium, although you might want to consider them for long international journeys.

Some trains split en route to their destinations. Be sure to get on the right set of cars and ask the conductor, to be certain. Destinations are sometimes—but not always—marked on the cars themselves. First-class cars are indicated with the numeral "1" near the door, and with a yellow stripe above the windows.

There is little in the way of **food service** on trains within Belgium, although many have a roving mini-bar offering snacks and beverages. You are better off purchasing refreshments in the station, or nearby, and bringing them on the train.

All but the most local of trains carry both first- and second-class accommodations. First class is, of course, a bit more comfortable and a whole lot less crowded during peak travel times, but most people will find second class to be perfectly adequate for the short journeys involved.

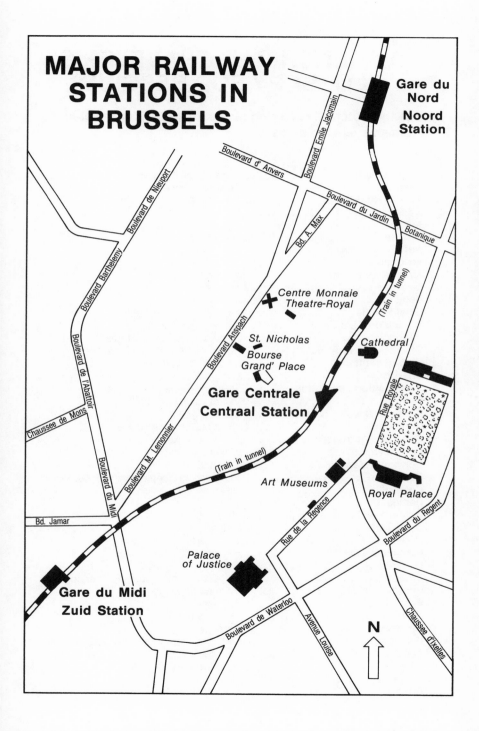

MAJOR RAILWAY STATIONS IN BRUSSELS

Gare du Nord
Noord Station

Boulevard d' Anvers

Boulevard Emile Jacqmain

Boulevard de Nieuport

Boulevard du Jardin

Botanique

Bd. A. Max

Boulevard Barthelemy

(Train in tunnel)

Centre Monnaie Theatre-Royal

Boulevard Anspach

St. Nicholas
Bourse
Grand' Place

Cathedral

Rue Royale

Gare Centrale
Centraal Station

Boulevard de l'Abattoir

Chaussee de Mons

Boulevard M. Lemonnier

(Train in tunnel)

Art Museums

Royal Palace

Boulevard du Midi

Rue de la Regence

Boulevard du Regent

Bd. Jamar

Palace of Justice

Gare du Midi
Zuid Station

Boulevard de Waterloo

Avenue Louise

Chaussee d'Ixelles

N

A FRENCH RAIL TRAVELER'S GLOSSARY FOR BELGIUM

Use the Dutch Glossary on pages 16 and 17 for travel in the Flemish-speaking areas

Abonnement . . . . .Season ticket or pass
Aller. . . . . .To go one way
Aller et Retour . . . . .Round trip
A Partir . . . . .From (date) on
Arrêt . . . . .Stop, halt
Arrivée . . . . .Arrival
Autobus, Autocar. . . . . .Bus
Autorail . . . . .Railcar
Avec Supplément. . . . . .With surcharge
Banlieue .Suburban (commuter trains)
Billet . . . . .Ticket
Billet Simple . . . . .Ordinary one-way ticket
Bureau de Change . . . . .Currency exchange
Cadencé .Regularly repeating interval
CFL . . . . .Luxembourg National Railways
Changement . . . . .Change (of trains)
Chariot . . . . .Luggage cart
Composition des Trains . . . . .Train make-up
Composteur . . . . .Ticket validating machine
Compostez votre Billet . . . . .Validate your ticket
Consigne . . . . .Checkroom, left luggage
Consigne Automatique . . . . .Luggage locker
Contrôleur . . . . .Ticket collector
Correspondence. . . . . .Connection
Couchette . . . . .Inexpensive sleeping car with bunks
Couloir . . . . .Aisle (seat)
Dames. . . . . .Women
Défense de Fumer . . . . .No smoking
Demi-Tarif. . . . . .Half fare
Départ. . . . . .Departure
Deuxième Classe . . . . .Second class
Douane . . . . .Customs
Emporter. . . . . .To take out, as in items from snack bar
Enregistrement. . . . . .To send baggage ahead
Entrée . . . . .Entrance
Entrée Interdite. . . . . .Do not enter
Étranger .Foreign
Facultatif .Optional, on request (train or bus stop)
Fenêtre . . . . .Window (seat)
Fêtes . . . . .Holidays
Fumeurs .Smoking
Gare . . . . .Station

Gare Routière	.Bus station
Grandes Lignes	.Main lines
Grève	.Strike of workers
Guichet	.Ticket window
Hommes	.Men
Horaire	.Timetable
Jusqu'au	.Until (date)
Libre	.Free, available
Libre Service	.Self service
Ligne	.Line
Location de Voitures	.Car rental
Métro	.Subway
Messieurs	.Men
Monter	.To board (the train)
Objets Trouvés	.Lost-and-found
Occupé	.Occupied
Place	.Seat
Plein Tarif	.Full fare
Poste-PTT	.Post office, telephone service
Pré-Métro	.Underground trams
Première Classe	.First class
Prochain	.Next (departure)
Quai	.Platform
Quotidien	.Daily
Remboursement	.Refund
Renseignements	.Information
Réseau	.Network, system
Réservation	.Reservation
Retardé	.Delay
Salle d' Attente	.Waiting room
Sauf	.Except
Sortie	.Exit
Sortie de Secours	.Emergency exit
SNCB	.Belgian National Railways
Tarif	.Fare
Tous les Jours	.Every day
Vers	.To
Voie	.Track
Voiture	.Car (of train or otherwise)
Voiture Directe	.Through train to indicated destination
Voyage	.Trip, travel
Voyager	.To travel
Voyageur	.Traveler, passenger
Wagon	.Railroad car
Wagon-Lit	.Sleeping car
Wagon-Restaurant	.Dining car

RAILPASSES can be a fabulous bargain if you intend to do any real amount of train travel. The Belgian National Railways *(SNCB* or *NMBS)* accepts the following passes:

EURAILPASS
EURAIL SAVERPASS
EURAIL FLEXIPASS
EURAIL YOUTHPASS
BENELUX TOURRAIL PASS

All of these are described on pages 13 and 14. In addition, Belgium offers its own national passes:

B-TOURRAIL PASS — Valid for use within Belgium only, this economical pass is available for 5 days of unlimited rail travel within a period of 17 days. The travel days do not have to be consecutive, allowing you to spend more time in your base city between daytrips. Both first- and second-class versions are available, and prices are different for adults or for juniors between the ages of 6 and 25. It is sold at train stations in Belgium and cannot be purchased overseas.

16-DAY PASS — Also referred to as an *Abonnement Réseau,* this is a very good deal for people who plan to explore Belgium in depth. Available all year round, it is valid for 16 consecutive days of unlimited rail travel throughout Belgium. There are both first- and second-class versions, and the pass is sold at train stations in Belgium only.

A **Half-Fare Card** valid for one month is also offered at a bargain price.

Remember that all railpasses must be used in accordance with the rules and instructions accompanying them, and that you must always be prepared to show your passport. When having passes validated, be certain that you agree with the dates *before* allowing the agent to write them in.

If you intend to take several of the daytrips in this book, and especially if one or two of them are to more distant places such as Oostende, a railpass will probably wind up saving you a considerable amount of money. Even if the savings are less than that, a pass should still be considered for the convenience it affords in not having to line up for tickets, and for the freedom of just hopping aboard trains at whim. Possession of a railpass will also encourage you to become more adventurous in seeking out offbeat destinations. It allows you to take longer and more circuitous routes, which might be more interesting. Should you ever manage to get on the wrong train by mistake, your only cost will be your lost time. Railpasses can even be used to cut your dining expenses just by riding to a nearby small town for dinner, where restaurants are usually less expensive than in large cities.

Those who have decided against a railpass may still be able to save some money on their train fares. The Belgian National Railways offers a variety of **excursion tickets** to popular tourist spots, some of which include entry to the various attractions. These are usually called "A beautiful day at . . ." *(Un beau jour à . . .)* or some similar name. Ask about them at the train information counters. A **Half-Fare Card**, entitling you to a 50% discount on all train tickets for travel within Belgium for a one-month period, is available all year round.

While English is commonly spoken by most of the railway employees you are likely to come in contact with, the signs in stations and on trains, as well as the words used on schedules, are in either French or Flemish. The **glossary** on pages 168–169 should help you with the French. For terms in Flemish refer to the Dutch glossary on pages 16–17.

Passengers flying in or out of Brussels National Airport (Zaventem) will be happy to know that there is direct, frequent rail service from the terminal itself to both Nord and Central stations in downtown Brussels.

BY CAR:

Driving on Belgium's superb highways and dense network of secondary roads is essentially the same as in North America, but there are a few national peculiarities. First, there is the confusing matter of place names. Many towns have both a Flemish and a French name, to say nothing of the English one you're familiar with. Thus Brussels is either *Bruxelles* or *Brussel*. This can be absolutely baffling when Tournai suddenly becomes *Doornik*, or Liège is spelled *Luik*. Road signs are usually only in the language of the region you happen to be in at the moment. You will have to learn both names for each town you intend to drive to, and be on the lookout for signs leading to them. Good road maps show the official local name in heavy type and the alternate name in parentheses. The chapter headings in this book use the name most familiar to English speakers, with other name(s) following in parentheses.

Another problem is that strange traffic rule imported from France called *priorité à droite,* by which vehicles coming in from the right have the right-of-way. This leads to cars dashing into the main stream of traffic from side streets without stopping or slowing down. The rule does not apply when you are on a highway marked with a black arrow inside a red triangle, but you must still be on your guard at all times, especially in built-up areas.

The maximum speed limit on four-lane highways is 120 kph (75 mph), on other roads 90 kph (56 mph), and in urban areas 60 kph (37 mph). Seat belts must be worn at all times, and children under 12 are

A FRENCH DRIVER'S GLOSSARY FOR BELGIUM

Use the Dutch Glossary on pages 20 and 21 for travel in the Flemish-speaking areas

Accotement non Stabilisé	Soft shoulder
Allumez vos Phares	Turn on headlights
Arrêt Interdit	No stopping
Attention	Caution
Au Pas	Slow
Autoroute	High-speed limited-access highway
Autres Directions	Other directions
Carte Grise	Car registration papers
Carte Routière	Road map
Céder le Passage	Yield
Centre Ville	To the center of town
Chaussée Déformée	Bad road surface
Chantier	Road construction
Chute de Pierres	Falling rocks
Circulation Interdite	No thoroughfare
Descente Dangereuse	Steep hill
Déviation	Detour (Diversion)
Douane	Customs
Eau	Water
École	School
Entrée Interdite	No entrace
Essence	Gasoline (Petrol)
Fin d'Interdiction	End of restriction
Fin de Limitation de Vitesse	End of speed restriction
Gravillons	Gravel road surface
Halte	Stop
Hauteur Limitée	Low clearance
Huile	Oil
Impasse	Dead-end road (Cul-de-sac)
Interdiction de Doubler	No passing
Interdiction de Stationner	No parking
Limitation de Vitesse	Speed restriction
Location de Voitures	Car rental (Hire)
Nids de Poule	Pot holes
Passage à Niveau	Grade crossing
Passage Interdit	Entry forbidden, no thoroughfare
Passage Protégé	Right-of-way at intersection ahead
Pente Dangereuse	Steep incline
Permis de Conduire	Driver's license
Piétons	Pedestrians
Piste Reservée aux Transports Publics	Lane reserved for public transport

Pneus	Tires
Poids Lourds	Truck (Lorry) route
Priorité à Droite	Vehicles coming from the right have the right-of-way
Priorité à Gauche	Vehicles coming from the left have the right-of-way
Ralentir	Reduce speed
Rappel	Previous sign still applies
Réservée aux Piétons	Pedestrians only
Réservée aux Transports Publics	(Lane) reserved for public transport
Route Barrée	Road closed
Route Étroite	Narrow road
Route Glissante	Slippery road
Sauf (Seulement) Riverains	(Private road) for residents only
Sens Interdit	Wrong direction
Sens Unique	One-way street
Serrez à Droite	Keep to the right
Serrez à Gauche	Keep to the left
Sortie	Exit
Sortie de Camions	Truck crossing
Stationnement Autorisé	Parking allowed
Stationnement Interdit	No parking
Tenez vos Distances	Keep your distance
Toutes Directions	All directions
Travaux	Road work
Verglas	Slippery road
Virages	Curves ahead
Voie de Dégagement	Private entrance
Voie Unique	Single-lane traffic
Voiture	Car, vehicle
Voiture à Louer	Rental car
Zone Bleue	Time-indicator disc required for parking
Zone Rouge	Tow-away zone

DAYS OF THE WEEK:

Lundi	Monday
Mardi	Tuesday
Mercredi	Wednesday
Jeudi	Thursday
Vendredi	Friday
Samedi	Saturday
Dimanche	Sunday
Aujourd'hui	Today
Demain	Tomorrow

SEASONS:

Saison	Season
Printemps	Spring
Été	Summer
Automne	Autumn
Hiver	Winter

APPROXIMATE CONVERSIONS

1 Mile = 1.6 km
1 km = 0.6 miles

1 U.S. Gallon = 3.78 litres
1 Litre = 0.26 U.S. Gallons

confined to the rear seat, if there is one. All that's needed to drive in Belgium is a valid driver's license from your own country, a passport, registration for the car, and evidence of insurance (Green Card). Should you have a breakdown or an accident you can summon help from the roadside emergency telephones or, if you're on a main highway, by opening your hood and waiting for a patrol car to come by. The national phone number for medical help is 900, while that for the traffic police is 901.

WHEN TO GO:

Any time is a good time to visit Belgium, as most of the attractions are open year-round. A few, however, close between about mid-autumn and early spring. Specific details are given for each daytrip. The best time to come is undoubtedly between mid-spring and early autumn. June, with its longer days, offers the most sunshine. Whatever the season, be prepared for changing weather, and always carry protection against an unexpected brief shower. A light jacket or sweater will come in handy, even in summer.

HOLIDAYS:

Public holidays *(Jours Fériés/Openbare Feestdagen)* in Belgium are:

New Year's Day
Easter Monday
Labor Day (May 1st)
Ascension Day (6th Thursday after Easter)
Whit Monday (7th Monday after Easter)
National Day (July 21st)
Assumption (August 15th)
All Saints' Day (November 1st)
Armistice Day (November 11th)
Christmas Day

When any of these fall on a Sunday, the holiday is observed on the following Monday. Expect trains to operate on holiday schedules.

LANGUAGE:

As you are undoubtedly aware of by now, Belgium is primarily divided into French- and Flemish-speaking zones. Brussels, although located within the Flemish area, is officially bilingual and is in fact predominantly French. There is also a small German-speaking zone in the east. Much has been made of Belgium's linguistic problems, but somehow the people have adapted to it and actually get along with each other rather well.

A surprisingly large number of Belgians speak excellent English, and do so willingly. This is especially true in Brussels and in the Flemish areas. **Flemish**, by the way, is actually Dutch, with identical spellings and slightly different pronunciations. The pocket-size *Dutch-English Dictionary* by Berlitz has a handy menu-translator section that includes traditional Flemish dishes. The **French** spoken in Belgium is almost the same as that in France, even if the Parisians don't think so. Again, English is widely understood by the *Walloons,* as the French-speakers call themselves. A little knowledge of French will be helpful in ordering meals in the south, although you can get along quite well without it.

MONEY:

The Belgian franc, usually abbreviated as BF or Bfr., is issued in notes of 50, 100, 500, 1,000, and 5,000; and in coins of 1, 5, 10, and 20 francs. Its value is on a par with the Luxembourg franc, but while the Belgian franc is legal tender in Luxembourg, the reverse is not true.

It is always best to change your money at a commercial bank. In Belgium, the bank's service charge for cashing travelers' checks remains the same regardless of the amount exchanged. The money exchange offices in major train stations are convenient and open for longer hours, but their rate of exchange is not quite as good. Avoid changing money at hotels, shops, and restaurants, where the rates can be atrocious.

FOOD AND DRINK:

Belgian cuisine is renowned throughout the world, and is one of the major reasons for visiting that country. Although basically French, it has its own specialties that you're almost certain to enjoy. To help you do that, several choice restaurants are listed for each destination in the next section of this book. Most of these are longtime favorites of experienced travelers and serve typically Belgian dishes, except where otherwise noted. Their relative price range, based on the least expensive full meal offered, is indicated by these symbols:

$ — Inexpensive, but may have fancier dishes available.
$$ — Reasonable. These establishments may also feature daily specials.
$$$ — Luxurious and expensive.
X: — Days or periods closed. ·

Those who take dining *very* seriously should consult an up-to-date restaurant and hotel guide such as the classic red-cover *Michelin Benelux,* issued annually around the beginning of each year. It is always wise to check the posted menus before entering, paying particular attention to any daily set-meal specials.

Belgians demand good food almost as a birthright, and get it at a bewildering variety of restaurants. Regular meals tend to be enormous and lengthy, perhaps as compensation for the small "continental" breakfasts. A great deal of fat is often used in traditional Belgian cooking, so you will probably want to limit yourself to one full meal a day. This is no hardship, since light meals are always available at cafés, and there are plenty of street vendors for snacks.

Some typically Belgian **meat dishes** are: *Carbonnades flamandes* (beef cooked in beer), *Biftek et frites* (beefsteak with French fries), *Jambon d'Ardennes* (smoked ham), *Rognons de Veau à la Liègeoise* (roast veal kidneys), and *Boudins Liège* (sausage). A wide choice of game dishes is available in season. The favorite **seafood** seems to be *moules* (mussels), served in such huge quantities that you won't have room for anything else. Shrimp is often prepared as *Tomates aux Crevettes* (stuffed in tomatoes) or as *Croquettes aux Crevettes* (deep fried in cakes). A great many other fish dishes are commonly found on menus. *Waterzooi*, a famous Flemish specialty, is either chicken or fish, stewed in a sauce with vegetables. Another **fowl** treat is *Oie à l'instar de Visé* (goose boiled and then fried). Among the **vegetables** usually featured are *Chicorée-witloof* (Belgian endive), *Asperges à la flamande* (white asparagus with egg sauce), and the ever-popular *choux de Bruxelles* (Brussels sprouts). The most common **snack**, sold everywhere, is *frites* (French fries, most often eaten with mayonnaise). Be sure to try *gaufres* (the famous Belgian waffles), and don't forget the sinfully rich chocolates.

Belgium is the land of glorious **beer**. No one, not even the Germans or the Dutch, make a better brew. Hundreds of different brands are produced in this small country, and there is a fantastic range of tastes and strengths (up to 12%!) available. Relatively little of this is exported, so here is your chance to try something different. A few of the more common types are: *pils* (similar to Dutch and other European beers), *gueuze* (with a strong winey taste), *kriek* (with a hint of cherries), *trappiste* (dark, malty, and often very strong, once made by monks), and *rodenbach* (bitter). No **wines** are made in Belgium, but Luxembourg is not far away and their white Moselles are both excellent and unusual. All kinds of French wines are available at quite reasonable prices. Finally, if you just want mineral water, you won't find a better one than the Belgian *Spa*.

SUGGESTED TOURS:

The do-it-yourself walking tours in the next section are relatively short and easy to follow. On the assumption that most readers will be traveling by train, they always begin at the local station. Those going by car can make a simple adjustment. Suggested routes are shown by heavy broken lines on the maps, while the circled numbers refer to attractions or points of reference along the way, with corresponding numbers in the text. Remember that in Brussels the streets have names in both French and Flemish.

Trying to see everything in any given town could easily become an exhausting marathon. You will certainly enjoy yourself more by being selective and passing up anything that doesn't catch your fancy in favor of a friendly café.

Information such as the opening times of various attractions is as accurate as was possible at the time of writing, but nothing is more certain in travel than change. You should always check with the local tourist office if seeing a particular sight is crucially important to you.

The amount of time that any segment of a walking tour will take can be estimated by looking at the scale on the map and figuring that the average person covers about 100 yards per minute.

TOURIST INFORMATION:

Virtually every town of any tourist interest in Belgium has its own information office, which can help you with specific questions. Known by a variety of names, they are almost always identified by the small letter "**i.**" Their locations are shown on the town maps in this book by the word "**info.**," and repeated along with the phone number under the "Tourist Information" section for each trip. To phone ahead from another town in Belgium you must first dial the area code, which always begins with 0 and is shown in parentheses, followed by the local number.

ADVANCE PLANNING INFORMATION:

The **Belgian Tourist Office** has branches throughout Western Europe and in a few other parts of the world. They will gladly provide maps and brochures as well as help in planning your trip. You can contact them at:

780 Third Ave.,
New York, NY 10017
U.S.A.
☎ (212) 758-8130, FAX (212) 355-7675

39 Princes Street
London W1R 7RG
England
☎ (0171) 629-0230

Brussels

(Bruxelles, Brussel)

Brussels is more than just the capital of Belgium. As the seat of the European Community, numerous other international agencies, and hundreds of multi-national corporations, it is truly regarded as the *de facto* capital of all Europe. Perhaps more to the point, Brussels is also the perfect base for exploring the entire country on one-day excursions. Before setting out on daytrips, however, you should really take a look at this lively and often surprising city. While only a few of its sights can really be called spectacular, there are many interesting attractions that lie hidden away amid the bustle of modern commerce. The "get acquainted" walking tour described in the next few pages will take you to some of the best of these, after which you might want to probe other sights beyond the city center.

Located at the strategic point where the ancient Cologne-Bruges road crossed the Senne River, Brussels developed into an important trading center as early as the 10th century. Then known as *Bruocsella*, the town had its origins in a much earlier settlement, of which little is known. It was granted its first charter in 1312, growing rapidly to a population of 43,000 by the 15th century, by which time it was ruled by the dukes of Burgundy. In the years to come, power shifted back and forth between the French, the Spaniards, the Austrians, and the Dutch. Belgium finally declared its independence in 1830, and Brussels became its capital.

GETTING THERE:

Trains connect Brussels' three major stations (see map on page 167) with nearly every other place in Belgium, and they run so frequently that reference to schedules is rarely necessary. Some typical running times are: Ghent—33 minutes, Antwerp—35 minutes, Bruges—58 minutes, and Liège—78 minutes. There are also good international services to Amsterdam, Luxembourg City, and Paris—each less than 3 hours away—and to other European cities as well.

By car, Brussels is only 30 miles from Antwerp, 34 miles from Ghent, 48 miles from Liège, and 60 miles from Bruges—all by superb modern highways. Recommended routes are shown in the chapters for these and other towns.

By air, Brussels is served with direct flights from every corner of Europe and the world. Its modern National Airport at Zaventem is only 9 miles from the city center and has its own train station right in the terminal, with frequent departures for the 20-minute ride to Brussels' Central Station.

GETTING AROUND:

You won't need public transportation for this walking tour, but it is essential for some of the outlying attractions that you might want to visit later. Consisting of subways *(Métro)*, trams, and buses, the system operates from 6 a.m. until midnight. One single fare takes you anywhere in the city, and you can save money by purchasing a 10-trip ticket or a 12-hour Tourist Ticket. Maps and information are available at the tourist office or in the subway stations. Be warned that taxis are quite expensive, although a tip is included in the metered fare.

WHEN TO GO:

Any time is a good time to visit Brussels, which is rarely over-crowded with tourists. The city is much more alive on a working day, but note that some of the major museums are closed on Mondays.

FOOD AND DRINK:

One of the great rewards of a trip to Brussels is the opportunity of dining well. The restaurants listed below are mostly in the area of the Grand' Place, with a few near the Place du Grand Sablon. Many superb establishments are not shown here because they are located well off the walking-tour route. For details on these you should consult a reliable restaurant guide such as the annual **Michelin Benelux**. Those on a tighter budget will be happy to know that a large variety of inexpensive cafés serving light lunches, cafeterias, and fast-food outlets are located along most of the suggested route.

> **Maison du Cygne** (Grand' Place 9) Elegant dining in one of Brussels' best restaurants. For reservations phone (02) 511-8244. X: Sat. lunch, Sun., Aug. $$$
>
> **Trente Rue de la Paille** (Rue Paille 30, just north of Place du Grand Sablon) Traditional dishes in a cozy atmosphere. Phone (02) 512-0715. X: Sat., Sun., holidays, July. $$$
>
> **Taverne du Passage** (Galerie de la Reine 30, 1 block northeast of Grand' Place) Fine Belgian dishes in an arcade. Phone (02) 512-3731. X: Wed., Thurs. in summer. $$

Aux Armes de Bruxelles (Rue des Bouchers 13, 2 blocks northeast of Grand' Place) Traditional Belgian cuisine. Phone (02) 511-5598. X: Mon. $$

La Roue d'Or (Rue des Chapeliers 26, 2 blocks south of Grand' Place) An inviting brasserie. Phone (02) 514-2554. $$

L' Ogenblik (Galerie des Princes 1, 3 blocks northeast of Grand' Place) Superb French cuisine in a simple setting. Phone (02) 511-6151. X: Sun. $$

't Kelderke (Grand' Place 15) A cellar restaurant right in the heart of things. Phone (02) 513-7344. $

Chez Léon (Rue des Bouchers 18, 2 blocks northeast of Grand' Place) A popular bistro noted for its Belgian cuisine. Phone (02) 511-1415. $

Le Roi d'Espagne (Grand' Place 1) A great casual place for snacks and beer, outdoor tables. $

TOURIST INFORMATION:

The tourist office for Brussels (T.I.B.), phone (02) 513-89-40, is in the Town Hall on Grand' Place. For information on all of Belgium, consult the main office at 61 Rue du Marché aux Herbes, one block northeast of the Grand' Place. Their phone number is (02) 504-03-90.

SUGGESTED TOUR:

The **Gare Centrale/Centraal Station** (1) is a convenient place to start this tour, although you may prefer to begin right at the ***Grand' Place**, just a short walk away. Regarded by many as the most beautiful square in Europe, it has been the center of life in Brussels since the 12th century. Without exception, all of the buildings surrounding it are extraordinary pieces of architecture, ranging in style from the Gothic to the baroque. With its many outdoor cafés, markets, and street entertainments, the square is a magnet attracting both visitors and residents alike.

The west side of the Grand' Place is totally dominated by the monumental **Town Hall** (*Hôtel de Ville*) (2), whose exquisite, delicate tower soars to a height of 314 feet and is topped by a copper weathervane of the Archangel Michael. Construction of this masterpiece began in 1402 and was completed by 1480, although a few alterations have been made since. The entrance under the tower is off-center, as it is actually part of an earlier 14th-century building. In 1695, the Town Hall was badly damaged during an artillery bombardment ordered by France's Louis XIV, which destroyed the other houses in the square. Everything was quickly rebuilt, however, accounting for the exuberantly baroque structures in what is otherwise a medieval setting. The splendid interior of the Town Hall, noted especially for its tapestries,

Façades on the Grand' Place

may be visited on guided tours that are conducted several times a day, on select days of the week. You may prefer to come back for this. The city tourist office is also in the Town Hall.

Directly across the square stands the **Maison du Roi** (3), which, despite its name, was built as a law court and never had anything to do with sheltering kings. First erected around 1515, it was severely damaged in the invasion of 1695, only partially repaired, and then neglected until the late 19th century, when it was completely reconstructed using old pictures as a guide. Today it houses the **Musée Communal** (Municipal Museum). Although this is devoted to the history of Brussels and contains a number of outstanding works of art, its most popular attraction is undoubtedly the **Manneken-Pis Room** on the top floor. Here you can see a vast collection of exotic costumes worn on different occasions by that world-famous statue of an impish little boy, whom you'll be meeting soon. The museum is open Mondays through Thursdays from 10 a.m. to 12:30 p.m. and 1:30–5 p.m., closing at 4 p.m. between October and the end of March; and on Saturdays and Sundays from 10 a.m. to noon. It is closed on a few major holidays.

The rest of the square is lined with magnificent **guild houses** erected between 1696 and 1700 after their predecessors had been demolished during the bombardment of 1695. Many of these now house restaurants and cafés, where you can sit outdoors while relishing the

Brussels

300 Yards

The Manneken-Pis

whole scene. You may want to stop in at number 10, which belonged to the brewers' guild and now contains the **Brewery Museum**. Step inside to discover how Belgium's favorite liquid was made in times gone by. A good place to taste the delicious result is at numbers 1 and 2, the Roi d'Espagne Café—whose rustic interior is strangely embellished with a stuffed horse.

Now leave the Grand' Place and follow the map to what is surely the most famous sight in Brussels. The **Manneken-Pis** (4) tells a lot about the Belgians and what they think of foreign invaders. Who else would have erected a two-foot-high statue of a little boy peeing? First carved in stone, "Little Julian" was redone in bronze in 1619 and has been periodically stolen, but always replaced. People from all over the world continue to follow the example of France's King Louis XV, who donated a splendid costume to keep the lad warm. The entire wardrobe, now numbering some 400 outfits, is on display in the Maison du Roi in the Grand' Place. These are worn on special occasions throughout the year, but most of the time Julian remains his happy naked self. The inevitable souvenir shops near the statue offer an imaginative range of slightly perverted gifts, some of which squirt wine.

Head back to the town center on Rue du Midi and stop at the delightful little **Church of St. Nicholas** (5). Almost completely abutted by shops, this strangely appealing church was begun in the 12th century and greatly altered throughout the centuries. Its atmospheric interior is usually open from 10 a.m. to noon and 4–6 p.m.

Rue de la Bourse leads past the Stock Exchange *(Bourse),* built in 1873 in the classical manner. Turn right on Boulevard Anspach, a busy shopping street, to Place de Brouckère. Surrounded by modern office buildings, this is the commercial heart of today's Brussels. From here stroll around to Place de la Monnaie, a vast open pedestrian area bordered by the **Théâtre Royal de la Monnaie** (6), the National Opera House. Opened in 1819 and later rebuilt, this was the scene in 1830 of a mass demonstration that led to Belgium's declaration of independence from Holland.

Return along the busy shopping street called Rue des Fripiers and turn left on Rue du Marché aux Herbes. This brings you into the center of medieval Brussels, a preserved area of antiquity known as **L'Ilot Sacré** (The Sacred Isle). Practically next door to the Grand' Place, its colorful narrow streets and passageways are lined with picturesque restaurants and craft shops.

Follow the map through the maze and enter the **Galeries Saint-Hubert** (7), a complex of glass-vaulted shopping arcades whose different sections are known as the Galerie des Princes, the Galerie du Roi, and the Galerie de la Reine. Opened in 1847, these were the first such structures in Europe, the concept later spreading to Paris, Milan, London, and other cities. In reality, it was the forerunner of the modern indoor shopping mall. Within its sunlit passages you will find several "outdoor" cafés and restaurants.

The route now leaves the Lower Town and begins a slight climb to the Upper Town. Along the way you will pass the massive ***Cathedral of St. Michael** (8), which serves as the national church of Belgium and which only achieved cathedral status in 1962. That was after a long wait, as construction of the present structure began in 1226 and was pretty well completed by the 15th century. Its somewhat austere interior is noted for the exceptionally fine 16th-century **stained-glass windows** in the choir, depicting Brussel's Burgundian, Austrian, and Spanish rulers. Some other features to look for are the **Chapel of the Holy Sacrament** to the side of the choir, and the fabulous 17th-century **pulpit** in the nave. The cathedral is presently undergoing renovation, but parts of it may be visited from the south transept entrance.

Continue uphill to Place du Congrés, where the tall 19th-century **Congress Column** (9) honors the national gathering that proclaimed a Belgian constitution after the 1830 revolution. An eternal flame marks the grave of unknown soldiers from both world wars. Step out onto the huge esplanade just beyond this for a splendid panoramic view across Brussels, with a close-up look at the modern administrative complex.

Now follow Rue Royale and turn left on Rue de la Loi. The 18th-century **Palace of the Nation** houses both chambers of the Belgian parliament and overlooks the **Parc du Bruxelles** (10), a rather formal public park in the French manner. Once a hunting preserve of the dukes of Brabant, it was the scene of fierce fighting between Dutch troops and the rebellious Belgians in 1830. Stroll through it to the **Royal Palace** (11), the official town residence of the king. Some of its interior, particularly the Throne Room, is usually open to the public between late July and early September.

Just downhill from this is the Place Royale, where two of the finest art museums in all of Europe are located. Known collectively as the ***Musées Royaux des Beaux-Arts de Belgique** (12), they are connected internally at the basement level, and since there is no admission charge, you can wander back and forth between them. The larger one, with its entrance on Rue de la Régence, is the **Museum of Classic Art** *(Musée d'Art Ancien)*. Its extensive collections are particularly rich in works by the Flemish masters such as Bruegel, Rubens, Memling, and Van der Weyden. The Dutch schools are represented by, among others, Bosch, Frans Hals, and Van Dyck. There are also masterpieces of the Italian, French, German, and Spanish schools from the 15th through the 18th centuries. An underground passage connects this museum with the **Museum of Modern Art**, much of which is housed in spectacular subterranean galleries first opened in 1984. The collections here cover the entire scope of 19th- and 20th-century art, with special reference to works by Belgian artists such as Ensor, Magritte, and Delvaux. Both museums are open Tuesdays through Sundays, from 10 a.m. to 5 p.m. Don't miss this special Brussels treat, especially since it's free.

Continue down Rue de la Régence to the **Square du Petit Sablon** (13), a delightful area lined with small bronze statues representing the medieval trade guilds. Across from this stands the **Notre-Dame du Sablon Church** (14). Dating from the 15th century, this is one of the most beautiful late-Gothic structures in Belgium. Step inside to see its famous 17th-century baroque **pulpit** and the magnificent stained-glass windows. The square below this, known as Place du Grand Sablon, is noted for its outdoor antiques market held on Saturdays from 9 a.m. to 3 p.m. and on Sundays from 9 a.m. to 1 p.m. There is also a large variety of cafés and restaurants around here.

You can return to the central train station, or to Grand' Place, via the route shown on the map.

ADDITIONAL SIGHTS:

Brussels is reputed to have a hundred museums, give or take a few. In addition, there are several other sights that you might want to visit on another day. Complete details on these are available at the tourist office or by purchasing a special guidebook to the city. Some of the more outstanding attractions are:

Waterloo. The site of the famous battle where Napoleon met his final defeat in 1815 has an enormous monument you can climb, and several museums explaining the battle. Get there by a local train leaving all three stations at half-hour intervals in the direction of Charleroi, or by bus route "W" from Place Rouppe.

Atomium. A remnant from the 1958 World's Fair, this strange structure represents an iron crystal molecule magnified 20 billion times. Consisting of nine spheres, each about 60 feet in diameter and connected by tubes to reach a height of 335 feet, it houses displays on nuclear energy and space travel as well as a restaurant. Travel within it is by elevator and escalators. More than a wee bit dated today, it is a great place to reminisce about the 1950s. Take the Métro to Heysel, or tram 18 or 81 to the north end of the line.

Royal Museum of Art and History. Located in the Parc du Cinquantenaire to the east of the center city, this museum has an enormous collection of classical antiquity and artifacts of mixed ages from all over the world. While there, you can also visit the Museum of the Blind and the Royal Museum of the Army and Military History—among others. Take the Métro to the Merode stop, or tram 81, or bus numbers 20, 28, 36, 61, 67, or 80.

Horta Museum. Brussels' favorite architect was Victor Horta, whose work in the Art Nouveau style is renowned throughout the world. You can see its splendors in his former home at Rue Américaine 25 in the southern part of the city. Bus number 54 or 60, or trams 81, 82, 91, or 92 go there.

Ghent

(Gent, Gand)

History may live on in Ghent, but this great Flemish industrial city most certainly does not dwell in the past. Although it may possess more venerable buildings than any other place in Belgium, it is hardly a preserved museum. Indeed, its medieval treasures have become an integral part of a dynamic urban center where the Middle Ages blend right into the 20th century.

Ghent began as an abbey founded by St. Bavon, about A.D. 630. During the 9th century, a castle was built at the confluence of the rivers Lieve and Leie, around which a town developed. By the 13th century, a growing textile industry made Ghent one of the largest cities in northern Europe, and a force to be reckoned with. Its economy declined after the Spaniards came to power in the 16th century, but was revived with the introduction of cotton-spinning machinery during the Industrial Revolution. A new canal opened the way to seagoing vessels, and today Ghent is the second-largest port in Belgium. The city has a curious connection with American history, for it was here that the treaty ending the War of 1812 was negotiated and signed.

GETTING THERE:

Trains depart Brussels' three major stations (see map on page 167) at half-hour intervals for the 33-minute ride to Ghent's St. Pieters Station. Return service operates until late evening.

By car, Ghent is 34 miles northwest of Brussels via the A-10/E-40 highway. Park as close to the cathedral as possible and drive to the Bijloke Museum and the Fine Arts Museum to avoid a long walk.

WHEN TO GO:

Avoid visiting Ghent on a Monday, when many of its most important sights are closed.

FOOD AND DRINK:

Some good restaurant choices are:

Waterzooi (Sint Veerleplein 2, near the castle) Famous for local dishes, phone (09) 225-0563. X: Wed., Sun. $$$

Graaf van Egmond (St. Michielsplein 21, 3 blocks west of the Belfry) Flemish specialties in a 13th-century townhouse on the river. Phone (09) 225-0727. $$

Het Cooremetretshuys (Graslei 12, on the ancient harbor) In a 14th-century house. Phone (09) 223-4971. X: Sun., Wed. $$

Raadskelder (Botermarkt 18, by the Belfry) Good Flemish food in the medieval vaults. Phone (09) 225-4334. $$

Cour St. Georges (Botermarkt 2, near the Town Hall) Flemish dining in a 13th-century inn. Phone (09) 224-2424. $$

Ghent is famous (or notorious!) for its traditional beer taverns *(kroegen)*, which serve up to several *hundred* different varieties of brew—some of which are very high in alcohol content. Among the more interesting places are:

Bieracademie Dulle Griet (Vrijdagmarkt 50) X: Sun., Mon. $

Tempelier (on the street just west of Vrijdagmarkt) X: Tues. $

Waterhuis aan de Bierkant (Groentenmarkt 9, on the water 2 blocks southeast of the castle) Outdoor tables. X: Mon. $

TOURIST INFORMATION:

The local tourist office, phone (09) 224-1555, is in the crypt of the Town Hall on Botermarkt. There is also a regional tourist office just across from the train station, whose phone number is (09) 222-1637.

SUGGESTED TOUR:

From **St. Pieters Station** (1) it is an uninteresting 1½-mile walk to the center of town, following the route on the map. You can avoid this by taking tram number 1, 11, or 12 to Korenmarkt or Centrum.

Begin at the **Belfry and Cloth Hall** *(Belfort en Lakenhalle)* (2), two adjoining medieval structures in the middle of a large open square. At one time these were hemmed in by houses, which have long since disappeared. The **Belfry** soars to a height of 312 feet and can be seen for miles around. Begun in 1321 and completed in 1339, it contains one of the best carillons in Belgium and may be climbed for a splendid view of the city. Ask at the nearby tourist office for current details. A ten-foot copper dragon, first cast in 1377 and twice replaced, tops the spire, while next to its base stands a 17th-century former jail called the *Mammelokken*. The adjacent **Cloth Hall** dates from the early 15th century and was originally an assembly room for wool and cloth merchants.

Step across the square to ***St. Bavon's Cathedral** *(St. Baafskathe-*

Ghent

500 Yards

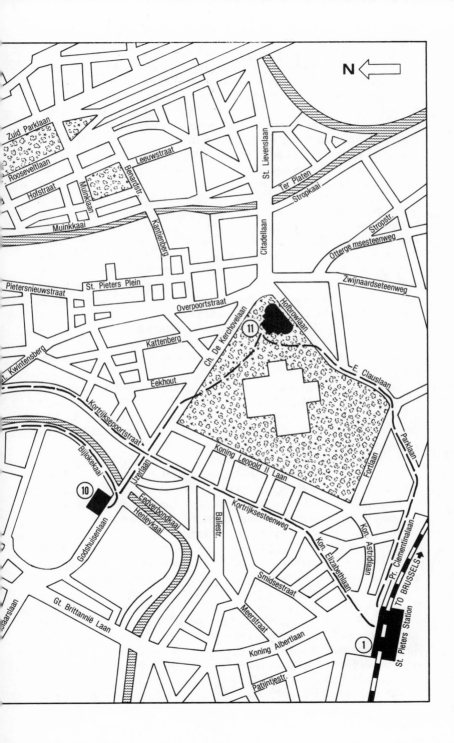

draal) (3), a magnificent Gothic structure, built between the 13th and 16th centuries on the foundations of an earlier Romanesque church. St. Bavon's is renowned throughout the world for the quality of its art treasures. Foremost among these is the **Adoration of the Mystic Lamb*, a large 15th-century altarpiece that is regarded as being one of the most important paintings in the history of art. It is supposedly a joint creation by Jan van Eyck and his older brother Hubert, but this is disputed by historians, as there is no evidence that the famous Flemish painter ever had a brother by that name. That the work exists at all is a miracle in itself. Phillip II tried to take it to Spain, and in 1566 it barely escaped destruction by the Calvinists, who considered it a symbol of idolatry. During the 18th century, its naked Adam and Eve proved offensive to the eyes of the Hapsburg emperor Josef II, who had those panels replaced by clothed figures. The French stole the painting in 1794 and didn't return it until after Napoleon's defeat at Waterloo, after which parts of it were sold to a Berlin museum. It was not until 1920 that all of its sections were reunited in Ghent, only to be partially stolen again. During World War II, the Nazis grabbed the whole thing and hid it in an Austrian salt mine, where it was discovered in 1945 by American soldiers. Happily, it is now in one piece, except for a small panel that has never been recovered and was replaced by a copy.

Other major masterpieces in the cathedral include the *Conversion of St. Bavon* by Peter Paul Rubens, the *Triptych of the Calvary* by Justus of Ghent, and a fabulously carved pulpit by Laurent Delvaux. Be sure to visit the 12th-century **crypt** with its famous frescoes and church treasures. The cathedral is open on Mondays through Saturdays, from 9:30 a.m. to noon and 2–6 p.m.; and on Sundays and holidays from 1–6 p.m. The hours are slightly reduced in winter. Entry to the church is free, but there's a charge for the *Mystic Lamb* and the crypt.

Return to the Belfry and turn right to the **Town Hall** *(Stadhuis)* (4), a peculiar jumble of architectural styles if ever there was one. Begun in the 15th century, its construction dragged on until the 18th. Part of it is flamboyant Gothic, another is sober Renaissance, a third Flemish baroque, and the final fourth is in the rococo style. Oddly enough, it all works, and the entire structure is actually quite handsome. The tourist office is in its basement; ask them about guided tours through the rooms above.

Now follow the map to the **Vrijdag Markt** (5), where a flea market is held on Fridays, hence the name. Traditionally the meeting place of the townspeople, this large square has seen more than its share of political violence and skirmishes between the trade guilds since at least the 14th century.

Continue on Meerseniersstraat to the Leie River, near which you

The Castle of the Counts

can see **"Mad Meg"** *(Dulle Griet)*, an enormous 15th-century cannon once used in Ghent's interminable wars. Cross the little bridge and turn left past some interesting façades to the **Museum of Folklore** *Museum voor Volkskunde* (6). Housed in a beautifully restored 14th-century children's home, the museum re-creates life among the common people of Ghent during the 19th century. Its picturesque courtyard is lined with 18 typical Flemish houses, complete with replica shops and period room settings. Visits to this enchanting place may be made on Tuesdays through Sundays, from 9 a.m. to 12:30 p.m. and 1–5:30 p.m., with slightly shorter hours in winter.

The route now leads to **'s Gravensteen** (7), the massive and foreboding ***Castle of the Counts**. Built in 1180 on the foundations of the original 9th-century castle, it was primarily used to keep the local citizens in line through sheer intimidation. You can climb all over its perfectly restored battlements for a great view, and visit (if you dare!) the terrifying torture chambers, where a vast assortment of hideous instruments of pain and death are on display. Just follow the arrows. The castle is open daily from 9 a.m. to 6 p.m., closing at 4 p.m. in winter. Don't miss this chilling adventure!

The square in front of the castle was used as a place of public execution, by burning or beheading, until the late 18th century. It also served as a fish market and is lined with impressive old buildings.

Cross the bridge and turn left to the **Decorative Arts Museum** *(Museum voor Sierkunst)* (8), where exhibitions of handicrafts and design are displayed in a fine 18th-century mansion. It is open on Tuesdays through Sundays, from 9:30 a.m. to 12:30 p.m. and 1:30–5:30 p.m.

Just a short stroll from this is the medieval harbor, bordered by a lovely stretch of old buildings called the **Graslei** (9). Short boat trips through the city's streams and canals are offered near the bridge on either side of the river. These leave frequently between April and the end of October, from 10 a.m. to 7 p.m. The cruises last about 35 minutes. Cross the bridge and stroll along the Graslei for a wonderful look at some marvelous ***guild houses** dating from the 13th through the 17th centuries. The bridge at its south end, the *St. Michielsbrug,* offers a stunning view of the urban scene.

From the nearby center of town you can return to St. Pieters Station by tram or continue walking along the river's edge to the **Bijloke Museum** (10), also called the Museum of Antiquities *(Museum voor Oudheden).* Housed in a still-functioning medieval abbey, the museum has a superb collection of the religious and applied arts, weapons, clothes, musical instruments, and so on, displayed in lovely room settings. It is open on Tuesdays through Sundays, from 9:30 a.m. to 12:30 p.m. and 1:30–5:30 p.m.

Those traveling on foot may want to return to the station via the **Fine Arts Museum** *(Museum voor Schone Kunsten)* (11), located in Citadel Park. Here you will find an excellent collection of Flemish and Dutch works by such masters as Bosch, Rubens, Van Dyck, Bruegel, and Frans Hals. There are also quite a few modern pieces by James Ensor, Rouault, Delvaux, Magritte, and others. It is open during the same hours as the Bijloke Museum, above. From here it is a short walk back to the train station.

*Bruges
(Brugge)

Time has long stood still in medieval Bruges, a romantic city that went to sleep in the Middle Ages and didn't wake up until this century. Virtually all of the events of modern history have passed it by, leaving behind a perfectly preserved gem that is today among the loveliest places in Europe. No visitor to Belgium should miss seeing it.

In its heyday Bruges was a very wealthy town, attracting great artists and erecting splendid houses. Built around a 9th-century castle, its position near the Zwin estuary made it an ideal inland port, well protected from the storms of the North Sea. By the 12th century it was one of the most important trading centers in Europe. Shiploads of wool from England arrived daily to be woven into cloth at Bruges.

Gradually, however, the Zwin began to silt up and at first, expensive efforts were made at dredging it. Around the same time, the English started to make their own cloth for export. The weavers at Bruges—defending their own privileges—prohibited this from entering their harbor, and so the trade naturally shifted to rival Antwerp. This was the beginning of the end. Investment in a canal, new harbor facilities, and a change in the guild rules might have saved the day, but the merchants of Bruges balked at the price, with the result that the town slowly declined and became known as "Bruges-la-Morte," or "the dead city."

Ironically, the necessary canal finally got built, and it opened in 1907, along with the splendid modern harbor of Zeebrugge. By then, however, the citizens of Bruges had discovered a gold mine in their own past and took steps to insure that the town's medieval appearance would forever remain intact to delight the tourists.

And Bruges does get more than its share of visitors. Everything is so well organized, though, that even in the peak travel season it remains an extraordinarily pleasant place and never seems overcrowded. The suggested walking tour, besides covering the basics, also takes you into parts of town that relatively few tourists ever get to see.

Incidentally, the town is known locally by its Flemish name of

Brugge, even if the English-speaking world continues to call it by the French Bruges.

GETTING THERE:

Trains depart Brussels' three major stations (see map on page 167) at half-hour intervals for the 58-minute ride to Bruges (Brugge). Return service operates until late evening.

By car, Bruges is 60 miles northwest of Brussels via the A-10/E-40 highway to exit 9. Park as close to the train station as possible and avoid driving in the Old Town.

WHEN TO GO:

Any time is a good time to visit Bruges, but note that some of the major attractions are closed on either Tuesdays or Wednesdays between October and the end of March.

FOOD AND DRINK:

Being a major tourist area, Bruges offers a wide range of restaurants and cafés in every possible price range. Some choices are:

Duc de Bourgogne (Huidenvettersplein 12, a block southeast of the Basilica of the Holy Blood) A world-famous inn with classic cuisine. Phone (050) 33-20-38 for reservations. X: Mon., Tues. lunch. $$$

't Pandreitje (Pandreitje 6, 2 blocks southeast of the Basilica of the Holy Blood) Classic French and Belgian cuisine. Phone (050) 33-11-90. X: Sun., Wed. $$$

't Bourgoensche Cruyce (Wollestraat 41, close to the Basilica of the Holy Blood) A small and very popular restaurant overlooking a canal. Phone (050) 33-79-26. $$$

De Witte Poorte (Jan van Eyckplein 6) Excellent seafood and other dishes. Phone (050) 33-08-83. X: Sun., Mon. $$$

De Karmeliet (Langestraat 19, 3 blocks south of the Jerusalem Church) Renowned French cuisine, phone (050) 33-82-59 for reservations. X: Sun. eve., Mon. $$$

't Kluizeke (Sint Jacobstraat 58, 3 blocks northwest of the Markt) In a quiet part of town. $$

Boudewijn ('t Zand, 2 blocks west of the Cathedral) An outstanding value. Phone (050) 33-69-62. $$

De Postiljon (Katelijnestraat 3, opposite the Memling Museum) Conveniently near the major attractions. X: Sun. eve., Tues. $

Malpertus (Eiermarkt 9, a block northwest of the Markt) Exceptional value. X: Thurs., July. $

TOURIST INFORMATION:

The highly organized local tourist office is at Burg 11, by the Town Hall. You can phone them at (050) 44-86-86.

SUGGESTED TOUR:

Leave the **Brugge Train Station** (1) and follow the map through a park to the **Minnewater** (2), popularly known as the "Lake of Love." During the Middle Ages this was the commercial harbor of the town, defended in part by the powder tower of 1398 at its south end.

Stroll along this peaceful scene and turn left into the ***Beguinage** (Begijnhof) (3), a sheltered world of meditation that has hardly changed since its foundation in the 13th century. In those days its tiny houses were occupied by single lay women, or widows who wished to live a religious life without taking formal vows. Today it is inhabited by Benedictine nuns wearing 15th-century costumes. Amble quietly through its courtyard and visit the small church, first erected in 1245 and rebuilt in 1605. The **house** at the northeast corner has been restored to its 17th-century condition and is open to visitors at the times posted. Don't miss this unusual treat. If the south gate to the Beguinage is closed, you can usually get in via the main north gate.

Now follow the map to the bridge on Katelijnestraat. This is one of the four places where you can take a delightful half-hour ***boat ride** through the town's picturesque canals. These depart whenever there are sufficient customers, between March and November, and are a "must" for all visitors to Bruges.

Just across the bridge stands the **Church of Our Lady** (Onze Lieve Vrouwekerk) (4). Built in a variety of styles between the 13th and 15th centuries, it has the tallest spire in the Low Countries. Step inside to see the famous ***Virgin and Child** statue by Michelangelo, one of the few pieces by that renowned artist to have left Italy during his lifetime. Among the many other works of art are the 16th-century monumental tombs of Mary of Burgundy and Charles the Bold. High above the north ambulatory there is an enclosed balcony that opens into the adjacent Gruuthuse Museum. The balcony was put there in the 15th century so the wealthy merchant who lived in that mansion could attend services without leaving home. The Church of Our Lady is usually open Mondays through Saturdays from 10–11:30 a.m. and 2:30–5 p.m. On Sundays it is open in the afternoon only.

Directly across the street from the church is the **Hospital of St. John** (St. Janshospitaal) (5), which houses the magnificent ***Memling Museum**. Founded in the 12th century to care for Bruges' sick and indigent, this former hospice contains a stunning collection of works

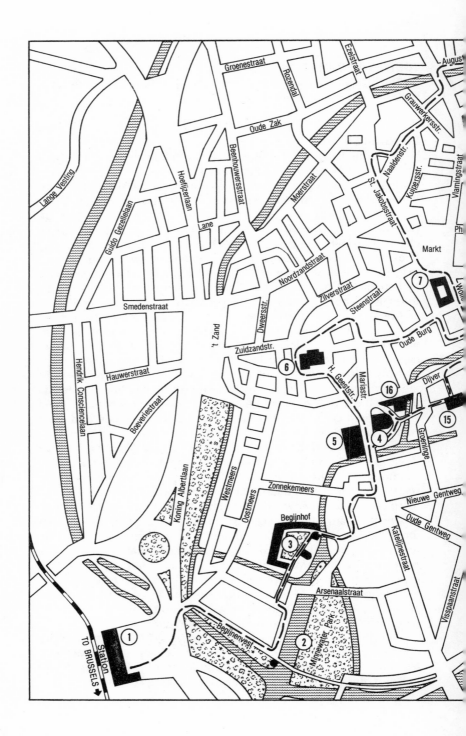

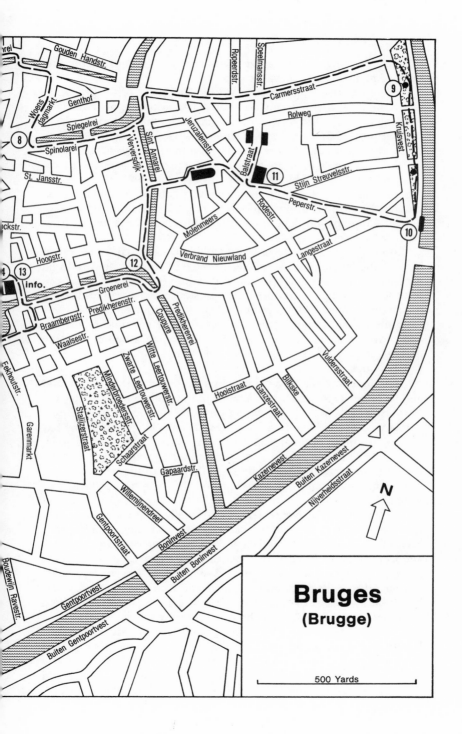

Bruges
(Brugge)

500 Yards

by Hans Memling, a 15th-century German-born painter who became the leading artist of medieval Bruges.

The most outstanding pieces are the **Reliquary of St. Ursala**, in which the legend of the saint and her 11,000 virgins being massacred in Cologne is depicted on the sides of an oak reliquary, and the **Mystical Marriage of St. Catherine**, a sublimely beautiful altarpiece dedicated to St. John the Baptist and St. John the Evangelist, the patron saints of the hospital. While there, be sure to visit the restored 17th-century Dispensary, which remained in use until 1971. The museum is open daily from 9:30 a.m. to noon and 2–6 p.m., but is closed on Wednesdays from October through March. You can purchase an economical combination ticket that also includes the Groeninge, Gruuthuse, and Brangwyn museums.

Continue along Mariastraat and Heilige Geeststraat to **St. Salvator's Cathedral** (6), an essentially Gothic structure grafted onto an earlier Romanesque base. Architecturally undistinguished, it has suffered much during the centuries of its existence and was only elevated to cathedral status in 1834. Nevertheless, its interior does have some exquisitely carved choir stalls and misericords, splendid tapestries, and a lovely baroque rood screen. The adjoining **Cathedral Museum** features some works by the old Flemish masters Dirk Bouts and Hugo van der Goes.

The route now follows a complicated but colorful path to the **Markt** and its rather extravagant and slightly askew 13th-century **Belfry** (7), the very symbol of Bruges. Soaring some 270 feet above the old marketplace, it may be climbed for a truly spectacular ***view** on any day from 9:30 a.m. to noon and 12:45–5 p.m., with slightly shorter hours in winter. On the way up you can glimpse the famous 47-bell **carillon** that plays tunes every quarter-hour. At the base of the belfry tower is the Halle, a 13th-century covered market that now houses local government agencies.

Stroll through the lively Markt, an unusually attractive square lined with restaurants and outdoor cafés. From here, the walking tour leaves the tourists behind and explores a quiet part of town where the atmosphere of the Middle Ages remains more intact. Follow the map through a series of narrow streets and alleyways to **Jan van Eyckplein** (8), named after the great 15th-century Flemish painter. This neighborhood was the center of commercial activities during the 13th and 14th centuries, and still retains much of that ambiance.

Continue along the canalside Spinolarei until you come to a bridge. At this point you could cut the tour short by turning right and following the map to the Basilica of the Holy Blood (14). If you prefer to see some more sights of an unusual nature, however, you should cross the bridge and turn down Carmersstraat to the outer ring canal.

The St. Janshuismolen

Here you will find several restored windmills, one of which may be visited. Known as **St. Janshuismolen** (9), it is of the stilt type and was rebuilt in 1770. You can climb up into its working mechanism for a good look on any day between May and the end of September, from 9:30 a.m. to noon and 12:45–5 p.m.

Now amble through the park to the early-15th-century **Cross Gate** *(Kruispoort)* (10), once a part of the ramparts that were largely demolished during the late 18th century. Head back into town on Langestraat and Peperstraat, which will take you to the 15th-century **Jerusalem Church** (11), supposedly built to the same plans as the Holy Sepulchre in Jerusalem. It is especially noted for its 15th-century stained-glass windows and its interesting crypt. Just north of this, in the medieval almshouses, is the popular **Lace Center** *(Kantcentrum)*. Sponsored by the state, this is where the ancient skills of lace making are passed on to younger generations. You can pay a visit Mondays through Saturdays, from 10 a.m. to noon and 2–6 p.m. Across the street is the Folklore Museum, which you might also want to see.

The route now continues on past St. Anne's Church and crosses a small canal. Turn left and follow around to one of the prettiest sights in Bruges, the **Groenerei** (12). From here you get a lovely view down

View of the Belfry from the Canal

the canal and into the old part of town. Stroll along the water and turn right on Blinde Ezelstraat to the flamboyant **Town Hall** *(Stadhuis)* (13). Begun in the 14th century, its magnificent façade is a veritable forest of statuary. Step inside to see its splendid Gothic Hall *(Gotische Zaal)*, decorated with murals depicting the history of Bruges, and its fantastic vaulted ceiling. Visits can usually be made daily, from 9:30 a.m. to noon and 2–6 p.m., closing a bit earlier in winter.

The large open square known as Burg, in front of the Town Hall, occupies the site of the original 9th-century castle around which Bruges developed. Also facing this is the **Basilica of the Holy Blood** *(Heilig Bloedbaziliek)* (14), where what is said to be blood washed from the body of Christ is venerated. The 12th-century basilica consists of a lower and an upper chapel, the lower being a dark Romanesque structure that remains virtually unchanged. The sacred relic is in the upper chapel, which was rebuilt in the Gothic style during the 16th century. On Ascension Day, it is carried through the city streets in a colorful procession. The Basilica is open nearly every day, from 9:30 a.m. to noon and 2–6 p.m., closing at 4 p.m. in winter.

Return across the canal and follow the map to the world-famous ***Groeninge Museum** (15). Covering the entire scope of Flemish art

The Bonifacius Bridge

from the 15th through the 20th centuries, this superb museum displays works by Jan van Eyck, Hans Memling, Rogier van der Weyden, Hugo van der Goes, Breugel, Bosch, and such moderns as Magritte and Delvaux. It is open daily from April through September, from 9:30 a.m. to 5 p.m.; and on Wednesdays through Mondays the rest of the year, from 9:30 a.m. to 12:30 p.m. and 2–5 p.m. Don't miss it.

Leave the museum by a side passage and stroll around to the tiny ***Bonifacius Bridge**, beyond which lies one of the most enchanting and evocative corners of old Bruges. From here it is only steps to the **Gruuthuse Museum** (16), housed in a fabulous 15th-century merchant's mansion. In it are displayed several thousand antiques of all sorts, covering the entire sweep of Bruges' history. As you wander through the complex of rooms, you may be startled to look out directly into the interior of the Church of Our Lady, reminding you that this tour has come full circle. The museum is open daily from 9:30 a.m. to 5 p.m. From October through March it has shorter hours and is closed on Tuesdays.

Oostende

(Ostende, Ostend)

The sparkling seaside resort of Oostende neatly bundles most of its considerable attractions into a compact area overlooking the North Sea. A busy passenger port with constant ferries to England's Ramsgate, a colorful fishing harbor and yacht marina, miles of sandy beaches, Belgium's largest casino, and a thriving shopping district all vie for the attention of visitors—many of whom come over from Britain. Connoisseurs of modern art will see a different aspect of Oostende, however, as this was the lifelong home of James Ensor, one of the major pioneers of Expressionism. Many of his strange works may be seen here, along with his fully restored home.

Although Oostende was founded in the 11th century and was a main departure point for the Crusades, it is today a thoroughly modern town, since little of its past survived the wars of this and previous centuries.

GETTING THERE:

Trains depart Brussels' three major stations at hourly intervals for the 80-minute ride to Oostende. Return service operates until midevening. Expect crowds on summer weekends.

By car, it's the A-10/E-40 highway all the way. Oostende is 72 miles northwest of Brussels.

WHEN TO GO:

Oostende is best visited between June and the end of September, when all of its attractions are open. A few of the museums are closed on Tuesdays. Good weather will make this trip much more enjoyable.

FOOD AND DRINK:

Being a popular seaside resort, Oostende has a great variety of restaurants and cafés in all price categories. Quite a few of these specialize in seafood. Some choices are:

> **Au Vigneron** (Koningstraat 79, 3 blocks southwest of the casino) Classic French cuisine in a former royal villa on the sea. Phone (059) 70-48-16 for reservations. X: Sun. eve., Mon. $$$

Along the Visserskaai

Villa Maritza (Albert I Promenade 76, 2 blocks southwest of the casino) Exquisite French cuisine in a villa overlooking the sea. Phone (059) 50-88-08 for reservations. X: Sun. eve., Mon. $$$
Old Fisher (Visserkaai 34, near the North Sea Aquarium) A comfortable place for both seafood and meat dishes. Phone (059) 50-17-68. X: Wed. eve., Thurs. $$
Chopin (A. Buylstraat 1, 2 blocks southeast of Ensor's House) Locally popular for seafood and steak. Phone (059) 70-08-37. X: Thurs. $$
Cardiff (St. Sebastiaanstraat 4, a block west of the Fine Arts Museum) A small hotel with a fine dining room. Phone (059) 70-28-98. $

TOURIST INFORMATION:

The local tourist office, phone (059) 70-11-99, is at Monacoplein 2, opposite the casino. During July and August there is a branch in the train station.

SUGGESTED TOUR:

The **train station** (1) is right on the harbor and connects directly with ferries to England. From here, stroll down along the old fishing harbor and the **Visserskaai**, a delightful fishermen's quay lined with seafood restaurants and cafés. Near its end is the **North Sea Aquarium**

(2), where living fish may be seen in a natural environment along with a fine collection of seashells. It is open daily from June through September, from 10 a.m. to 12:30 p.m. and 2–6 p.m. During April and May the hours are shorter, and for the rest of the year it is open on weekends only.

A walk out on the **Western Jetty** *(Westerstaketsel)* (3) affords good views and the opportunity of taking a short **cruise**, which departs hourly after 10:45 a.m., every day from June through mid-September.

Return to the Visserskaai and continue along the broad Albert I Promenade, which looks out over the sea. This leads to the modern **Casino** *(Kursaal)* (4), complete with a concert hall, nightclub, restaurant, and gambling rooms. The latter open daily at 3 p.m. and require payment of a membership fee.

Now follow the map to the ***James Ensor House** (5) on Vlaanderenstraat. One of the most original artists of modern times, Ensor was born in Oostende in 1860 and died there in 1949, having seldom left the town. His father was English, thus the name. The house was previously used by his aunt and uncle as a souvenir shop, the ground floor of which is now preserved. Upstairs, the studio and living quarters have been maintained as they were in his time, although the works of art on display are all copies, as the originals are in major museums. What is most striking about his work is its sense of grotesque satire, a legacy that can be traced back to earlier Flemish painters such as Bruegel and Bosch. You may love or hate these paintings, but you will never forget them. The house is open from June through September, Wednesdays through Mondays, from 10 a.m. to noon and 2–5 p.m.; and also on some off-season holidays.

Continue straight ahead to Wapenplein, the main square of Oostende. This is dominated by the **Festival and Culture Palace** *(Stedelijk Feest en Kultuurpaleis)* (6), which houses two interesting museums. The first of these is the **"De Plate" Folklore Museum**, where the history of the town from prehistoric to relatively recent times is on display, with artifacts and period room settings. It is open daily, except on Tuesdays, from July through September, 10 a.m. to noon and 3–5 p.m. During other months it is open on Saturdays only.

On the floor above this is the **Fine Arts Museum**, devoted primarily to the artistic trends of the last hundred years. Pride of place is naturally given to Oostende's own James Ensor, who is represented by a large collection of his earlier works. These may be seen any day except Tuesdays and a few holidays, from 10 a.m. to noon and 2–5 p.m.

The route now goes through an attractive pedestrians-only shopping area and turns left to the **Church of St. Peter and St. Paul** (7). First built in the 14th century, it was rebuilt in the neo-Gothic style

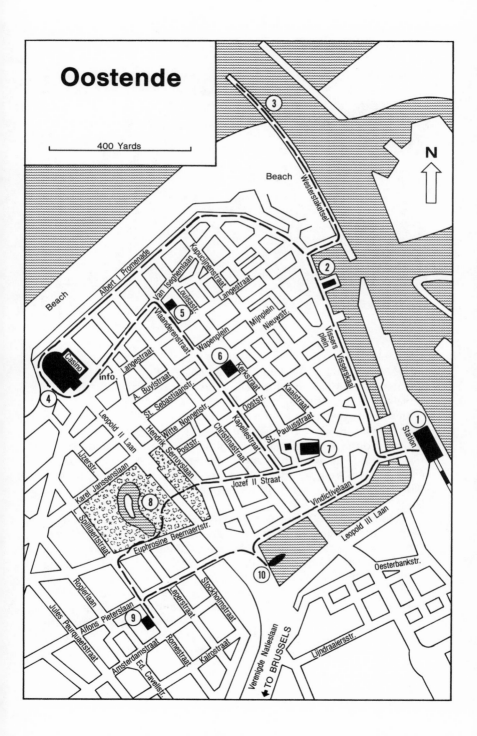

Oostende

400 Yards

N

Beach

Westerstakketsel

Beach

Albert I Promenade

Van Iseghemlaan
Kapucijnenstraat
Louisastr.
Langestraat
Mijnplein
Nieuwstr.
Vlaanderenstraat
Wapenplein
Vissers plein
Visserskaai

Casino
info.
Langestraat
A. Buylstraat
St. Sebastiaanstr.
Kerkstraat
Kaaistraat
Ooststr.
Leopold II Laan
Witte Nonnenstr.
Hendrik Serruyslaan
Poststr.
Christinastraat
Kapellestraat
St. Paulusstraat
Ijzerstr.
Karel Janssenslaan

Station

Jozef II Straat

Vindictivelaan

Spilliaertstraat
Euphrosine Beernaertstr.
Leopold III Laan
Oesterbankstr.

Rogierlaan
Jules Peurquaetstraat
Alfons Pieterslaan
Lepestraat
Stockholmstraat
Amsterdamstraat
Ed. Cavelstr.
Romestraat
Kairostraat
Verenigde Natieslaan
Lijndraaiersstr.

TO BRUSSELS

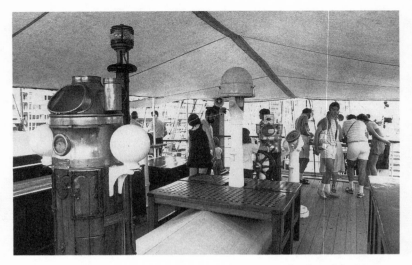

On Board the Mercator

in 1907 and contains the tomb of Belgium's first queen, who died in Oostende in 1850. Behind it stands the Peppermill Tower, the only remaining part of the original medieval church.

A stroll westward on Josef II Straat soon brings you to the **Leopold Park** (8) with its flower clock, pond, bandstand, and miniature golf course. Continue through this and follow Spilliartstraat and Romestraat to the **Provincial Museum for Modern Art** (9), which explores contemporary Belgian art in all of its aspects, including sculpture, film, and video. It is open daily except on Tuesdays, from 10 a.m. to 6 p.m.

Return on Alfon Pieterslaan to what is perhaps Oostende's most exciting attraction. Moored at the end of the yacht basin is the ****Mercator*** (10), a splendid three-masted former training ship of the Belgian Merchant Navy. Launched in 1932, it made voyages throughout the world until 1960, when it was retired as a museum. You can climb all over this proud sailing ship and explore below decks as well, examining the items collected during its many adventures to exotic ports. Visits may be made daily from April through September, and on weekends the rest of the year. The hours vary, but in summer it is usually open until 6 or 7 p.m. From here it is a short walk back to the station.

Kortrijk
(Courtrai)

Although it boasts no world-famous tourist attractions, Kortrijk does offer the opportunity to get off the beaten path and enjoy a thoroughly delightful Flemish town with a rich history. This easy daytrip includes a visit to what may be the most charming *béguinage* in the Low Countries, to an important 13th-century church with two outstanding works of art, to a splendid town hall, and to an excellent museum of local history. More than that, Kortrijk is an unusually pleasant shopping center for the region, with pedestrianized streets and a good selection of places to eat and drink. The town lies just six miles from the French border.

Known as *Cortoriacum* in Roman times, Kortrijk was always an important road junction. Ever since the Middle Ages it has prospered as a result of the unusually soft water in its river, the Leie. This was ideal for making linen from the locally grown flax, and set the stage for the town's textile industry of today.

Kortrijk will always be remembered in history as the site of the Battle of the Golden Spurs, which occurred in 1302 and marked the beginning of the end of the Age of Chivalry. Fought between the Flemish weavers and a large army of French knights, it was the first time that ordinary citizens had ever defeated a professional force in armor.

GETTING THERE:

Trains leave Brussels' three major stations at hourly intervals for the 70-minute ride to Kortrijk *(Courtrai)*. Return service operates until mid-evening.

By car, leave Brussels on the A-10/E-40 highway west towards Ghent to exit 15, then take the A-14/E-17 southwest to Kortrijk exit 3. The total distance from Brussels is 56 miles.

WHEN TO GO:

Kortrijk may be visited at any time, but note that the museum is closed on Mondays. Some other sights are closed or have shorter hours during the off-season, especially on weekends.

FOOD AND DRINK:
You will find a good selection of restaurants and cafés in Kortrijk. Among them are:

> **Broel** (Broelkaai 8, near the museum) Both indoor and outdoor meals by the river. Phone (056) 21-83-51. X: Sat., Sun. $$

> **Gasthof Den Tuin** (Spoorweglaan 5, a block east of the station) An exceptional value for lunch. Phone (056) 21-55-45. $ and $$

> **Center Broel** (Graanmarkt 6, a block south of the Town Hall) Good-value meals in a small hotel. Phone (056) 21-97-21. $ and $$

> **Belfort** (Grote Markt 52) A small hotel with a recommended restaurant. Phone (056) 22-22-20. $ and $$

TOURIST INFORMATION:
The local tourist office, phone (056) 23-93-71, is at Schouwburg-plein, between the train station and the Grote Markt. Ask them about the nearby National Flax Museum, accessible by bus or car.

SUGGESTED TOUR:
Leave the **train station** (1) and follow the map past the tourist office to the **Grote Market** (2). In the middle of this large open market square stands the 14th-century **Belfry**, the only remaining part of a medieval cloth hall that was destroyed by bombing during World War II. The two figures under its center pinnacle strike the hours on the town clock.

Facing the northwest corner of the square is the **Town Hall** *(Stadhuis)* (3), of 14th-century origin but rebuilt around 1520 with both Gothic and Renaissance elements. Several alterations have occurred since, the latest being a complete renovation in 1962. The many statutes of the counts of Flanders that embellish its façade are modern reproductions. Step inside to see the Aldermen's Chamber *(Schepenzaal)* on the ground floor, which has a splendid 16th-century fireplace in the flamboyant Gothic style. The room is now used for weddings and receptions. Upstairs, the Council Chamber *(Oude Raadzaal)* has an even more magnificent 16th-century mantlepiece, decorated with figures of the virtues and the vices of mankind. All around, the sculptures, murals, and stained-glass windows merit close examination, as some of the scenes depicted are more than a little satirical. The Town Hall may usually be visited on Mondays through Fridays, from 9 a.m. to noon and 2–5 p.m.

Now stroll through the square to the **Church of St. Martin** (4), begun in the 13th century and rebuilt at the beginning of the 15th. In its choir, there is a beautifully carved gilded stone tabernacle, and in the center nave a baroque pulpit.

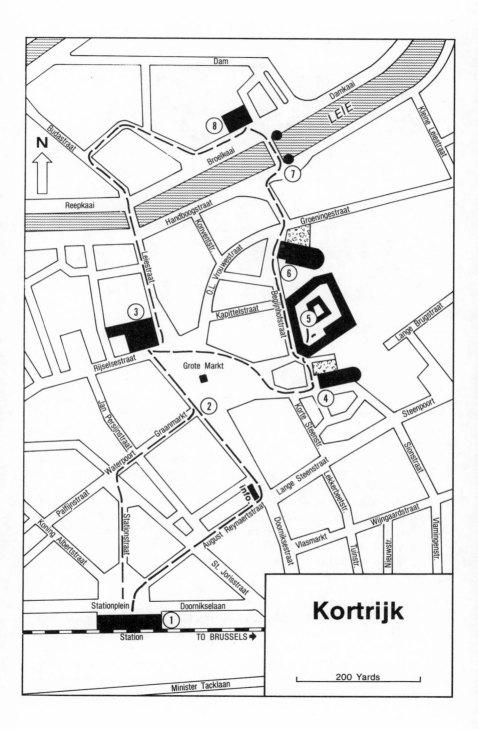

In the Béguinage

Close to this is the entrance gate to the **Béguinage** *(Begijnhof)* (5), a place of surprising calm in the center of a busy town. These tiny spiritual communities were founded in the Middle Ages and were especially prevalent in Belgium, which at one time had 94 of them. The Béguines were lay women who lived devout lives of chastity, simplicity, and obedience, but who did not take perpetual vows. Their numbers were high as a result of the surplus of women caused by constant wars, which killed off many of the available men to whom they would otherwise have been married.

Although it was founded in 1238, the 40 tiny houses that still exist in the Béguinage are mostly from the 17th century. Near the entrance is a chapel, dating perhaps from the 15th century, that has a nice interior with an air of restrained elegance. The Mother Superior's House contains a small museum of life in the Béguinage in former times. Stroll through the narrow winding streets, and be sure to notice the miniscule Chapel of Our Lady of the Snow, where pious people come to pray for relief from mental stress.

Continue on to the ***Church of Our Lady** *(Onze Lieve Vrouwkerk)* (6), the oldest building in town and once part of its fortifications. Built in the 13th century, it was altered several times since and is noted for its two great artistic treasures. One of these is the 14th-century alabaster statue of St. Catherine, and the other is the masterful *Raising of the Cross* of 1631, one of the last paintings done by Van Dyck before

The Broel Towers

he left Flanders for England. The church is generally open Mondays
through Saturdays, from 7:30 a.m. to noon and 2–7 p.m.; and on Sundays and holidays from 9 a.m. to noon and 6–7 p.m. During the winter, it is open in the late afternoons only and is closed on Sundays.

Continue on to the **Broel Towers** (7), two fortifications from the
12th and 15th centuries that once guarded the river crossing. In the
center of the bridge stands a statue of St. Nepomucenus, the patron
saint of the drowned.

Beyond this is the **Municipal Museum** *(Stedelijk Museum)* (8), located in an 18th-century mansion. Its interesting collections include
relics from the Battle of the Golden Spurs, ancient artifacts, local lace
and damask, the applied arts, and paintings by regional artists. Visits
may be made daily except on Mondays, from 10 a.m. to noon and 2–
5 p.m.

The small shopping area just west of this has several attractive
cafés where you can relax before returning to the station.

Mechelen
(Malines)

Travelers with a particular interest in cathedrals and churches in general will surely enjoy a visit to Mechelen, the religious capital of Belgium and the seat of its archbishop primate. Located just a few miles north of Brussels, it is a thoroughly Flemish town that has preserved a great deal of its medieval atmosphere.

Mechelen grew around an 8th-century abbey, founded by St. Rombout, and soon became part of the Bishopric of Liège. After a period of independence it passed to the dukes of Burgundy, reaching a peak of prosperity in the early 16th century when it was chosen as the residence of Margaret of Austria, who governed the Low Countries as regent for the infant Charles V. A brilliant court of artists and scholars lived in Mechelen in those days, but the glory faded in 1531 when the government moved to Brussels. During World War I it held out heroically against the invading Germans, finally succumbing and suffering much damage. This and the ravages of World War II have since been repaired, with the town today being an exceptionally pleasant place to visit.

GETTING THERE:

Trains depart Brussels' three major stations frequently for the 20-minute ride to Mechelen *(Malines)*. Return service operates until late evening.

By car, Mechelen is 17 miles north of Brussels on the A-1/E-19 highway.

WHEN TO GO:

You can stroll around Mechelen at any time in good weather, but don't plan on seeing the cathedral on Sundays or holidays until 1 p.m. The museums have various closing dates, and an outdoor market is held in the Grote Markt on Saturday mornings.

FOOD AND DRINK:

Some good restaurant choices in Mechelen are:

D'Hoogh (Grote Markt 19, upstairs) Classic French cuisine. Res-

The Town Hall in the Grote Markt

ervations needed, phone (015) 21-75-53. X: Sat. lunch, Sun. eve., Mon. $$$

Mytilus (Grote Markt 23, near the tourist office) Indoor/outdoor dining, with mussels in season. Phone (015) 20-19-52. $$

Convent (Nonnenstraat 40, a block northwest of the Béguinage Church) Dining in a 17th-century dwelling. Phone (015) 20-01-86. X: Tues. $$

Gulden Anker (Brusselsesteenweg 2, a block southwest of the Brussels Gate) Noted for its seafood. Phone (015) 42-25-35. X: Sat. lunch, Sun. eve. $$

There are quite a few cafés on the Grote Markt.

TOURIST INFORMATION:

The local tourist office, phone (015) 29-76-55, is in the Town Hall on Grote Markt.

SUGGESTED TOUR:

Express trains from Brussels stop at Mechelen's **main station** (1). From there, follow the map to the **Grote Markt** (2), a lovely market square lined with gabled houses from the 16th through the 18th centuries. In its center stands a statute of Margaret of Austria, whose 16th-century regency briefly brought fame to Mechelen, then the effective capital of the Low Countries. A colorful outdoor market is still held here on Saturday mornings.

The east side of the square is totally dominated by the **Town Hall** *(Stadhuis)*, composed of two very different buildings. The larger one to the right, which houses the tourist office and whose Gothic arch leads to a nice inner courtyard, is the former *Lakenhal*, or Cloth Hall. Begun in 1320, it was rebuilt after a fire in 1342 and acquired its octagonal turrets only in the 16th century. At the same time, its left wing was torn down to make space for a palace, but work on this soon ceased when the court moved to Brussels. The flamboyant structure you see here today, which appears to be many centuries old, was actually built in 1911 to the original plans. Together, the ensemble makes a dramatic sight.

While at the Town Hall, stop in at the tourist office to ask about which of the town's several small (and unusual) museums are open today, and how to get to them.

Leave the square and follow Befferstraat to the **Palace of Margaret of Austria** (3), erected in the Gothic and Renaissance styles during the 16th century. It now serves as a law court. Try to get a look at its magnificent inner courtyard. Across the street is the 17th-century **Church of St. Peter and St. Paul**, whose interior is graced with lovely oak confessional boxes, carved with allegorical sculptures.

The route now leads to the **Hof van Busleyden**, a beautiful early-16th-century mansion that houses the **City Museum** *(Stedelijk Museum)*. Its collections are concerned with local history and especially with the musical art of the carillon, for which Mechelen is famous. The museum is open on Tuesdays through Fridays, from 10 a.m. to noon and 2–5 p.m.; and on weekdays and holidays from 2–6 p.m. Adjacent to it is the Carillon School, whose students come from all over the world.

Just around the corner stands **St. Janskerk** (5), a 15th-century church noted for its exquisite triptych, the *Adoration of the Magi*, one of the finest works by Rubens. Unfortunately, the church is often closed, but if it's open be sure to stop in.

Now follow the map to **St. Catherine's Church** *(St. Katelijnekerk)* (6), built in 1336. Its rather austere interior is quite lovely and features some exceptional confessionals and an interesting pulpit. Continue on through an old part of town to the baroque **Béguinage Church** (7). Built in 1629, it contains a number of superb art works, but is rarely open.

The route on the map soon brings you to the ***Cathedral of St. Rombout** (8), a truly remarkable Gothic structure whose 15th-century tower soars to a height of 318 feet and contains two carillons. The older of these is partly from the 15th century, while the newer is a recent addition. Construction on the cathedral itself began in 1217 and continued into the 16th century.

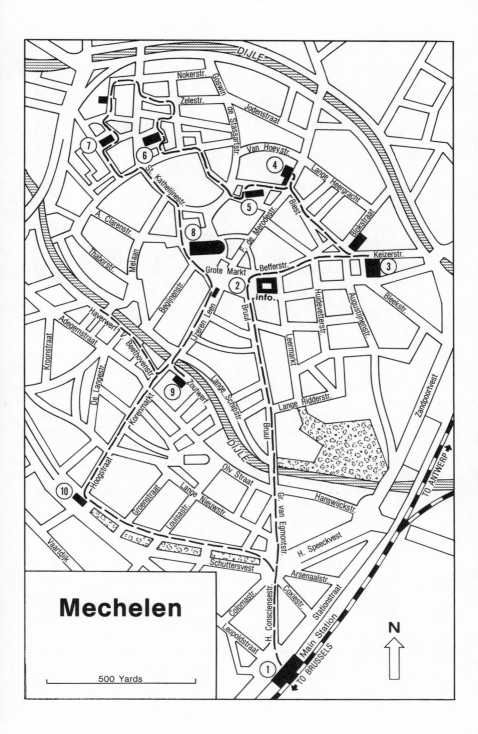

Nokerstr.

Goswin de Stassartstr.

Zelestr.

Jodenstraat

DIJLE

7

6

St. Kathelijnestr.

Van Hoeystr.

Lange Heergracht

4

Biest

Blokstraat

5

A. Clarenstr.

Thaborstr.

Melaan

E. de Merodestr.

Keizerstr.

3

8

Grote Markt

Befferstr.

2

info.

Bruul

Huidevetterstr.

Augustijnenstr.

Bleekstr.

Beginenstr.

Haverwerf

Adegemstraat

IJzeren Leen

Leermarkt

Kroonstraat

V. Beethovenstr.

De Langestr.

Korenmarkt

Zoutwerf

Lange Schipstr.

Lange Ridderstr.

9

Bruul

DIJLE

Olv Straat

Hoogstraat

Groenstraat

Lange Nieuwstr.

Louisastr.

Hanswijckstr.

Zandpoortvest

TO ANTWERP

10

Vaartdijk

Schuttersvest

Gr. van Egmontstr.

H. Speeckvest

Arsenaalstr.

Stationstraat

Colomastr.

H. Consciensestr.

Coxstr.

Main Station

TO ANTWERP

Mechelen

1

TO BRUSSELS

500 Yards

N

The Brussels Gate

Step inside to see the 17th-century high altar and the tombs of the archbishops. A series of paintings in the ambulatory depicts the life of St. Rombout, while other works of art in the south transept include Van Dyck's magnificent *Crucifixion* of 1627. The cathedral is open Mondays through Saturdays, from 9:30 a.m. to 4 p.m. (6 p.m. in summer); and on Sundays and holidays from 1–6 p.m.

Stroll over to the Grote Markt and turn right on the IJzerenleen, an attractive shopping street that begins at the handsome 14th-century *Schepenhuis*, Mechelen's first town hall. The bridge on the Dijle River, known as the Grootbrug, dates from 1298 and has three irregular arches. Once across it, you could make an interesting little side trip down Van Beethovenstraat, a small street named for the composer's grandfather, who was born in Mechelen. It leads through a brewery to the river's edge, where some 16th-century houses grace the area near the next bridge.

A left turn at the Grootbrug brings you to **De Zalm** (9), the House of the Salmon, a handsome Renaissance structure built in the 16th century for the Fishmongers' Guild. The nicest way back to the train station takes you past the imposing 14th-century **Brussels Gate** *(Brusselpoort)* (10), the only remaining part of the medieval town walls. From there just follow the map to the station.

*Antwerp
(Antwerpen, Anvers)

If you haven't already discovered it, a visit to Antwerp should come as a wonderful surprise. Belgium's second-largest city and major seaport is not only a great cultural center, it is also a highly entertaining, beautiful, vital, and immensely likeable place. Don't miss this urban Flemish treat!

Legend has it that Antwerp began during the Roman era with the riverside castle of a giant named Druon Antigonus, who extracted tolls from passing ships and cut off the hands of sailors who refused to pay, which he then threw into the Schelde—thus the name *Handwerpen*, meaning "to throw a hand." Historians, however, offer a less picturesque theory, insisting that the name derives from *Aan de Werpen*, literally "at the wharf." Whatever the truth of the matter, Antwerp's reason for existence has always been its strategic location on a deep river that runs through Dutch territory to the North Sea.

Actually, there has been a settlement here since the 2nd century A.D., and it acquired a fortress in the 9th century. Towards the end of the 15th century, Antwerp took over much of the trade of rival Bruges, whose outlet to the sea had silted up. The city was sacked by the Spaniards in 1576, and its economy was later ruined by the Dutch, who blocked access to the Schelde estuary for nearly 150 years, an act of aggression that ended only under Napoleon's assumption of power in 1795. Belgium's declaration of independence in 1830 led to Holland charging a toll for "their" river, but this was settled in 1863. Since then, Antwerp has regained its position and is once again one of the leading ports of Europe.

Antwerp's most famous citizen was Peter Paul Rubens (1577–1640), the German-born painter who spent most of his life in Antwerp and left behind an astonishing legacy of art that graces the city today. You'll be seeing much of this along the walking tour, although the city possesses far more masterpieces than can possibly be seen in one day. For this reason, and for the other attractions as well, it may be a good idea to stay over for a few days, or to come back at a later time to continue your exploration of this magnificent place.

GETTING THERE:

Trains depart Brussels' three major stations frequently for the 35-minute ride to Antwerp's Centraal Station. Return service runs until late evening.

By car, the easiest route is to take the A-1/E-19 highway through Mechelen. Antwerp is 32 miles north of Brussels. Park as close to the Rubens House as possible, to cut down your walking distance.

WHEN TO GO:

Antwerp is a pleasure to visit at any time, but note that some of the main museums are closed on Mondays and/or major holidays. The harbor cruises operate from Easter through September.

FOOD AND DRINK:

There are a great many wonderful restaurants and cafés all over Antwerp. A few of the better choices in the areas covered by this walking tour are:

Between Centraal Station and the center:

Rimini (Vestingstraat 5, 2 blocks west of Centraal Station) Italian cooking. Phone (03) 226-0608. X: Wed., Aug. $$

Bistrot Bouillon (Lange Nieuwstraat 25, a block west of St. Jacobskerk) A popular bistro that's open late. Phone (03) 231-8440. X: Sat. lunch, Sun. $$

Panaché (Statiestraat 17, 2 blocks northwest of Centraal Station) A sandwich to a full meal, quick service in a deli. $

In the center of town:

't Fornuis (Reyndersstraat 24, 2 blocks southwest of the cathedral) Traditional food in a rustic atmosphere. Phone (03) 233-6270 for reservations. X: Sat., Sun. $$$

Den Gulden Greffoen (Hoogstraat 37, 2 blocks south of the Town Hall) Regional cuisine in an elegant 15th-century house. Phone (03) 231-5046. X: Sun. $$$

In de Schaduw van de Kathedraal (Handschoenmarkt 17, opposite the cathedral) Delicious Belgian specialties. Phone (03) 232-4014. X: Mon., Tues. $$$

De Gulden Beer (Grote Markt 14) Italian cuisine right on the main square, both indoors and out. Phone (03) 226-0841. X: Wed. $$$

Rooden Hoed (Oude Koornmarkt 25, just south of the cathedral) The oldest restaurant in town, specializing in seafood but with other dishes. Phone (03) 233-2844. X: Wed. $$

De Peerdestal (Wijngaardstraat 8, 3 blocks northeast of the cathedral) A large country-style restaurant with a broad menu. Phone (03) 231-9503. X: Sun. $$

The Town Hall in the Grote Markt

TOURIST INFORMATION:
The local tourist office is located at Grote Markt 15, phone (03) 232-0103.

SUGGESTED TOUR:
Centraal Station (1) is located about one mile east of the Old Town's center, where the sights begin. The entire distance from station to center is along a series of attractive shopping streets, but if you prefer to ride you can take the underground tram *(Pre Métro)* to Groenplaats.

The ***Cathedral of Our Lady** (2) is just north of the Groenplaats, once the town graveyard and now a pedestrian area with a statue of Rubens. Although it is the largest Gothic church in Belgium, it is so hemmed in by houses, built right up to its walls, that its immense size does not become immediately apparent. The present cathedral was begun in 1352 and was essentially finished during the 16th century. Its fantastically ornate north tower soars some 404 feet above the street, while the south tower was never completed.

The cathedral's spacious interior is undergoing a long-term restoration, so many of its art treasures are moved around from time to time. Three masterpieces by Rubens to be on the lookout for are his *Elevation of the Cross*, the *Descent from the Cross*, and the *Assump-*

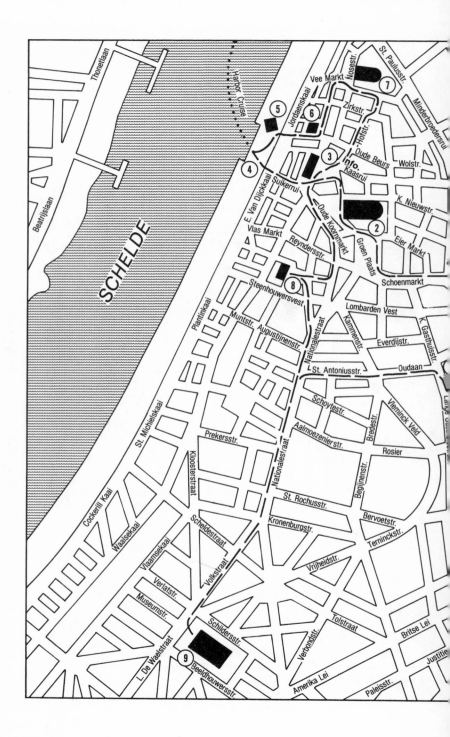

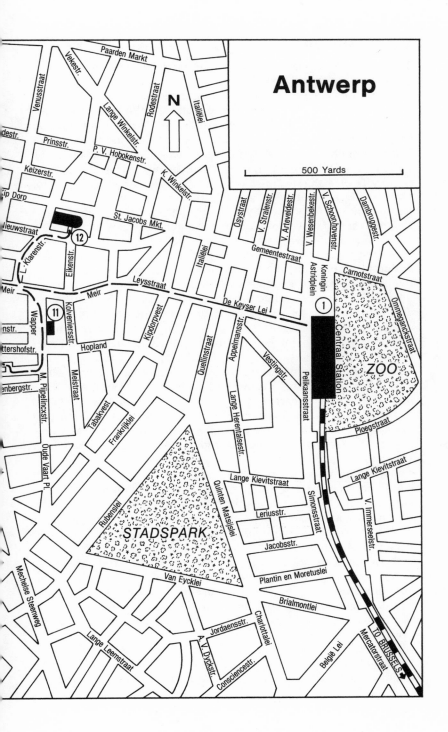

Antwerp

500 Yards

N

tion. Visits may be made on Mondays through Fridays from 10 a.m. to 5 p.m., on Saturdays from 10 a.m. to 3 p.m., and on Sundays and holidays from 1–4 p.m.—but not during services.

Continue on to the nearby **Grote Markt** (3), the impressive main square of Antwerp. In its center stands the Brabo Fountain, atop which the legendary hero Silvius Brabo tosses the hand of Antigonus into the Schelde, thus saving the town from the evil giant's tyranny. The entire west side of the square is occupied by the magnificent 16th-century **Town Hall** *(Stadhuis),* whose essentially 19th-century interior may usually be visited on any day except Sundays. Ornate guild houses, mostly from the 16th century, line the other sides of the square. Many of these now contain restaurants or cafés, contributing to the generally festive atmosphere.

A short stroll down Suikerrui brings you to the Schelde River. ***Harbor cruises** offered by the Flandria Company depart frequently from the landing stage at **Steenplein** (4). These are a lot of fun, although only the longer trips get into the modern port, as it is quite a distance downstream. Still, the views are interesting, and refreshments are available on board. Most of the cruises are for either 50 or 80 minutes, but a few last much longer. The boats generally operate from Easter through September.

At the north end of Steenplein stands a forbidding medieval fortress called the **Steen** (5), whose foundations date from the 9th century. The remaining parts of the castle itself were built around 1250 and have been altered many times since. Originally the residence of the ruling counts, it was later used as a notorious prison and now houses the **National Maritime Museum** *(Scheepvaartmuseum Steen).* The modern statue at its entrance is of the "Lange Wapper," a giant who was the scourge of drunkards. Inside, the museum has a fascinating collection of nautical artifacts, ship models, and displays concerning Antwerp's maritime development. There is a colorful café in the basement, and an outdoor collection of real boats and barges adjacent to the castle. The museum is open daily, except on major holidays, from 10 a.m. to 5 p.m.

Now follow the map to the **Vleeshuis** (6), a masterful gabled and turreted mansion, built for the Butchers' Guild in 1503. Its elegant interior today houses an excellent museum for the applied arts that is especially noted for its collection of old musical instruments. Visits may be made on any day, except Mondays and some major holidays, from 10 a.m. to 5 p.m.

Continue on to Veemarkt, the former cattle market, and **St. Pauluskerk** (7), a late Gothic church of the 16th century ornamented with a 17th-century baroque tower. Its lovely interior contains some fine

The Steen and the Lange Wapper *Statue*

woodcarvings, choir stalls, and confessionals. There are also several paintings by Rubens and other local artists.

The route now leads through a charming old part of town and returns to the Grote Markt. Head south on Oude Koornmarkt and follow around to Vrijdagmarkt, where an antiques market is held on Wednesday and Friday mornings. Facing this is the ***Plantin-Moretus Museum** (8), an absolutely essential stop for anyone who loves books. The publishing firm founded in 1555 by Christopher Plantin grew to become the most important in Europe, was taken over by his son-in-law Jan Moretus, and remained in business until 1867. The complex of buildings in which it is housed served as both the family mansion and as printing shops. Step inside to see the vast collection of publishing artifacts, including examples of the development of alphabets, a type foundry, printing presses, many rare volumes, and a Gutenberg Bible. There are also several paintings by Rubens, who was a family friend. Don't miss this special treat, which is open daily, except for a few major holidays, from 10 a.m. to 5 p.m.

From here, you can make a **side trip** on foot or by bus or tram to the Royal Museum of Fine Arts, or you could skip that and head straight for the Mayer van den Bergh Museum.

The ***Royal Museum of Fine Arts** *(Koninklijk Museum voor Schone Kunsten)* (9) is easily among the most impressive in the Low Countries. Its monumental collections include works by such masters as Van Eyck, Van der Weyden, Memling, Dirk Bouts, and Quentin Massys, among others. Rubens gets two entire galleries to himself, and his contemporaries, such as Van Dyck and Jordaens, are well represented. You'll also find paintings by Bruegel, Cranach, Frans Hals, and Rembrandt. Modern art is well covered with works by such Belgian luminaries as Ensor, Magritte, and Delvaux. Admission to the museum is free, except for special shows. It is open daily, except on Mondays and some major holidays, from 10 a.m. to 5 p.m.

Return via the route on the map and turn east to the **Mayer van den Bergh Museum** (10), where a small but absolutely exquisite collection of medieval and Renaissance art is displayed in a reconstructed 16th-century town house. The most important piece here is Bruegel's *Dulle Griet* (Mad Meg), an astonishing painting that touches on the supernatural. Visits may be made daily, except on Mondays and major holidays, from 10 a.m. to 5 p.m.

Continue on to what is probably Antwerp's most popular attraction, the ***Rubens House** (11). The great painter Peter Paul Rubens began construction on this large townhouse and studio around 1610 and lived there until his death in 1640. After that it deteriorated badly, and by the time it was acquired by the city in 1937 there was not much left beyond the framework. A meticulous reconstruction was finished and it opened to the public in 1946. None of its present furnishings actually belonged to Rubens, but they are all authentic antiques from his time and show just how well this prosperous artist, diplomat, and scholar really lived. Be sure to get out into the garden, laid out as it appeared in his paintings. The house is open daily, except for a few major holidays, from 10 a.m. to 5 p.m.

While on the subject of Rubens, you may want to visit the nearby **St. Jacobskerk** (12), a patrician church where the artist and his family are buried. Above the altar in the Rubens Chapel is one of the master's last works, *Our Lady Surrounded by Saints,* in which he depicted himself as St. George, his two wives as Martha and Mary, his father as St. Jerome, and his son as Christ. The church is open April through October, from 2–5 p.m.; and during the rest of the year from 9 a.m. to noon; but not during services.

From here, you can walk or take a tram back to the station. Antwerp has a great many other attractions, such as the extraordinary zoo and the Diamond Museum, on which the tourist office will be happy to give you brochures for your next visit.

Leuven
(Louvain)

It seems appropriate that the oldest university in the Low Countries should be in a town famous for its beer. Leuven—dare it be called the Heidelberg of Belgium?—excels both at education and at having fun. An easy daytrip here will reward you with some outstanding art and architecture, lovely gardens, an unusually picturesque béguinage, and a lively student scene in the old marketplace.

Located on the medieval trade route between Cologne and Bruges, Leuven became an important town in the 12th century, when it was the capital of Brabant and a leading center of cloth weaving. Shifting trade patterns and internal political strife caused a rapid decline during the 14th century, but the town's prosperity was renewed in 1425 by the founding of the university. At first a leading center of liberal thought, with such renowned scholars as Erasmus and Mercator, the school turned to more traditional Catholic values in reaction to the Reformation. Another fundamental change occurred in 1968 when its French-speaking faculty and students moved south to form their own university in Walloon territory. The Flemish-speaking school at Leuven presently has about 22,000 students spread throughout the city and in the immediate surroundings.

GETTING THERE:

Trains depart Brussels' three major stations at half-hour intervals for the 25-minute ride to Leuven *(Louvain)*. Return service operates until late evening.

By car, Leuven is 16 miles east of Brussels via the A-3/E-40 highway to exit 22. Park as close to the Grote Markt as possible.

WHEN TO GO:

Avoid going to Leuven on a Monday, when most of the sights are closed. On Sundays and holidays they are open from 2–5 p.m. only. Good weather will make the outdoor cafés and gardens of the town much more enjoyable.

FOOD AND DRINK:

Leuven has a good range of restaurants and cafés in all price ranges. Some choices are:

> **Belle Epoque** (Bondgenotenlaan 94, a block west of the station) Classic French cuisine, indoors or out. Phone (016) 22-33-89. X: Sun., Mon. $$$

> **De Zeester** (Mechelstraat 22, a block northwest of St. Pieterskerk) Specializes in seafood, with good-value lunch specials. Phone (016) 23-44-01. X: Sat. lunch, Sun. $$

> **Y Sing** (Parijsstraat 18, 2 blocks southwest of St. Pieterskerk) Chinese and Thai cuisine. Phone (016) 22-80-52. X: Wed. $

> **De Blawe Schuit** (Vismarkt 16, 3 blocks northwest of St. Pieterskerk) A popular student hangout. $

The many outdoor cafés on the Oude Markt cater to students and tourists alike. Be sure to try the products of the local Artois Brewery, whose many brands include the popular Stella Lager.

TOURIST INFORMATION:

The local tourist office, phone (016) 21-15-39, is on the Naamsestraat side of the town hall.

SUGGESTED TOUR:

Leave the **train station** (1) and walk or take a bus a half-mile down Bondgenotenlaan to Fochplein, the center of town. In the middle of the square stands the modern "Fonske" Fountain, in which a student attempts to pour knowledge into his head but sometimes only succeeds in wetting the passersby. Behind him is one of the most astonishing structures in Belgium, the unbelievably ornate **Town Hall** *(Stadhuis)* (2), a miracle of the 15-century Flamboyant Gothic style. Its richly sculpted façade is decorated with turrets, pinnacles, and no fewer than 236 statues. The latter were planned from the start but not actually added until the early 19th century. Guided tours of the sumptuous interior are usually available once or twice a day; ask at the tourist office along the west side of the building. The Town Hall also contains an interesting **Brewery Museum**, where the local specialty is celebrated Tuesdays through Saturdays, from 10 a.m. to noon and 2–5 p.m.

Just across the Grote Markt square stands ***St. Pieterskerk** (3), a splendid 15th-century late Gothic church that has been repaired after severe wartime damage. Its interior has some truly remarkable art treasures, foremost of which is the magnificent triptych, *The Last Supper,* a 15th-century masterpiece by the local painter Dirk Bouts. This and other superb pieces may be seen Tuesdays through Saturdays, from 10 a.m. to noon and 2–5 p.m.; and on Sundays and holidays in summer from 2–5 p.m.

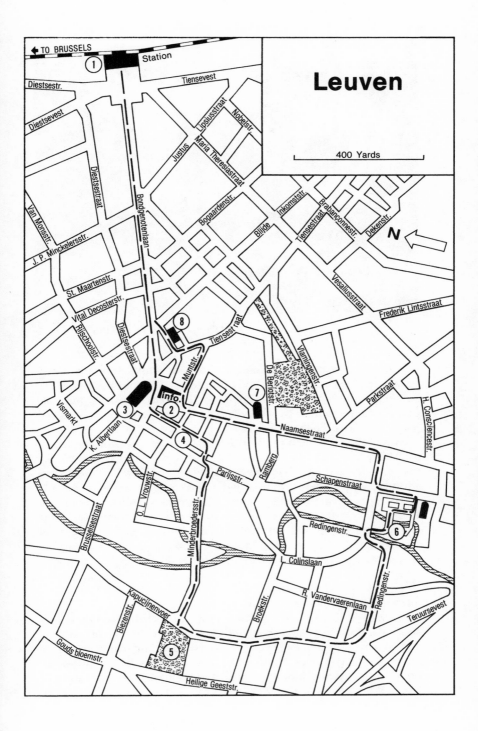

The "Fonske" Fountain and the Town Hall

From here, it is a short stroll into the **Oude Markt** (4), a large open square lined with old houses and bordered on the south by university buildings. Much of this pedestrian area is filled with delightful outdoor cafés frequented by students, making it a particularly attractive place to sample the local brew.

Now follow the map to the **Botanical Gardens** *(Kruidtuin)* (5), an especially lovely spot where even tropical plants flourish. From here, the route leads to the **Great Béguinage** *(Groot Begijnhof)* (6), an enclosed town-within-a-town founded in the early 13th century. Among its oldest surviving buildings are a 14th-century church and several 16th-century houses. Its narrow streets and tiny stream make it a highly picturesque place to explore, perhaps the most inviting of all the béguinages in the Low Countries. Recently restored, it is now used to accommodate university students and faculty.

Return via Naamsestraat, perhaps stopping at the baroque St. Michielskerk (7) or the nearby St. Donatus Park, where you can see remains of the 12th-century ramparts.

Turn right just before the Town Hall and visit the **Municipal Museum Vanderkelen-Mertens** (8), which features paintings of the 15th- and 16th-century Leuven School, Gothic statues, and many other local art treasures. It is open Tuesdays through Saturdays, from 10 a.m. to noon and 2–5 p.m.; and on Sundays and holidays in summer from 2–5 p.m. From here, you can take a bus or walk back to the train station.

Bokrijk

Europe has an ever-increasing number of outdoor folk museums where the rural past is brought back to life, but perhaps none of them surpass Bokrijk in sheer entertainment value. Although it may have certain "cultural" overtones, for the foreign tourist a visit here is just plain fun.

Farm structures, village houses, churches, schools, country inns, wind and water mills, and even urban buildings have been brought here from all over the Flemish provinces of Belgium and reassembled into typical villages as well as a small corner of a city. Dating from the 12th through the late 19th centuries, many of the preserved buildings are furnished with authentic antiques to appear as they would have in times past. The old crafts and farming methods continue to be practiced as a way of keeping ancient traditions alive.

Located in the large Provincial Domain of Bokrijk (an estate once owned by an abbey and purchased by the province of Limburg in 1938 as a nature preserve), the Flemish Open-Air Museum opened in 1958 as one of the largest outdoor folk museums in Europe. An English-language guide booklet with a map is available at the entrance so you can explore the entire area on your own, traveling by foot or riding one of the horse-drawn wagons. Authentic rural inns with outdoor tables, serving real country beer and home-cooked meals make for pleasant stops along the way. The suggested route described here takes you past all of the interesting highlights, which are numbered and described in great detail in the guide booklet.

GETTING THERE:

Trains bound for Genk depart Brussels' three major stations at hourly intervals for the 1½-hour ride to Bokrijk. Be sure to get on a car marked for Genk, as the trains split en route. Bokrijk has no station, but the trains stop at a platform close to the museum entrance. Return service runs until mid-evening.

By car, leave Brussels on the A-3/E-40 and go east, almost to Leuven, then take the A-2/E-314 northwest to exit 30 and follow signs south to Domein Bokrijk Openluchtmuseum. The total distance is 52 miles.

WHEN TO GO:

The open-air museum at Bokrijk operates between April and Mid-October, daily from 10 a.m. to 6 p.m. Good weather is essential for this trip.

FOOD AND DRINK:

There are several places to eat and drink within the open-air museum, as well as a good restaurant just outside the entrance. They are:

St. Gummarus Inn (#5 on map) A huge inn with a turn-of-the-century ambiance. Indoor and outdoor tables. Very popular. $

Dolphin Inn (#6 on map) A 17th-century inn with a good food selection, outdoor tables available. $

In't Paenhuys (#4 on map) An old country brewery with a small choice of snacks and beers. Outdoor tables. $

Bierkelder (#8 on map) A typical beer cellar from Antwerp. A huge variety of beers are available, but only snack food. $

't Koetshuis (Bokrijklaan, outside the entrance) In a mock castle near the open-air museum. Regional cuisine in a rustic atmosphere. X: Tues. off season. $$

TOURIST INFORMATION:

The provincial tourist office, phone (011) 23-71-11, is at Universiteitslaan 1 in Hasselt.

SUGGESTED TOUR:

Leave the **train halt** (1) and walk a short distance to the ***Flemish Open-Air Museum** *(Openluchtmuseum)* entrance (2), where you can purchase a guide booklet in English along with your ticket. From here follow the map to a **South Limburg Village** (3), complete with a 17th-century farmstead, a 16th-century granary, a laborer's cottage, a 19th-century school, an 18th-century chapel, and more.

Continue on to a 17th-century country brewery that now houses a café called the **In't Paenhuys** (4). Grouped around this is a 17th-century half-timbered house, an especially nice pigsty, a bakehouse with a latrine, and a small chapel. Head towards the octagonal windmill of the 18th century, the 12th-century Romanesque church, the archers' mast, and the cave hut.

Turn left at the next windmill and left again at another farmstead. You are now in a village typical of Antwerp Province. Opposite the pillory is the **St. Gummarus Inn** (5), an 18th-century structure restored to its condition of 1900. This is a great place for simple meals and especially for the local Bokrijk's Hoevebier—a full-bodied and tasty brew. A souvenir shop is nearby, as is the 18th-century vicarage. Also

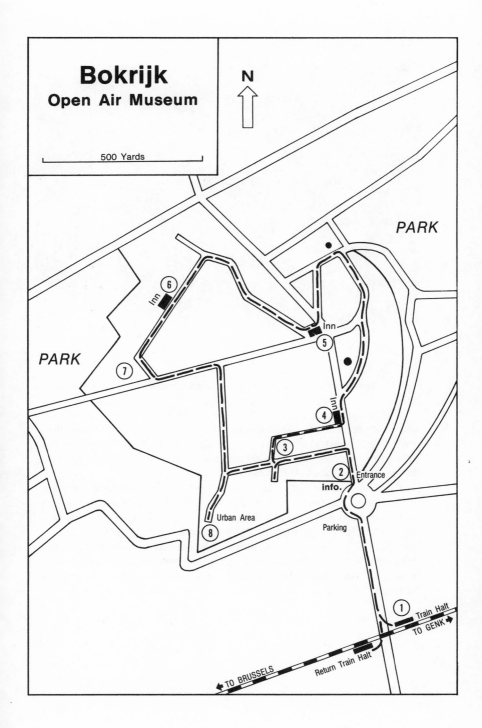

A Horse Wagon Passes the Dolphin Inn

nearby are more pigstys and outhouses, and a 17th-century farm-house.

The route now leads past an ancient abbey farmstead, a water mill, and more farms to the **Dolphin Inn** (6), a 17th-century meeting place from West Flanders. Restored to its early-20th-century condition, it now offers a good selection of regional dishes and brews, including the very strong black Abbey beer.

Continue on through a rural area typical of **West Flanders** (7) and an undeveloped part of the museum to the **Urban Section** (8). City buildings from Antwerp are being moved here brick by brick to save them from the wrecker's ball. Dating from as far back as the 15th century, the ones that are now finished house exhibitions as well as a delightful and very popular beer cellar that features a fabulous choice of brews. This is the perfect place to relax before heading back to the train-halt.

Liège
(Luik)

Quaint it's not, but Liège is the very heart and soul of French-speaking Wallonia. Snuggled into a narrow valley of the Meuse River, this large industrial city has its own distinctive way of life, characterized by a fierce sense of independence and a taste for lusty living. Its main attraction for tourists lies in its splendid museums, which cover an unusually broad range of subjects.

Liège was founded in the 8th century as the seat of a bishop and prospered as a center of learning. During the 14th century it was the capital of a principality ruled by prince-bishops and aligned with the Holy Roman Empire. In the 15th century nearly all of Belgium was captured by the dukes of Burgundy, but Liège put up a fierce resistance, falling at last to Charles the Bold, who exacted revenge in 1468 by destroying everything except a few churches. That is why so few medieval structures remain in the town.

Regaining its independence in 1477 and later rebuilding over the ruins, Liège prospered with the development of coal mining, ironworks, and a world-famous armaments industry. The French Revolution brought an end to dominance by the prince-bishops, and since Belgian independence in 1830 the city has been self-governing. The opening of the Albert Canal in 1939 has made it one of the major inland ports of Europe.

GETTING THERE:

Trains leave Brussels' three major stations at half-hour intervals for the ride of slightly over an hour to Liège's Guillemins Station. Return service operates until mid-evening.

By car, Liège is 60 miles east of Brussels via the A-3/E-40 highway to exit 32. Park as close to the cathedral as possible.

WHEN TO GO:

Avoid going to Liège on a Monday, when most of its sights are closed. Some of the smaller museums may be closed on Tuesdays instead.

FOOD AND DRINK:

You can always dine well in Liège. The restaurant choices below are in the area covered by the walking tour.

Vieux Liège (Quai de la Goffe 41, 4 blocks southeast of the Museum of Walloon Life) Superb cuisine in a 16th-century riverside building. Phone (041) 23-77-48. X: Wed. eve., Sun., holidays, Aug. $$$

Chez Max (Place de la République Française 12, by the Royal Theater) An elegant brasserie with traditional French cuisine. Phone (041) 22-08-59. X: Sat. lunch, Sun. $$ and $$$

As Ouhès (Place du Marché 21, a block east of the Palace of the Prince-Bishops) Seafood and traditional local dishes. Phone (041) 23-32-25. X: Sat. lunch, Sun. $$

Robert Lesenne (Rue de la Boucherie 9, 3 blocks northeast of the Town Hall) A good place for meat dishes. X: Sat. lunch, Sun. $$

Shanghai (Galeries Cathédrale 104, just north of the cathedral) Chinese cuisine. X: Tues. $

TOURIST INFORMATION:

The city tourist office, phone (041) 21-92-21, is at Féronstrée 92, 2 blocks southwest of the Church of St. Barthélemy. There is also a branch office in front of the Guillemins Train Station.

SUGGESTED TOUR:

From the **Guillemins Train Station** (1) to the center of town is a pleasant walk of about one mile. It is also possible to get there by taking bus number 1 or 4. However you go, the ***Cathedral of St. Paul** is a good place to start your tour. Founded in the 10th century, the present Gothic structure dates partly from the 14th century but mainly from the 16th. It became a cathedral in 1801 after the former Cathedral of St. Lambert was destroyed in the French Revolution. Inside, there are several fine 16th-century stained-glass windows in the south transept, along with some interesting sculptures. The real gems, however, are in the ***Treasury** *(Trésor)*. These include the marvelous gold reliquary donated by Charles the Bold in a fit of conscience after destroying the city, and the majestic 16th-century reliquary of St. Lambert. To see them you will have to ask the sacristan at 2a Rue St. Paul, adjacent to the cathedral, from 10 a.m. to noon and 2–5 p.m.; but not during services. He's expecting you, and it's really worth the slight effort.

Now follow the map through a series of pedestrian shopping streets and galleries and pass the imposing Royal Theater of 1818. Rue Joffre leads into Place St. Lambert, a large open square built over the site of the former Cathedral of st. Lambert. On the north side of this

Palace of the Prince-Bishops

stands the enormous **Palace of the Prince-Bishops** *(Palais des Princes-Evêques)* (3), now used as the Court of Justice. First built in the 11th century as the seat of government, it was reconstructed in 1533 and given a new façade in 1737. You can usually walk through the entrance to see one of the interior Gothic courtyards, a quite impressive sight.

Just beyond the palace is the lovely Place du Marché, with its famous 17th-century Perron Fountain symbolizing the city's communal freedoms. Opposite this stands the 18th-century Town Hall *(Hôtel de Ville)*, whose entrance lobby is richly decorated.

Continue on the nearby ***Museum of Walloon Life** *(Musée de la Vie Wallonne)* (4), easily one of the best folk museums in Belgium. Housed in a 17th-century convent, it features period room settings, workshops, a huge collection of everyday objects relating to past life in the region, a puppet theater, and even a rather elaborate guillotine. Be sure to ask at the cloakroom about going down into the reconstructed coal mine in the basement. The museum is open Tuesdays through Saturdays, from 10 a.m. to 5 p.m.; and on Sundays and holidays from 10 a.m. to 4 p.m.

The route now threads around to the tiny Impasse des Ursulines (5). Architectural elements from the past are on display in this 17th-century convent. If you feel up to it, you can climb the very steep steps up the Montagne de Bueren for a panoramic view from the

Citadel (6), following the route taken in 1468 by local citizens in a futile effort to defeat Charles the Bold. Otherwise, you can follow Rue Hors Château to the next destination.

Whichever way you get there, the **Church of St. Bartholomew** *(Eglise St.-Barthélemy)* (7) contains one of the greatest art treasures of Belgium. The ***Baptismal Font**, cast in bronze in 1118, is a stunning example of the metalworker's art with its sculpted baptismal scenes supported on the backs of ten small oxen in extremely high relief. You can see it on Mondays through Saturdays, from 10 a.m. to noon and 2–5 p.m.; and on Sundays and holidays from 2–5 p.m.

Stroll around to the nearby **Ansembourg Museum** (8), housed in an 18th-century mansion noted for its fine interiors. The displays here, in a rich setting, are of the decorative arts, including furniture and tapestries. The museum is open on Tuesdays through Sundays, from 1–6 p.m.

One of the more unusual attractions of Liège is the **Museum of Arms** (9), just around the corner on Quai de Maestricht. Long a major industry of the city, armaments for both sporting and military uses have been collected from all over the world and displayed here in a mansion that twice housed Napoleon. The exhibitions range from 14th-century firearms to contemporary weaponry. Anyone with an interest in guns should not miss this treat, which is open on Mondays, Thursdays, and Saturdays from 10 a.m. to 1 p.m.; and on Wednesdays and Fridays from 2–5 p.m. It is also open on the first and third Sundays of the month from 10 a.m. to 1 p.m.

Almost next door to this is the **Curtius Museum** (10), which occupies a fabulous mansion built in 1610. It contains one of Belgium's best collections of medieval decorative arts along with a rich assortment of archaeological artifacts from prehistoric, Gallo-Roman, and Merovingian times. Among its treasures is the famous 10th-century gospel book of Bishop Notger, covered in exquisitely carved ivory. Within the same institution is the **Museum of Glass** with its interesting displays of glass objects from all over the world, dating from Classical to modern times. Visits may be made on Mondays, Thursdays, and Saturdays from 2–5 p.m.; and on Wednesdays and Fridays from 10 a.m. to 1 p.m. It is also open on the second and fourth Sundays of the month, from 10 a.m. to 1 p.m.

Now follow the map past the main tourist office to the **Îlot St.-Georges** (11), where you will find the **Museum of Walloon Art**. Specializing in the arts of Belgium's southern provinces from the 16th through the 20th centuries, it is open on Tuesdays through Saturdays, from 1–6 p.m.; and on Sundays and holidays from 11 a.m. to 4:30 p.m. There you will also find the **Salle St.-Georges**, a venue of notable art exhibitions.

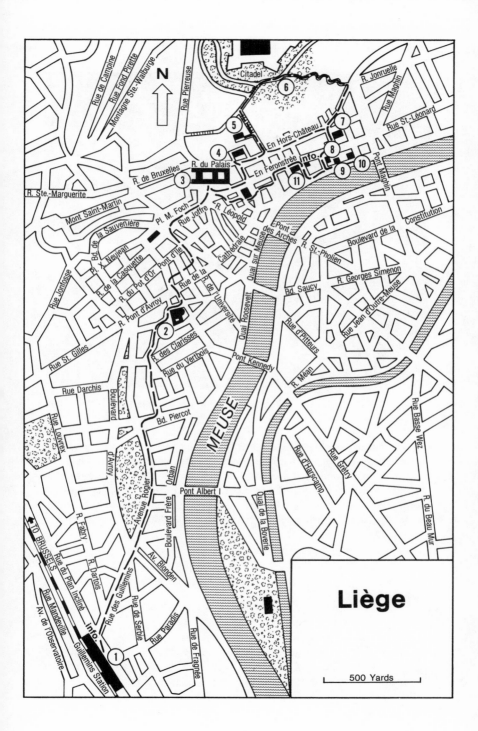

Liège

500 Yards

The Baptismal Font in the Church of St. Bartholomew

The route now leads through some old and sometimes very narrow streets back to Place St. Lambert, where you can get a bus back to the station. If you would rather walk there it may be more pleasant to follow along the banks of the river. Liège, by the way, has quite a few other museums and interesting churches scattered all over town, which the tourist office will be happy to tell you about.

Namur

(Namen)

Guarding the confluence of the Meuse and Sambre rivers and acting as the gateway to the Ardennes, Namur has always been a strategic military bastion. Its enormous citadel originally dates from Roman times and has been frequently rebuilt throughout nearly 2,000 years of an often violent history. Today it is a major tourist attraction, reached by cable car or by a long, winding road. The town itself is unusually pleasant, with several good museums and a wealth of 17th- and 18th-century buildings.

By eliminating the museums, this trip could easily be combined in the same day with one to Dinant, described in the next chapter.

GETTING THERE:

Trains depart Brussels' three major stations at half-hour intervals on weekdays and hourly intervals on weekends for the 54-minute ride to Namur. Return service operates until mid-evening.

By car, Namur is 40 miles southeast of Brussels via the A-4/E-411 highway. Park as close to the station as possible.

WHEN TO GO:

The most important attraction of Namur, its Citadel, is open daily from Easter through late October. Some of the museums are closed on Tuesdays, while others have various closing days. Good weather is essential for this trip.

FOOD AND DRINK:

Some good restaurant choices in Namur are:

Château de Namur (Ave. Ermitage 1, at the top of the cable car) Good food with a wonderful view. Phone (081) 74-26-30). $$$

La Bruxelloise (Ave. de la Gare 2, near the station) A good value, with mussels in season. Phone (081) 22-09-02. $$

La Soupière (Rue Saint-Loup 8, 2 blocks southwest of Museum of Old Namur) In the center of town. X: Sun. $

La Petite Fugue (Pl. Chanoine Descamps 5, 2 blocks east of Felicien Rops Museum) An exceptional value. X: Sun. $

TOURIST INFORMATION:

The local tourist office *(Syndicat d' Initiative)*, phone (081) 22-28-59, is at Square Léopold, just east of the station.

SUGGESTED TOUR:

Leave the **train station** *(Gare)* (1) and follow Avenue de la Gare to the tourist office, then turn down Rue de Fer to the **Museum of Old Namur Arts** *(Musée des Arts Anciens du Namurois)* (2). Housed in an 18th-century mansion, the collections here are predominantly sculptures, paintings, and metalwork of the region, from both the Middle Ages and the Renaissance. The museum is open on Wednesdays through Mondays, from 10 a.m. to 12:30 p.m. and 1:30–5 p.m.

Now follow the map to the **Convent of the Sisters of Our Lady** *(École des Soeurs de Notre-Dame)* (3), which houses Namur's greatest art treasures. The collection of early-13th-century gold plate by the master Brother Hugo of Oignies is a superb example of the stylistic lengths to which reliquaries, chalices, crosses, and other items of religious art could be carried. They may be seen daily from 10 a.m. to noon and 2–5 p.m., but not on Thursdays, holidays, or on Sunday mornings.

The route leads across a bridge to the lower station of the **Cable Car** *(Téléférique)* (4) that carries you slowly and gently to the heights of the Citadel. The cars operate daily from Easter through late October, from 10 a.m. to 6 p.m. You can also drive or walk up.

Once at the **top** (5), stroll down Avenue d'Artois and into the woods to the **Museum of the Forest** *(Musée de la Forêt)* (6), a charming rustic structure from 1910 in which subjects such as forestry, hunting, and fishing are explored along with samples of the flora and fauna of the Ardennes region.

Continue on past a sports stadium to the entrance of the ***Citadel** (7), a massive complex of fortifications spread over an area of 20 acres. It is believed that a stronghold has stood on this site since at least Roman times, but most of what exists today is from the 17th through the 19th centuries. Parts of it remained in use by the Belgian Army until 1975, and the whole fortress was opened to the public in 1978. You can visit it on foot or by riding the little "tourist train;" or you can take a guided tour. Either way, be sure to visit the small museum in the former barracks *(Caserne)*. The Citadel is open daily from Easter through late October.

Return to town via the cable car or on foot. Just across the bridge is the **Archaeological Museum** (8), housed in a 16th-century meat hall. The collections here are particularly rich in prehistoric, Gallo-Roman, Merovingian, and Early Christian artifacts from the region. It

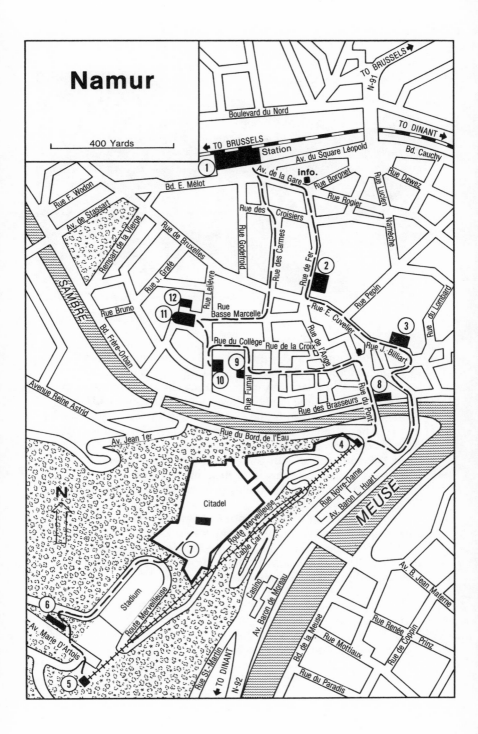

The Citadel from the River

is open on Mondays and Wednesdays through Fridays, from 10 a.m. to 5 p.m.; and on weekends from 10:30 a.m. to 5 p.m.

Stroll ahead to Place d'Armes and turn left near the 14th-century **Belfry**, once part of the medieval town walls. The route leads through a delightful part of town to the **Félicien Rops Museum** (9) at Rue Fumal 12, where some 600 works by the popular 19th-century artist can be seen daily except on Tuesdays. Continue on to the **Hôtel de la Croix Museum** (10), an 18th-century mansion with a splendid interior. It contains some marvelous local paintings and other artworks from the 17th and 18th centuries, and is open daily except Tuesdays, from 10 a.m. to noon and 2–5 p.m.

Close to this is the **Cathedral of St. Aubain** (11), a neo-classical structure of the 18th century, built on the site of churches dating back to the 3rd century. Just behind it is the **Diocesan Museum** (12) with a notable collection of medieval religious art and artifacts. From here walk back through the town to the train station.

Dinant

Dinant's spectacular location at the foot of a cliff overlooking the strategic Meuse River has long made it a prime destination for visitors. Not all of these have been friendly, as its bloody history will attest. Every war that ever raged in this area has left the little town in ruins, but always its lovely setting brought the people back to rebuild once again.

During the 15th century, Charles the Bold sacked Dinant and had 800 of its inhabitants bound back-to-back and tossed into the river. In what is nearly a repeat of that brutal action, the Germans, in 1914, executed 674 of its civilians and then put the town to the torch. Towards the end of World War II it became the target of American artillery fire as the Nazis were driven out of their stronghold in the Citadel.

But all of that is in the past, and hopefully will remain there. Dinant today is an exceptionally beautiful and very popular place with several outstanding attractions. By rushing a bit, a visit here could be combined in the same day with one to Namur, described in the previous chapter.

GETTING THERE:

Trains depart Brussel's three main stations hourly for the 90-minute ride to Dinant, with no weekend service in winter. Additionally, there is frequent year-round service to Namur, with connecting trains to Dinant on weekends and holidays from October through May. Return service operates until mid-evening.

By car, leave Brussels on the A-4/E-411 highway and follow it to Namur, where you change to the N-91 and N-92 roads to Dinant. The total distance is 58 miles southeast of Brussels.

WHEN TO GO:

Dinant's major attraction, the Citadel, is open every day from March through October. Between November and the end of February it is open daily, except on Fridays and a few holidays. The other attractions are generally open daily from April through September or October. Good weather is essential for enjoyment of this trip.

FOOD AND DRINK:

Being a major tourist area, Dinant has an enormous selection of restaurants and cafés. Some choices are:

Le Jardin de Fiorine (Rue Cousot 3, along the river just southeast of town) A local favorite for fine cuisine. Phone (082) 22-74-74. X: Wed., Sun. eve. $$

Les Baguettes du Mandarin (Ave. Winston Churchill 3, near the bridge) Chinese cuisine. Phone (082) 22-36-62. X: Tues. $$

Couronne (Rue Adolphe Sax, under the Citadel) A small hotel and tavern with good meals. $$

Thermidor (Rue de la Station 3, just southeast of the station) Excellent local cuisine. Phone (082) 22-31-35. X: Tues. $ and $$

TOURIST INFORMATION:

The local tourist office *(Syndicat d'Initiative),* phone (082) 22-28-70, is at Rue Grande 37.

SUGGESTED TOUR:

Leave the **train station** (1) and follow the map across a bridge to the foot of the **Citadel Cable Car** *(Téléférique)* (2). Here you can buy a combination ticket for the round-trip cable car and the Citadel; or, buy one for the Citadel alone and climb the 408 exhausting steps on foot. Those with cars can also drive there via Rue St. Jacques.

The **Citadel Fortress** (3) offers a fabulous view of the town and the scenic Meuse Valley. A castle has occupied this spot since around 1050, both guarding the town and making it liable to enemy attack. The present massive structure was built by the Dutch in 1821 and has played a combat role in all the wars since. Guided tours through the entire complex are conducted frequently, although you may still want to purchase an illustrated guide booklet in English to make more sense of what you're seeing. Among the sights shown are the carriage of Madame de Maintenon (who stayed here while Louis XIV was attacking Namur), the military prison dungeons, the kitchens and workshops, an arms collection, and a reconstructed trench and destroyed shelter from World War I, which you can climb through.

At the end of the tour you have a choice of going back down to the town by cable car, or following the map across the top of the hill to the next destination, which can also be reached from the town level by a chair lift *(Télésiège).* However you get there, the **Mont-Fat Park** (4) has a number of attractions, including the 14th-century Montfort Tower, from which there are magnificent views. There is also a restaurant and a self-service outdoor café.

From here, you can walk down a stepped path to the **Prehistoric Caves** *(Grotte de Mont-Fat)* (5), an intriguing subterranean world that

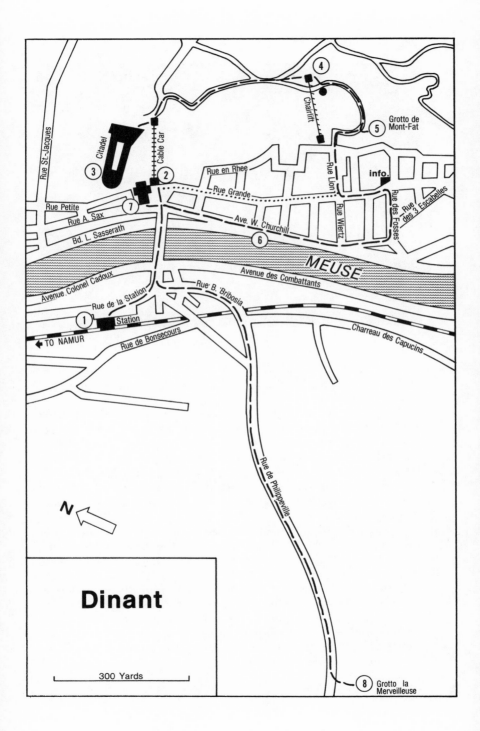

Dinant

Rue St.-Jacques

Citadel

③

Cable Car

②

⑦

Rue Petite

Rue A. Sax

Bd. L. Sasserath

Rue en Rhee

Rue Grande

④

Chairlift

⑤

Grotto de
Mont-Fat

Rue Lion

info.

Rue Wiertz

Rue des 3 Escabelles

Rue des Fosses

Ave. W. Churchill

⑥

MEUSE

Avenue Colonel Cadoux

Rue de la Station

Rue B. Bribosia

Avenue des Combattants

Charreau des Capucins

① Station

← TO NAMUR

Rue de Bonsecours

Rue de Philippeville

N

⑧ Grotto la
Merveilleuse

300 Yards

View of the Citadel and the Church

can be visited on guided tours conducted about hourly from April through September.

Continue downhill to the town and stroll around to the **river bank** (6), where **boat rides** lasting from 45 minutes to several hours are conducted by a few different companies.

Next to the bridge stands the strange-looking **Church of Notre-Dame** (7), first built in the early 13th century and many times destroyed, but always rebuilt to the original plan. Its weird bulbous spire is a trademark of the town, and its interior contains some good paintings by a local artist.

If you feel up to it, a 15-minute walk on the other side of the river will bring you to the **Grotto of Dinant "La Merveilleuse"** (8). Noted for its beautiful white stalactites and underground waterfalls, these caves are among the most fantastic in this part of Europe. They are open from March through November, daily from 10 a.m. to 6 p.m. Allow an hour for the tour. Two additional sights within hiking distance (or an easy drive) of the town are the **Museum of Copper**, where antique and modern examples of copperware are exhibited; and the **Abbey of Leffe**, where you can visit the resident monks daily at 4 p.m. Ask the tourist office about these.

Tournai
(Doornik)

The five unique towers of Tournai's great cathedral crown an ancient Roman town that gave birth to the French monarchy. It was here that Clovis was born around A.D. 465, and it was from here that he set out to conquer the many little kingdoms to the south and consolidate them into what is now France. Although the capital was soon moved elsewhere, Tournai retains much of its regal past, despite the many wars it has endured.

Always the survivor, its magnificent 12th-century cathedral is regarded as the finest in Belgium and easily among the most interesting in Europe. The town itself, although badly damaged in past conflicts and brutally bombed during World War II, has been restored along traditional lines and is today an utterly delightful place to visit.

GETTING THERE:

Trains leave Brussels' three major stations hourly for the 65-minute ride to Tournai. Be sure to get on the correct car, as the trains split en route. Return service operates until mid-evening.

By car, head south from Brussels on the N-6 to Halle, then west on the A-8 and southwest on the N-7 to Tournai. The total distance is 53 miles.

WHEN TO GO:

Avoid going to Tournai on a Tuesday, when nearly everything of interest other than the cathedral is closed.

FOOD AND DRINK:

Tournai has a fine selection of excellent restaurants and cafés, among them being:

Au Carillon (Grand' Place 36) An excellent choice right on the main square. Phone (069) 21-18-48. X: Sat. lunch, Sun. eve., Mon., Aug. $$$

Le Pressoir (Vieux Marché aux Poteries 2, by the cathedral entrance) Regional cuisine in a 17th-century building. Phone (069) 22-35-13. X: Tues., Aug. $$

Charles Quint (Grand' Place 3) A nice restaurant with a view of the Belfry) Phone (069) 22-14-41. X: Wed. eve., Thurs. $$

Aux Trois Pommes d'Orange (Rue de la Wallonie 28, just east of the Belfry) Good-value Portuguese cuisine. $

TOURIST INFORMATION:

The local tourist office, phone (069) 22-20-45, is opposite the Belfry.

SUGGESTED TOUR:

Leave the **train station** (1) and follow the map to the small **Rue Barre St. Brice** (2), where you will find two of the oldest private houses in Europe at numbers 12 and 14. Dating from the 12th century, these Romanesque dwellings are remarkably well preserved. Close to them are some nice Gothic homes from the 13th century. At the south end of the street stands the 12th-century Church of St. Brice, built next to an old cemetery where King Childeric, the father of Clovis, was buried in 481. His tomb was discovered in 1653 and its relics removed to Paris.

Now cross the Schelde River, here called the Escaut, and stroll around to the ***Cathedral of Notre-Dame** (3). Built on the site of earlier churches, the present structure combines elements of both the Romanesque and Gothic styles and was consecrated in 1175. Its five towers are highly unusual as they crown the crossing rather than the west front. The best view of the cathedral is from the square facing the north transept.

Step inside to see the arcaded triple nave, whose St. Louis Chapel has superb stained-glass windows and a wonderful *Crucifixion* by Jordaens. Under the crossing stands an elaborate 16th-century Renaissance rood screen, which marks the entry into the graceful Gothic choir. A heavily restored painting of *Souls in Purgatory* by Rubens hangs in a chapel off the south ambulatory. Just beyond this is the **Treasury**, where one of Europe's great collections of medieval religious art is on display. You will discover many other interesting objects as you wander around inside the cathedral, which is open daily from 10 a.m. to noon and 2–6 p.m.; closing at 4:30 p.m. from November to Easter. Hours on Sundays and religious holidays are shorter.

Exit from the south transept and walk over to the **Belfry** *(Beffroi)* (4). The first such structure in Belgium, it was built between the 12th and 14th centuries to celebrate the town's freedom. You can climb it for a great view of the cathedral, and it is not necessary to go all the way to the top, as there is an open balcony halfway up. It is open daily, except on Tuesdays, from 10 a.m. to noon and 2–5:30 p.m.

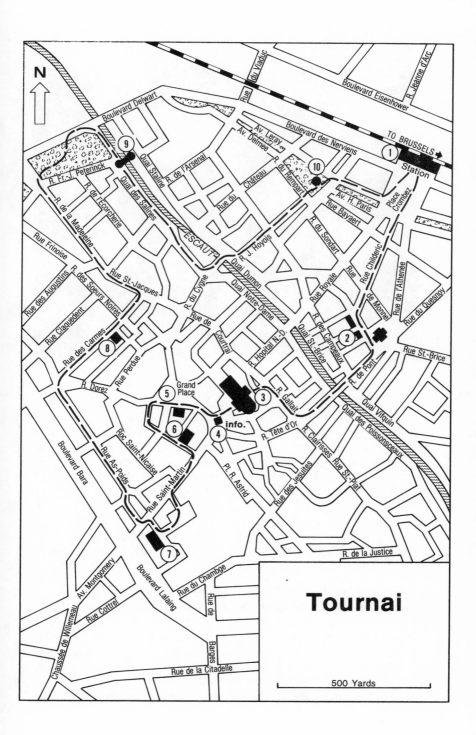

Tournai

500 Yards

The Belfry and the Cathedral Towers

Next to this is the triangular **Grand' Place** (5), a lively marketplace lined with ancient structures that were rebuilt following World War II destruction. The Cloth Hall on its south side is particularly impressive.

Stroll around to the ***Folklore Museum** in the picturesque 17th-century *Maison Tournaislenne*. Life in old Tournai is re-created through a series of authentic room settings, shops, and other displays. This highly evocative and very interesting museum is open daily, except on Tuesdays, from 10 a.m. to noon and 2–5:30 p.m.

Two other museums in the immediate vicinity might interest you. They are the **Tapestry Museum** on Place Reine Astrid, and the **Porcelain Museum** on Rue Saint-Martin. Both are open at the same times as the Folklore Museum.

Now follow the map to the **Museum of Fine Arts** *(Musée des Beaux-Arts)* (7), which houses in its splendid 1928 structure designed by Victor Horta a large and generally excellent collection of works by such renowned artists as Tournai's own Rogier van der Weyden, Bruegel, Rubens, and others. Among the moderns represented are Manet, Seurat, Van Gogh, Monet, and James Ensor. The museum is open during the same times as the Folklore Museum, above.

The route now leads through some quiet old streets to the **Mu-**

The Pont des Trous

seum of History and Archaeology (8). The collections on display here include local Roman artifacts, medieval sculptures, books, manuscripts, and many other fascinating objects. It is open during the same times as the Folklore Museum, above.

Continue on and go through a small park to the **Pont des Trous** (9), a 13th-century fortified bridge that once guarded the river approach to Tournai. Well restored, it now houses a café that can be reached by steps inside the towers. **River cruises** lasting about an hour depart from the landing stage near the bridge—ask the tourist office for current schedules.

Stroll along the river's edge to the next bridge and cross it. From here, you can return to the station via the **Henry VIII Tower** (10), built in 1515 after the English king had captured Tournai. The rest of his citadel was demolished by France's Louis XIV, but this massive circular keep remains and now houses the **Museum of Weapons** *(Musée d'Armes)*. Climb inside to examine the large collection of World War II arms used by the American, British, and German forces, as well as by the Belgian Resistance. It's open at the same times as the other museums. A short walk along a tree-shaded avenue brings you back to the station.

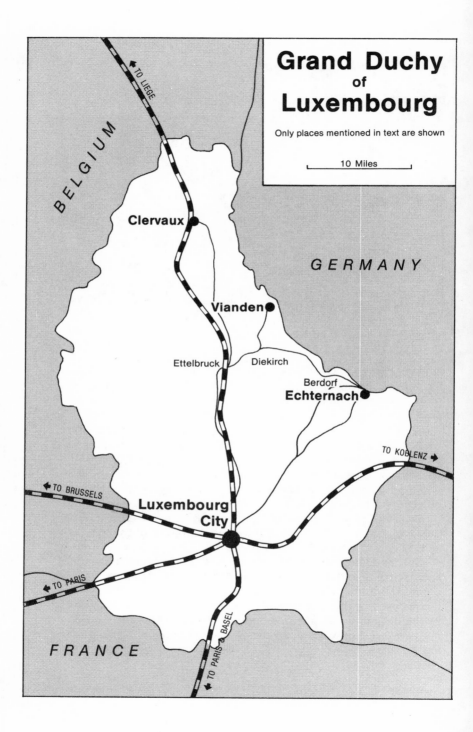

Getting Around Luxembourg

It may be tiny, but the Grand Duchy of Luxembourg packs a surprising amount of magnificent scenery into its 999 square miles. Medieval castles look down from their hilltop perches over unspoiled forests and idyllic valleys. Both its industries and its only city are located in the south, leaving the rest of the country in a largely undisturbed state of natural beauty. While it has little in the way of major tourist sights, Luxembourg offers the perfect interlude in your European adventures. It is also a popular gateway for low-cost flights from North America.

The many castles and fortifications dotting the landscape are mute testimony to a violent past. Throughout its long history, Luxembourg was the battleground for countless invading armies. Conquered by Caesar's legions, ruled by Charlemagne, fought over by the Germans, the French, the Spaniards, the Dutch, and just about everyone else who tried to establish hegemony over one of Europe's most strategic crossroads, this miniscule nation has changed its boundaries many times while struggling to retain its identity. Twice in the 20th century it has been the scene of terrible warfare, the most recently during the decisive Battle of the Bulge in 1944–45.

Today the people of Luxembourg still cling to their ancient motto *"Mir woelle bleiwe wat mir sin"*—"We want to remain what we are." And what they are today is something worth noting. With one of Europe's highest standards of living and a *per capita* industrial output that rivals just about any country on earth, Luxembourgers remain intimately bonded to the land and to the rhythms of nature. They care deeply about their countryside, always maintaining it in a state of pristine beauty.

Luxembourg City is a much more cosmopolitan place than its size would suggest. A major international banking center, it is also the headquarters of the Secretariat of the European Parliament, the European Court of Justice, and the European Investment Bank. For three months of each year, it is the meeting place of the Council of Ministers of the Common Market. By basing yourself in one of the city's many hotels or other accomodations, you can easily explore the entire Grand Duchy on comfortable daytrips.

TRANSPORTATION:

The four one-day adventures in Luxembourg described in this book can all be made either by train, by bus, or by car. Some facts to consider in making a choice are:

BY RAIL AND BUS:

The **Luxembourg National Railways** (*Société Nationale de Chemins de Fer Luxembourgeois,* or CFL) operates a network of both trains and buses, covering more than 870 route-miles. They serve virtually every locality in the Grand Duchy, making it quite easy to get around without a car.

Train service to Brussels and much of Belgium is excellent, and there are good schedules to France and Germany as well. Unfortunately, direct rail connections with Holland are fairly poor, so you may be better off going to Amsterdam by way of Brussels.

Both trains and buses for destinations throughout Luxembourg depart from the train station in Luxembourg City *(Gare de Luxembourg).* You can get **information** and **schedules** from the Railtour center in the station's main hall, or phone them at 49-24-24 (7 a.m.–8 p.m. daily). **Reservations** cannot be made for travel within the country but you may want to consider them for long international journeys. There is no food service on domestic trains, so bring your own snacks. First-class cars are identified with the numeral "1" near the door, and with a yellow stripe above the windows. Some trains do not carry first-class cars, but second class is perfectly adequate for the short journeys involved. English is widely spoken, so you will have no trouble with language. The French Rail Traveler's Glossary on pages 168–169 will help you decipher any signs or notices.

Railpasses can be a wonderful bargain if you plan on making many trips by train throughout Holland, Belgium, and Luxembourg, and other European countries. The Luxembourg National Railways (CFL) accepts the following passes for **both trains and buses** (except for local buses within Luxembourg City and the Luxair airport bus):

EURAILPASS
EURAIL SAVERPASS

EURAIL FLEXIPASS
EURAIL YOUTHPASS
BENELUX TOURRAIL PASS

All of these are described on pages 13 and 14. In addition, Luxembourg offers its own national passes:

NETWORK TICKET — *(Billet réseau)*, a one-day pass for all trains and buses (except city and airport buses) within the Grand Duchy, but not to border points. It is worthwhile for both the Vianden and Clervaux daytrips. Travel on trains is in second class. Buy it at the station.

5-DAY NETWORK PASS — Called an *Abonnement réseau de cinq jours*, this economical pass is valid for unlimited travel on any five days within a period of one month on all lines of the CFL train and bus network. Train rides are in second class, and it is not good for city or airport buses. This is a very good deal for those staying in Luxembourg for four or more days. It is sold at the stations.

Remember that all railpasses must be used in accordance with the rules and instructions accompanying them, and that you must always be prepared to show your passport. When having passes validated, be certain that you agree with the dates *before* allowing the agent to write them in.

If you have decided against a railpass, you may still be able to save some money on tickets. The Luxembourg National Railways offers weekend and holiday round-trip tickets at half price and has a 50% reduction for senior citizens over the age of 65, subject to certain conditions. Groups traveling together in second class are entitled to a variety of discounts if arranged in advance.

Buses between Findel Airport and Luxembourg City are operated by Luxair and meet all flights. You can also take the cheaper city bus, although they may refuse passengers with luggage during rush hours. Neither of these services accept railpasses.

BY CAR:

Driving in the Grand Duchy is easy, and you should encounter no problems. A valid driver's license from your own country and a vehicle registration are all that you need. Except for the few motorways around Luxembourg City, the roads tend to be narrow, and there is not too much traffic to contend with. The speed limit on motorways is 120 kph (75 mph), on country roads 90 kph (56 mph), and in built-up areas 50 kph (31 mph). Seat belts must be worn in the front seat and the horn used for emergency situations only. A parking time-disc is needed for parking in marked "blue zones" in the city and larger villages.

WHEN TO GO:

The best time to visit Luxembourg is between May and mid-October, when the weather is at its best. Many of the attractions are closed during the off-season, as is noted in the town descriptions that follow. June, with its longer days, offers the most sunshine. Luxembourg has a more sheltered climate than either Holland or Belgium—but you should still carry protection from rain or chill.

HOLIDAYS:

Public holidays in Luxembourg are:

New Year's Day
Shrove Monday
Easter Monday
Labor Day (May 1st)
Ascension Day (6th Thursday after Easter)
Whit Monday (7th Monday after Easter)
National Day (June 23rd)
Assumption (August 15th)
All Saints' Day (November 1st)
Christmas Day
Boxing Day (December 26th)

LANGUAGE:

The native language, learned from birth, is *Letzebuergesch* (or *Luxembourgeois*)—a weird and unpronounceable mixture of low German and old French. This would present problems for a country that relies on international trade for its living were it not for the fact that everyone learns German and French in school. The government and most institutions function in French, but English is widely spoken by a great many people. You won't have any language problem in Luxembourg.

MONEY:

The Luxembourg franc, usually abbreviated as LF, has exactly the same value as the Belgian franc. Belgian currency may be used in Luxembourg, and you are very likely to get it in change. The reverse is not true, however. Be sure to get rid of any Luxembourg francs *before* leaving the Grand Duchy, as they are nearly impossible to exchange in any other country. As always, you are better off doing your currency exchanges at a commercial bank. Avoid changing money at hotels, shops, or restaurants.

FOOD AND DRINK:

Virtually any kind of cuisine, from the most elegant French to American fast-food, can be found in Luxembourg. The **local specialties**, however, are very well worth trying, as you are not likely to find them elsewhere. Usually hearty and copious, the dishes to look for are: *Jambon d'Ardennes* (smoked ham with a difference), *Quenelles de foie de veau* (calf's liver dumplings), *Treipen* (black pudding and sausages with potatoes), *Jud mat gardebo'nen* (smoked pork with broad beans), and *Cochon de lait en gelée* (suckling pig in aspic). Seafood lovers will appreciate the local trout, pike, and crawfish. Luxembourg pastries are renowned for their richness.

The white **Moselle wines**, rarely exported, are superb. These are also made in a sparkling version, similar to champagne. **Beer** from the Grand Duchy is similar to that of Germany, and some popular brand names are Mousel, Diekirch, Funck, and Bofferding. Fruit liqueurs are also produced locally.

Several restaurant choices are suggested for each daytrip destination. Most of these are longtime favorites of experienced travelers and serve regional cuisines unless otherwise noted. Their price range, based on the least expensive meal offered, is indicated by these symbols:

$ — Inexpensive, but may have fancier dishes available.

$$ — Reasonable. These establishments may also feature daily specials.

$$$ — Luxurious and expensive.

X: — Days or periods closed.

Those who take dining *very* seriously should consult an up-to-date restaurant and hotel guide such as the classic red-cover *Michelin Benelux,* issued annually around the beginning of each year. It is always wise to check the posted menus before entering, paying particular attention to any daily set-meal specials.

SUGGESTED TOURS:

The do-it-yourself walking tours in the next section are relatively short and easy to follow. Some of them include simple country walks for which suitable shoes are required. On the assumption that most readers will be traveling by train or bus, they always begin at the local station or bus stop. Those going by car can make a simple adjustment. Suggested routes are shown by heavy broken lines on the maps, while the circled numbers refer to attractions or points of reference along the way, with corresponding numbers in the text.

Virtually every locality of tourist interest has its own information office. You may want to check ahead with them if seeing a particular sight is crucially important to you, since it may be closed for one reason or another. These offices are shown on the town maps in this book by the word "**info.**," and mentioned along with the phone number in the text.

*OUTSTANDING ATTRACTIONS:

An * asterisk before any attraction, be it an entire daytrip or just one item in a museum, denotes a special treat that in the author's opinion should not be missed.

ADVANCE PLANNING INFORMATION:

The **Luxembourg National Tourist Office** has offices overseas that will gladly provide maps and brochures as well as advice concerning your trip. You can contact them at:

17 Beekman Place
New York, NY 10022
U.S.A.
☎ (212) 935-8888, FAX (212) 935-5896

122 Regent Street
London, W1R 5FE
England
☎ (0171) 434-2800, FAX (0171) 734-1205

Luxembourg City

Other European towns built walls and castles to defend themselves during the turbulent Middle Ages, but Luxembourg City went a step further and made the whole place into one massive fortress, literally the "Gibraltar of the North." Dramatically sited on a high plateau overlooking deep ravines, the city is a natural stronghold if ever there was one. Most of its fortifications were dismantled in the late 19th century, but enough of them remain to make this a very intriguing place to explore. The Old City itself is exceptionally pleasant, with a fine cathedral, a palace, an excellent museum, and a delightful main square lined with outdoor cafés.

Although a settlement of sorts has existed on this spot since at least the 4th century, the present city traces its origins to a castle built in 963 by Count Sigefroi, around which a town developed. By the 15th century, this covered roughly the same area as today's city. Changing hands many times between the Burgundians, the French, the Spaniards, the Austrians, and the Germans, it was always a pawn on the chessboard of European power struggles. The Grand Duchy was freed from foreign domination in 1867 in return for a proclamation of neutrality and the partial dismantling of its fortresses.

As a transportation hub and with its wide choice of accommodations, Luxembourg City is the obvious base for daytrips throughout the entire country.

GETTING THERE:

Trains connect Luxembourg City with Belgium, France, Germany, and beyond. Service to Brussels operates at about 2-hour intervals and the ride takes less than 3 hours. There is very little direct service to Amsterdam. Paris is 3½ hours away by express, and Koblenz, in Germany, only 2 hours.

By car, Luxembourg City is 136 miles southeast of Brussels, 243 miles southeast of Amsterdam, and 233 miles northeast of Paris. Most of these distances are over superb modern highways.

By air, Luxembourg's Findel Airport has convenient flights to many of Europe's major cities as well as inexpensive service to North America via Iceland.

WHEN TO GO:

The best time to visit Luxembourg City is from March through October, when the Bock Casemates are open. Note that the State Museum is closed on Mondays, and that the palace is closed for restorations until 1996. Good weather is essential for this largely outdoor trip.

FOOD AND DRINK:

The city is blessed with a huge variety of good restaurants in all price ranges. Some choices on or near the suggested walking route are:

Saint-Michel (Rue de l'Eau 32, behind the Ducal Palace) An atmospheric upstairs restaurant with superb cuisine. Phone 22-32-15 for reservations. X: Sat., Sun., holidays. $$$

Speltz (Rue Chimay 8, a block south of Place d'Armes) Traditional cuisine in an old town house. Phone 47-49-50. X: Sat., Sun. $$ and $$$

Am Pays (Rue du Curé 20, east of Place d'Armes) Renowned for its seafood. Phone 22-26-18. X: Sat. lunch, Sun. $$

Roma (Rue Louvigny 5, a block south of Place d'Armes) A wide range of Italian dishes, indoors or out. Phone 22-36-92. X: Sun. eve., Mon. $$

Caesar (Ave. Monterey 18, 3 blocks west of Place d'Armes) A brasserie with French and Italian cuisine. Phone 47-09-25. X: Sun. $ and $$

Céladon (Montée du Grund 28, between the Holy Ghost Citadel and St. Michael's Church) Exotic food of Thailand. Phone 47-49-34. X: Sat. lunch, Sun. $ and $$

TOURIST INFORMATION:

The city tourist office, phone 22-28-09, is at Place d'Armes in the center of the Old Town. For the rest of the country, you should contact the National Tourist Office in the Air Terminal next to the train station. Their phone number is 48-11-99.

SUGGESTED TOUR:

Those staying at one of the many hotels near the **train station** *(Gare)* (1) should follow Avenue de la Liberté to the Pont Adolphe Bridge and cross it to the real starting point of this walk, the **Place de la Constitution** (2). The views across the Pétrusse Valley from here are quite spectacular, although it is difficult to understand how such a miniscule stream could have cut a gorge as deep as this.

The Grand Ducal Palace

Next to a kiosk near the center of the square is the entrance to the **Pétrusse Casemates**, a part of the old fortifications that can be seen on half-hour guided tours conducted at posted times from July through September. While not quite as exciting as the Bock Casemates that you will come to later on, these do offer a fascinating plunge into a subterranean world of tunnels where cannons peer out of loopholes, as you climb down through levels built by the Spaniards, the French, and the Austrians during the 17th and 18th centuries. Some 15 miles of underground passages still honeycomb the Old City, and were used as bomb shelters during World War II. The tour descends all the way down to the river level and comes back up via a different route, returning you to the same place.

Close to the square is the **Cathedral of Notre-Dame** (3), begun as a Jesuit church in 1613 when the Gothic style was still in vogue this far north. An extension, through which you enter, was added in the 1930s. The somewhat austere interior is in keeping with the needs of the Jesuit order, while the modern crypt contains the mortal remains of Count John the Blind, killed in the Battle of Crécy in 1346. There are also the tombs of the Grand Ducal royal family and an interesting treasury that can be seen on request.

Leave the cathedral by way of its Renaissance front portal and stroll around to Place Guillaume, where a colorful market is held on Wednesday and Saturday mornings. The statue in its center is of Wil-

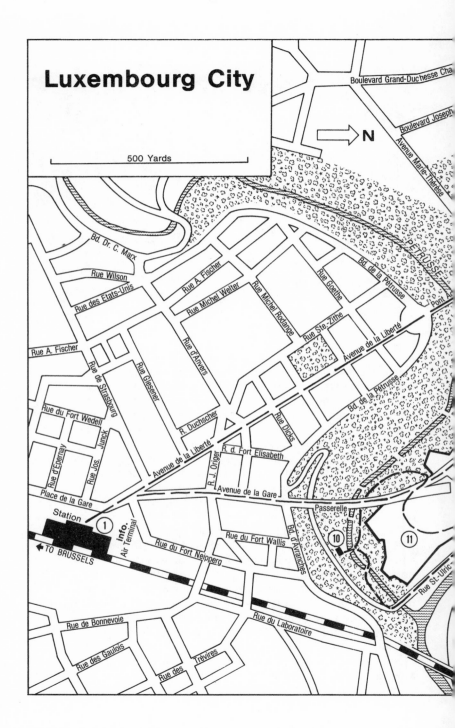

Luxembourg City

500 Yards

N

Boulevard Grand-Duchesse Cha

Boulevard Joseph

Avenue Marie-Thérèse

PÉTRUSSE

Pont A

Bd. Dr. C. Marx

Rue Wilson

Rue des Etats-Unis

Rue A. Fischer

Bd. de la Pétrusse

Rue A. Fischer

Rue Michel Welter

Rue Michel Rodange

Rue Goethe

Rue Ste.-Zithe

Avenue de la Liberté

Rue d'Anvers

Rue Glesener

Rue de Strasbourg

Rue du Fort Wedell

Junck

R. Duchscher

Avenue de la Liberté

Bd. de la Pétrusse

Rue Dicks

Rue d'Epernay

Rue Jos.

R. J. Origer

R. d. Fort Elisabeth

Avenue de la Gare

Place de la Gare

Station

Info.

Air Terminal

① ← TO BRUSSELS

Rue du Fort Neipperg

Rue du Fort Wallis

Passerelle

Bd. d'Avranches

⑩

⑪

Rue St-Ulric

Rue de Bonnevoie

Rue du Laboratoire

Rue des Gaulois

Trévires

Rue des

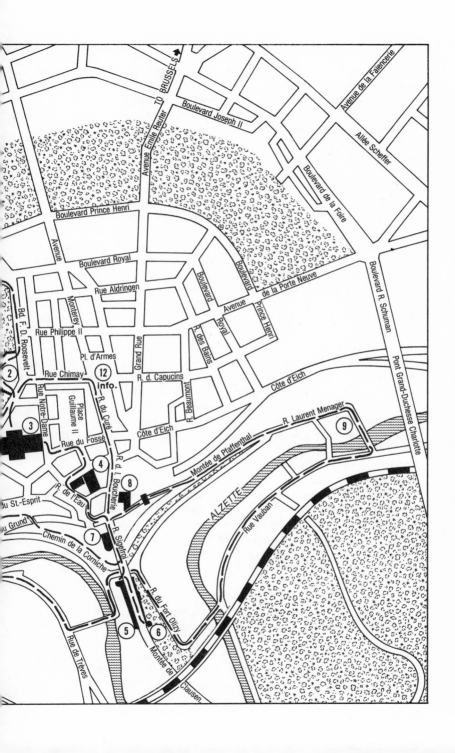

liam II, King of the Netherlands and Grand Duke of Luxembourg in the mid-19th century.

Just a block away stands the **Grand Ducal Palace** (4), originally the Town Hall and now the official city residence of the Grand Duke, Luxembourg's head of state. Most of the present structure dates from 1573 and has a fine Renaissance façade, although additions were made in the 19th century.

Continue on past the adjacent Chamber of Deputies and through some narrow old streets in the most ancient part of town to the Rocher du Bock, a rocky promontory that juts out into a loop of the Alzette River. This is where Sigefroi built his castle in 963. The entire rock is honeycombed with the city's most fascinating fortifications, the ***Bock Casemates** (5), which are entered by steps to the right. You can explore as many of the tunnels and gun placements as you feel up to, following the printed diagram and explanatory notes in English that are given to you at the entrance. Try to make it all the way to the end (section "G"), which is the most intriguing part, even though doing this entails some steep subterranean climbs. The loopholes through which the cannons were fired were greatly enlarged when the fortress was dismantled, and they now provide excellent views across both sides of the valley. The Bock Casemates are open daily from March through October, from 10 a.m. to 5 p.m.

The top of the rock, where a fortress once stood, now carries a road. To one side of this are ruins of the original 10th-century castle, and on the other side is the **Dent Creuse** (6), a broken bit of a 17th-century defensive tower. Return to town via Rue Sigefroi. **St. Michael's Church** (7) was first built as the castle chapel in 987, but has been restored several times since then. Its present 17th-century porch was a gift from Louis XIV.

Just across the old Fish Market *(Marché aux Poissons)* is the ***State Museum** *(Musée de l'État)* (8), which has wonderful displays of art, artifacts, history, and science. Be sure to see the model of the Bock Castle and the city as it appeared in its heyday, as well as the reconstructed room interiors from different eras. There is a great deal of art, both contemporary and ancient, some of which is priceless. The museum is open Tuesdays through Fridays, from 10 a.m. to 4:45 p.m.; on Saturdays from 2–5:45 p.m.; and on Sundays from 10–11:45 a.m. and 2–5:45 p.m. Admission is free. While there, check out the brand-new **Museum of the History of Luxembourg City**, a first-rate attraction opening nearby in 1995.

You can now head directly for Place d'Armes (12), a charming square lined with inviting outdoor cafés, or continue with an exploration of the lower town, down in the valley. The latter choice involves

Inside the Bock Casemates

a fairly long walk with a stiff climb at its end, but takes you through some interesting neighborhoods that few tourists see.

If you decide to push forward, follow Rue Wiltheim through the old town gates to the Trois Tours, a major 11th-century fortification with a good view across the Alzette. Continue downhill via the Montée de Pfaffenthal and cross the river on the fortified **Tours Vauban footbridge** (9). Just above this, the modern Pont Grande-Duchesse Charlotte spans the entire valley in one giant leap.

Return along Rue Vauban and go under the Bock fortifications, then turn left and follow the map across another footbridge and through the lower town to the **Chapel of St. Quirin** (10). Hewn out of the living rock, this is the oldest sanctuary in town and may originally date from pagan times. Now re-cross the ridiculously narrow Pétrusse stream and go under the 19th-century Viaduct. A strenuous climb returns you to the upper town and the ruins of the **Holy Ghost Citadel** (11).

From here, the Chemin de la Corniche path offers stunning panoramic views as it takes you back to the Bock Casemates (5). It is now only a short walk through the Old Town to **Place d'Armes** (12), where you can sit down at an outdoor café for some very welcome refreshments. Those heading back to the station may prefer to follow the route across the Viaduct, as shown on the map.

*Vianden

Towering high above a romantic village, the fairytale castle of Vianden casts its spell on the narrow, cobbled streets below. This is, quite
simply, the most picturesque little town in the Grand Duchy, and the
most enticing destination for a daytrip from Luxembourg City. In addition to its recently restored medieval castle, it offers a visit to the exile
home of Victor Hugo, an excellent folklore museum, magnificent scenery, and a delightful atmosphere that attracts visitors from all over
Europe.

The story of Vianden is the story of its castle. A small fort has existed on this hill since Roman times, and a castle was built over it in
the 9th century. This was greatly enlarged during the 11th, 12th, and
15th centuries and became an ancestral home of the House of
Orange-Nassau, the dynasty that supplies both the kings and queens
of the Netherlands as well as the grand dukes of Luxembourg.

Although you should really devote an entire day to enjoying Vianden, it is possible to combine a daytrip there with one to either Clervaux or Echternach, described in the next two chapters. Doing this is
much more practical by car, even though there is direct bus service
between Vianden and Echternach. To reach Clervaux involves a bus
to Ettelbruck and then a train.

GETTING THERE:

Trains depart the Luxembourg City Station several times in the
morning for the half-hour ride to **Ettelbruck**, where you change to a
connecting bus for Vianden. The bus ride takes about 30 minutes and
railpasses are accepted. Return service operates until early evening—
be sure to check times, so you don't get stranded.

By car, head north from Luxembourg City on the N-7 road to Diekirch, then follow local roads to Vianden. The total distance is 27
miles.

WHEN TO GO:

Vianden may be visited on any fine day from April through October. During the winter season, the castle is open on weekends and
holidays only.

The Castle of Vianden

FOOD AND DRINK:

Le Châtelain (Grand Rue 126, just below the castle) A popular restaurant with an outdoor terrace. Phone 84-90-96. X: Mon., Tues. off-season. $$

Heintz (Grand Rue 55, near the parish church) A small hotel with good food in an ancient building. Phone 84-155. X: Wed. except in summer. $

Auberge du Château (Grand Rue 74, near the folklore museum) Good-value meals at an attractive inn. Phone 84-574. X: Tues., Wed. lunch. $

TOURIST INFORMATION:

The local tourist office *(Syndicat d'Initiative)*, phone 84-257, is in the Victor Hugo House.

SUGGESTED TOUR:

Leave the **bus station** *(Gare Routière)* (1) and stroll down Rue de la Gare to the **Victor Hugo House** (2). The great French writer loved Vianden and stayed there several times, including a period of political exile in 1871. Reconstructed after World War II damage, the house is

Inside the Castle of Vianden

now a small museum containing some of the author's belongings, and documents relating to his visits. It also houses the local tourist office and is open daily from April through October, from 9:30 a.m. to noon and 2–6 p.m. During April, May, September, and October it is closed on Tuesdays.

Just before the bridge there is a bust of Victor Hugo. In the middle of the span you'll see a statue of St. Nepomuk, the patron saint of bridges. Continue across the Our River and head up Grand Rue to the **Parish Church of the Trinitarians** (3), a Gothic structure with a double nave dating from 1248. It is one of the oldest religious buildings in Luxembourg and is noted for its fine rococo altar. A short visit here is definitely worthwhile, as are a few moments spent in the 14th-century cloisters behind it.

The route now leads uphill and climbs steeply to the ***Castle of Vianden** *(Château)* (4), one of the great architectural treasures of the region. Until a few decades ago it lay in a state of semi-ruin, but a major restoration project has revived its former medieval splendor. The roof is back on, and many of the rooms are again furnished with period pieces. A printed diagram in English will be given to you at the entrance. The castle is open daily from March through December, and on weekends in January and February.

Return to the village and follow the very charming Vieille Rue until

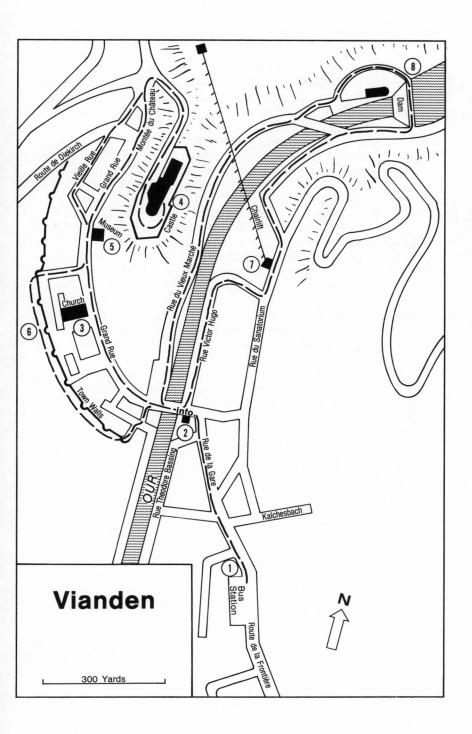

Vianden

300 Yards

N

it joins Grand Rue. Across the street is the **Folklore Museum** *(Musée d'Art Rustique)* (5), where local crafts, antiques, household items, and puppets are displayed in a charming old house. It is open daily from Easter to October, from 10 a.m. to noon and 2–6 p.m., and closed on Mondays the rest of the year.

You could easily return to the river by strolling down Grand Rue, but a more interesting (if slightly rugged) way to get there is by following the remnants of the ancient **Town Walls** (6). Now recross the bridge and turn left on Rue Victor Hugo, which brings you to the **Chairlift** *(Télésiège)* (7). From here, you can take an enjoyable ride across the river and up to the top of a hill overlooking the valley, town, and castle. The lift operates daily from April to September, but not in bad weather.

Ambitious walkers may want to continue on to the **Dam** *(Barrage)* (8). This forms the lower reservoir of a vast pumped-storage hydro-electric complex. During the night, when demand for power is low, surplus electricity is used to pump water from here to a higher reservoir. During peak-use periods this is released, turning generators on its way down. If you have a car, you might want to drive about three miles beyond the dam to the underground turbine rooms, which may be visited. Ask at the tourist office for details.

Walk across the top of the dam and follow the trail past the 17th-century Church of St. Rochus. From the bottom of the hill, Rue du Vieux Marché brings you back to town, where you can stop for some refreshment before heading out to the bus station.

Clervaux

Deep in the hilly Ardennes forest, in what nearly amounts to a wilderness area, lies the medieval village of Clervaux. Now a popular resort, it is still dominated by its 12th-century castle and by its Benedictine Abbey. There are several interesting things to see, including the Battle of the Bulge Museum, but mostly this is a place to get away from civilization for a few hours and go for a walk in the woods. Maps and suggested trail routes are available from the tourist office, or perhaps you would prefer to stick to the simple walk outlined here and spend more time in the restaurants and outdoor cafés. Either way, you're sure to enjoy a carefree visit to Clervaux.

GETTING THERE:

Trains depart the Luxembourg City Station several times in the morning for the lovely hour-long scenic ride to Clervaux. Return service operates until mid-evening.

By car, head north from Luxembourg City on the N-7 road to Marnach, then take the N-18 west into Clervaux. The total distance is 39 miles.

WHEN TO GO:

The castle at Clervaux is open daily from mid-May until mid-September. During the rest of the year it is open on Sundays and some holidays only, but closed during January and February. Good weather is essential for this trip.

FOOD AND DRINK:

Being a popular resort, Clervaux has a good number of restaurants and cafés, most of which are in small hotels. A few choices are:

Grand Hôtel Central (Place Maria Theresia 9, below the castle) A small hotel in the center of things. Phone 91-105. X: Tues. $$

Le Claravallis (Rue de la Gare 3) An attractive hotel near the station. Phone 91-034. $ and $$

L'Ilot Sacré (Grand Rue 42, beneath the castle) Good food at modest prices. Phone 92-706. $

TOURIST INFORMATION:

The local tourist office *(Syndicat d'Initiative)*, phone 92-072, is in the castle complex.

SUGGESTED TOUR:

Leave the **train station** *(Gare)* (1) and follow the map past several small resort hotels to the **pedestrian zone** (2). This very pleasant area is filled with shops, restaurants, and outdoor cafés—a fine place to return to after seeing the castle.

Steps lead from the market square to the **Castle** *(Château)* (3). Parts of this date from the 12th century, while other sections were added during the 15th and 17th centuries. The presence near its entrance of an American army tank and an artillery piece remind you that the castle played a significant role during World War II and was severely damaged in December, 1944. Now restored, the castle houses three interesting exhibitions as well as the local tourist office. You might want to stop in here to ask about walks that can be taken in the surrounding forest.

The first entrance leads to several rooms filled with scaled architectural models of the castles of Luxembourg, several of which include the surrounding villages and immediate countryside. A door at the second courtyard opens into the permanent home of a famous photographic exhibition that traveled to museums around the world during the 1950s. Assembled by the famous photographer Edward Steichen, a native of Luxembourg who made his career in America, the **"Family of Man"** show consists of several hundred poignant photos on the human condition by photographers all over the globe. Although the black-and-white images may seem a bit dated today, their power to stir the emotions remains intact.

A separate entrance in the castle's courtyard brings you into the ***Battle of the Bulge Museum**. Correctly known as the Battle of the Ardennes Forest, this was the final major conflict of World War II in Europe, and raged around Clervaux and in neighboring parts of Belgium during December of 1944 and January of 1945. The museum displays weapons, uniforms, personal effects, and other reminders of the war from both the American, British, and German forces. Visits to the castle may be made daily between mid-May and mid-September, from 10 a.m. to 5 p.m. During the rest of the year it is open on Sundays and some holidays only, from 1–5 p.m., but not during January or February.

From here, you may want to take one of the walks suggested by the tourist office or continue on to the Abbey and return to the station. To do this, just follow the map to the **Parish Church** (4), built in 1910 in the Rhenish Romanesque style to harmonize with the castle.

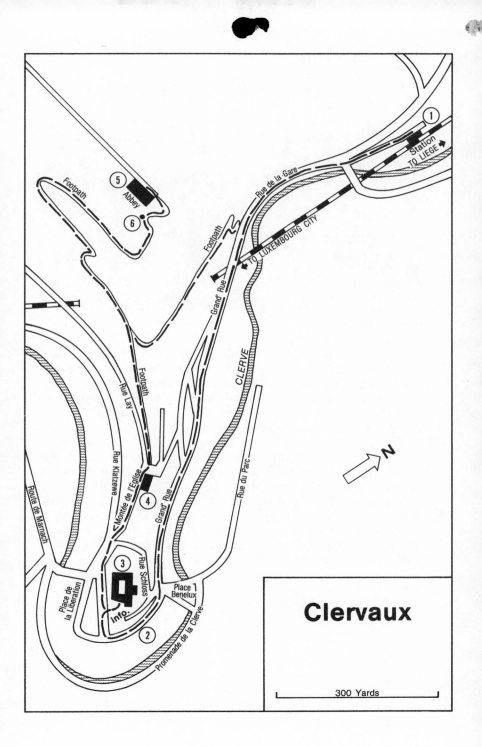

Clervaux

300 Yards

Outside the Castle of Clervaux

Steps opposite this lead up to a woodland trail marked "Abbaye," also identified as path "G." Follow it around to the **Benedictine Abbey of St. Maurice** (5), a Neo-Romanesque structure high above the village. The present abbey was constructed in 1910 after the monks moved here from France. You can visit their exhibition of contemporary monastic life, which is located in the crypt and is open daily from 9 a.m. to 7 p.m.

At the foot of the abbey is the **Monument to the Peasants' War** (6), honoring the local farmers who lost their lives fighting the French Revolutionary Army in the late 18th century. Trails lead directly from here to Rue de la Gare, returning you to the train station. This path, however, is a little bit rough and not too well marked, although certainly passable. Otherwise, you can return to town the way you came, and perhaps stop at one of the inviting outdoor cafés before walking back to the station.

Echternach

People who love walking in the woods will really enjoy this daytrip, which combines a marvelous medieval town on the German border with the most spectacular sylvan splendor in the Grand Duchy. Echternach is the center of a region known as the "Little Switzerland of Luxembourg," a name obviously coined by Dutch tourists who have never seen a real mountain. Although not very high, the hills around here are indeed rugged and permeated with fantastic rock formations. The deep, narrow ravine of the Gorge du Loup is perhaps the most famous of these and can be reached on foot from the town in considerably less than an hour.

Originally a Roman camp, Echternach developed around an abbey founded here in 698 by the Anglo-Saxon missionary St. Willibrord. Until the French Revolution it was ruled by the local abbots, but has since been secularized. Following wholesale destruction in World War II, it was rebuilt along the old lines and is today a favorite destination for visitors from Germany, which lies just across the town bridge.

GETTING THERE:

Buses depart from the front of the Luxembourg City Train Station (to the left as you leave it) about hourly for the hour-long ride to Echternach. These are operated by the railroad (CFL) and accept railpasses. Return buses run until early evening.

By car, Echternach is 22 miles northeast of Luxembourg City via the E-27 road. A detour through Berdorf will take you into the most spectacular scenery.

WHEN TO GO:

Echternach may be visited at any time in good weather, preferably between May and October. Those intending to hike in the Gorge du Loup should wear suitable shoes. Bring your passport if you want to stroll into Germany.

FOOD AND DRINK:

This popular resort has a wide selection of restaurants and cafés, among them being:

Quatre Saisons (Rue Haut-Ruisseau 2, behind the Old Town Hall) Quality cuisine at reasonable prices. Phone 72-80-39. X: Wed., Thurs. lunch. $$

Hôtel de la Basilique (Place du Marché 7) Indoor or outdoor dining around the Old Town Hall. Phone 72-94-83. $

Du Commerce (Place du Marché 16) An exceptional value near the Old Town Hall. Phone 72-301. $

TOURIST INFORMATION:

The local tourist office, phone 72-230, is next to the entrance of the Basilica.

SUGGESTED TOUR:

Leave the **bus station** *(Gare Routière)* (1) and follow the main shopping street, Rue de la Gare, to Place du Marchè, the old marketplace and the center of the town's activities. On its north side stands the **Old Town Hall** *(Hôtel de Ville,* locally called *Denzelt)* (2), a fabulous arcaded structure from the early 16th century.

Continue on to the **Basilica of St. Willibrord** (3), a part of the former abbey founded in 698 by the Anglo-Saxon missionary who first brought Christianity to this part of Europe. The present basilica originally dates from the 11th century, but was altered in the 13th century, very badly damaged during World War II, and reconstructed in 1952. Still a place of pilgrimage, it is regarded as the most important religious structure in Luxembourg. Its 9th-century ***Crypt**, a part of a former church on the site, has survived more or less intact and still contains the sarcophagus of St. Willibrord, which you can see.

The adjoining abbey, also rebuilt after World War II destruction, is now a state school. It does, however, have a small **Abbey Museum** with some fine illuminated manuscripts and items pertaining to the monastic life. Be sure to stop into the **Tourist Information Office** just outside the basilica, where you can obtain maps for a walk in the nearby Gorge du Loup or other woodland trails.

Just across the street is the 18th-century **Orangerie** (4), a formal garden of great beauty, which can be seen through the ornate gate. Now continue around to the **Municipal Park** with its splendid **Pavilion** (5) in a pure Louis XV style. A lovely walk along the Sûre River—which is the national boundary—leads to a bridge built on Roman foundations. The far side of this is in Germany.

Heading back towards the marketplace, you'll arrive at the **Museum of Prehistory** (6), which you might want to visit. It's open on

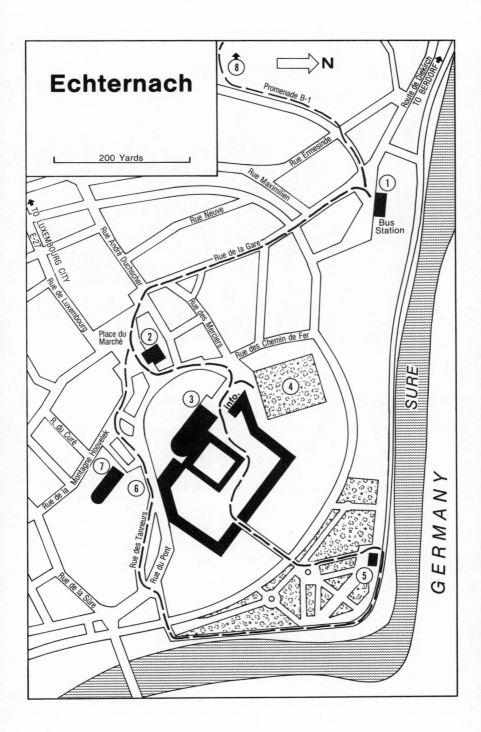

The Old Town Hall

Tuesdays through Sundays, from 10 a.m. to noon and 1–5 p.m. Close to it stands the **Parish Church of St. Peter and St. Paul** (7), reputed to be the oldest Christian sanctuary in the country. First built in the 7th century on the remains of a Roman fortress, it has been reconstructed many times since but still retains traces of the original structure.

The most popular woodland hike in this region is to the ***Gorges du Loup** *(Wolfschlucht)* (8, off the map). The trail to this leaves from near the bus station (1) and is identified as *Promenade B-1*. You can reach its most rugged and spectacular part in about a half-hour or so, but remember to allow enough time to get back to the bus station before the last departure for Luxembourg City.

Index

Boat Trips, Castles & Fortresses, Country Walks, Flower Markets & Gardens, Museums, Palaces, and Windmills are listed individually under those category headings. *Names of persons are in italics.*

Daytrips

● OTHER TITLES NOW AVAILABLE ●

DAYTRIPS LONDON
Explores the metropolis on 10 one-day walking tours, then describes 40 daytrips to destinations throughout southern England—all by either rail or car. 5th edition, 336 pages, 57 maps, 94 photos.

DAYTRIPS FRANCE
Describes 45 daytrips—including 5 walking tours of Paris, 23 excursions from the city, 5 in Provence, and 12 along the Riviera. 4th edition, 336 pages, 55 maps, 89 photos.

DAYTRIPS GERMANY
55 of Germany's most enticing destinations can be savored on daytrips from Munich, Frankfurt, Hamburg, and Berlin. Walking tours of the big cities are included. 4th edition, 336 pages, 62 maps, 94 photos.

DAYTRIPS ITALY
Features 40 one-day adventures in and around Rome, Florence, Milan, Venice, and Naples. 2nd edition, 288 pages, 45 maps, 69 photos.

DAYTRIPS ISRAEL
25 one-day adventures by bus or car to the Holy Land's most interesting sites. Includes Jerusalem walking tours. 206 pages, 40 maps, 40 photos.

DAYTRIPS WASHINGTON, DC
50 one-day adventures in the Nation's Capital, and to nearby Virginia, Maryland, Delaware, and Pennsylvania. Both walking and driving tours are featured. 352 pages, 60 maps, 48 photos.

DAYTRIPS NEW YORK
100 easy excursions by car throughout southern New York State, New Jersey, eastern Pennsylvania, Connecticut, and southern Massachusetts. 336 pages, 42 maps, 42 photos.

"Daytrips" travel guides, written or edited by Earl Steinbicker, describe the easiest and most natural way to travel on your own. Each volume in the growing series contains a balanced selection of enjoyable one-day adventures. Some of these are to famous attractions, while others feature little-known discoveries. For every destination there are historical facts, anecdotes, usually a suggested do-it-yourself walking tour, a local map, travel directions, time and weather considerations, and concise background material.

SOLD AT LEADING BOOKSTORES EVERYWHERE

Or, if you prefer, by mail direct from the publisher. Use the coupon below or just jot your choices on a separate piece of paper.

Hastings House
141 Halstead Avenue
Mamaroneck, NY 10543

Please send the following books:

_____copies   **DAYTRIPS LONDON** @ $14.95   _____
(0-8038-9367-1)

_____copies   **DAYTRIPS FRANCE** @ $14.95   _____
(0-8038-9370-1)

_____copies   **DAYTRIPS GERMANY** @$14.95   _____
(0-8038-9369-8)

_____copies   **DAYTRIPS HOLLAND, BELGIUM**   _____
        AND LUXEMBOURG @$14.95
(0-8038-9368-4)

_____copies   **DAYTRIPS ITALY** @$12.95   _____
(0-8038-9343-4)

_____copies   **DAYTRIPS ISRAEL** @$12.95   _____
(0-8038-9342-6)

_____copies   **DAYTRIPS WASHINGTON DC** @$12.95   _____
(0-8038-9349-3)

_____copies   **DAYTRIPS NEW YORK** @$12.95   _____
(0-8038-9332-9)

New York residents add tax: _____

Shipping and handling @ $2.50 per book: _____

Total amount enclosed (check or money order)   _____

Please ship to: _____

_____

_____

ABOUT THE AUTHOR:

EARL STEINBICKER is a born tourist who believes that travel should be a joy, not an endurance test. For nearly 30 years he has been refining his carefree style of daytripping while working in New York, London, Paris, and other cities, first as head of a firm specializing in promotional photography and later as a professional writer. Whether by public transportation or private car, he has thoroughly probed the most delightful aspects of countries around the world—while always returning to the comforts of city life at night. A strong desire to share these experiences has led him to develop the "Daytrips" series of guides, which he continues to expand and revise. Besides this book, these now include London, France, Germany, Italy, Israel, Washington DC, and New York. He pounds his word processor in rural Pennsylvania when not exploring new destinations or revisiting old ones.